PERSONAL AND ORGANISATIONAL TRANSFORMATIONS

through action inquiry

DALMAR FISHER

Woods College of Advancing Studies
Boston College, USA

DAVID ROOKE

Harthill Consulting Ltd
United Kingdom

BILL TORBERT

Carroll School of Management
Boston College, USA

2003
Edge\Work Press

PUBLISHED BY
EDGE\WORK PRESS

BRITISH LIBRARY CATALOGUING IN PUBLICATION DATA

Torbert, William R.
Personal and Organisational Transformations: through Action Inquiry

I. Title II. Fisher, Dalmar and Rooke, David III. Series 658.562

Fourth Edition

ISBN 0-9538184-0-3

First published 1995: McGraw-Hill
Fourth (revised) edition published 2003: Edge\Work Press

Printed by the Cromwell Press, Trowbridge, Wiltshire.

TABLE OF CONTENTS

ACKNOWLEDGEMENTS

We wish to thank all of the evening and international MBA students at Boston College, as well as the executive participants in BC's Leadership for Change program and our Harthill workshops who have so enthusiastically tested out the ideas in this book in their everyday work lives. As the reader will discover, many of their accounts of their experiments have been included, with their permission (and under fictional names), in the following pages as illustrations and as encouragements for you, our reader, to engage in this process of personal testing in your own daily actions.

We would also like to thank the various companies and their senior managements in Europe and America whose transformational stories appear in the pages to follow. They too have been willing to take many a real-time risk in applying the ideas presented here to their own executive development and to restructuring their whole company.

Among our scholarly colleagues, we are particularly grateful for the wise guidance, support and conversation we have enjoyed with Susann Cook-Greuter, Paul Gray, Christine Harris, Jackie Keeley, Judi Marshall, Richard Nielsen, Joseph Raelin, Peter Reason, and Sandra Waddock about issues of learning, development, and consulting.

As their names on the title pages of Chapters 9 and 10 attest, we were pleased to have Barbara Davidson and Melissa McDaniel join in our research at Sun Health Care and very much appreciate their collaboration in the writing of those chapters. Several other research assistants over the past dozen years helped us with studies that contributed to this book. We are grateful to Kathleen Beale, Kelly Crowther, Jennifer Leigh, Keith Merron, Larry Pike, Paul Skilton, and Rosemary Tin.

We are all deeply grateful for the solace we receive from our families.

PUTTING THE IDEAS INTO PRACTICE

An increasing number of consultants and organisations are using the ideas embodied in this book. The authors are delighted by this because we see these ideas as vital to the creative future of individuals and the sustainable well being of organisations and society.

You can find out more and get active support for the processes of personal and organisational transformation from the contact points below.

For information about the Leadership Development Framework and Profile for use with individuals, teams and organisations visit the Harthill website at www.harthill.co.uk

UK

| David Rooke | Email | david@harthill.co.uk |
| | Web | www.harthill.co.uk |

USA

| Bill Torbert | Email | torbert@bc.edu |
| | Web | www2.bc.edu/~torbert |

NOTES ABOUT THE SECOND TO FOURTH EDITIONS

The first edition was published by McGraw Hill in 1995. Future editions contain some modifications to stage descriptions and the inclusion of three new chapters. Several chapters have also been reworked. Perhaps the most significant change from the first edition is the replacement of the term 'continual quality improvement' to 'developmental action inquiry'. This reflects the centrality of the importance of action inquiry to our understanding of the developmental process in people and organisations.

In addition, we have not interrupted the flow of the chapters with footnotes and references. Instead, the reader will find relevant references to related work in the chapter by chapter Endnotes.

The changes are designed to make the book more accessible and usable. The key messages remain unchanged.

INTRODUCTION

Learning is the key challenge in management today. Never before has so much information and data inundated managers. Never before has the intensity of international competition impacted so keenly on daily decisions. Never before has there been such rapid change, growth, and transformation in the organisational world. Tomorrow's successful companies will be those in which people today are learning most rapidly and deeply. How in the midst of the pace of action can managers hope to learn?

The current focus on managerial learning is at least two decades old, and we make it clear in this book that learning is not just another passing management fad. Managerial learning is an essential capacity that is utterly indispensable to developing quality and effectiveness in the art and science of managing. But managerial learning before and after the action of the day is not enough. Managerial learning at the very moment of action is at once the least understood and least practised, yet the most valuable and the most powerful form of managerial learning.

This book offers a fresh and highly useful approach to helping managers to learn even as they are involved in the cut and thrust of daily action. We introduce action inquiry as a highly usable process that creates the possibility of a manager simultaneously learning at several levels and modifying their actions as a continual process. This process not only allows us to correct errors before they have negative consequences for business outcomes and trust, but also has the effect of creating a positive climate for others' learning and for appropriate group and organisational change as well.

Action inquiry also offers managers who participate in this way of asking questions, reflecting and acting (and action enquiry encompasses all of these and more, it is a total approach to being and doing for those who care to make it so!) a tool to support their own development. This is because action inquiry places you the person at the very centre of questions about the quality and effectiveness of your actions and the actions of others. Action inquiry is deeply developmental. More fully we might describe it as developmental action inquiry - the manager develops through a process of inquiry into his or her intentions, plans, actions, and effect that these have.

The challenge for top executives and leaders at all organisational levels is a great one. Not only do they need to be action inquirers, weaving together skilled strategic and interpersonal actions with high levels of attention to the impacts of their actions, with ever changing and growing personal mastery and understanding. They also need to be able to create learning organisation, in which developmental action inquiry is at the very heart of the organisation.

Action inquiry is an up-ending journey, and there is no end to the journey. It is endless because there is always scope for improving and refining one's own way of operating and it is upending because to inquire, 'what did I do, how did I do it, why did I do it and what impact did it have?' is likely to lead to thinking and acting differently in the future. We offer three propositions to explain why this lengthy action inquiry journey is necessary:

Proposition 1

Action inquiry (as the name suggests) requires integrating inquiry with action. The modern world separates the 'real world' of action from the 'ivory tower' of reflective inquiry. Why? So as not to paralyse action and not to bias inquiry. But action inquiry calls for flexibility and correction of errors at the very moment of seeking to make a sale, or in the midst of a management meeting. This requires a heightened awareness that inquires and corrects itself in the midst of action. Modern science and professional education do not cultivate this kind of heightened awareness. To do so requires that we transform our basic assumptions about the relation of action and inquiry. We must learn to speak in such a way as to combine action and inquiry at the same time. This way of speaking will be clearly defined and illustrated in Chapter 1.

Proposition 2

Action inquiry requires the exercise of an unfamiliar type of power - transforming power. Transforming people's basic assumptions cannot be accomplished by force, diplomacy, or other traditional forms of power commonly used to influence external behaviour. These types of power are likely to generate conformity, dependency, or resistance, not transformation. Transforming power is a rare, little understood type of power that invites mutuality, seeks contradiction, and requires heightened awareness of the present. The exercise of transforming power makes everyone present (including the person exercising the power) vulnerable to transformation.

Developmental action inquiry can be sustained only if it begins to transform the way you as a manager (or parent, or team member) use power. If the current power possessors - the chief executive officer (CEO), the board of directors, and top management - say that they favour action inquiry, but they use power in unilateral or otherwise manipulative ways, they will generate resistance to an inquiring approach. If you yourself, whatever your position, say you favour inquiry, but use power in manipulative ways, you too will generate resistance. Only as executives engage in awareness-heightening inquiry in the midst of action, and use power differently, will action inquiry become a credible and effectual activity within their organisation.

Proposition 3

In order for an individual manager to transform his or her assumptions about power and working relationships to the point of truly and continually engaging in developmental action inquiry, the manager will very likely need to work through several personal developmental transformations. According to developmental measures of managers, which we will describe later, the typical manager is three step changes away from the stage where transforming power is fully understood and practised. Moreover, each personal transformation requires a minimum of two years, and some three to five years are usually spent consolidating one's competencies at the next stage before one begins to appreciate its limits and wish to grow beyond them.

Each of these three propositions alone, and certainly all three taken together, suggest why establishing developmental action inquiry within any given organisation will, realistically, require at least a decade. This may seem daunting or discouraging. The reader may well ask, "Are transformation and action inquiry really worth the effort?" We think the examples in this book of individuals who have begun to reap the rewards of personal and organisational transformation will help answer this question. Furthermore, developmental progress and its accompanying pay-offs, can begin in small ways immediately, as the following example shows.

Amy, a systems analyst in the Claims division of an insurance company, wanted to increase her personal effectiveness and her visibility to her managers with an aim to moving up to a managerial position. Although she approached the challenge of personal change very tentatively, she nonetheless approached it.

> My experiments were by no means a threat to my job, but were my way of beginning to dabble in the 'art' of action inquiry.

Amy served as a member of a committee developing new software and claims processing procedures for her division, Claims Processing. The committee's members included George, the vice-president of the division, her own manager, John, and senior managers from other divisions. She saw her position on the committee as an obvious opportunity to work on her developmental goal and set as a specific objective,

> to participate more fully in committee meetings by asking questions to clarify directives and my specific responsibilities, instead of waiting and assuming someone would let me know what tasks I should be doing.

She went on to describe this effort.

> The full committee has met only once in recent months. In that meeting, Property Division personnel felt we were ready to begin to use the new software with actual incoming claims. Some members of the Motor Insurance Division expressed concern that we had not tested the software and procedures enough. During this meeting, I attempted to ask questions and clarify the concerns of the Motor Insurance people. Being ingrained in the software development and the claims handling processes, it was difficult for me to understand their hesitation.

> In another meeting with George, John, and two other Property Division managers, we discussed claims handling procedures. The procedure manual had been written and reviewed, but George was not yet fully comfortable with it. Training for the first unit member

using the system and procedures was scheduled for the next week. In the meeting, many ideas about how to process newly assigned claims were laid on the table. I realised the ideas were all good ones and we needed to have the best possible procedures in place. But I was feeling very stressed during this discussion because training was due to start and we needed to make a decision about what procedure to follow. The procedure manual had to be ready for the training. I spoke up in the meeting stating that at some point this manual had to be finished, but that training and the start of handling live claims would help us find the areas which needed to be examined and redesigned.

The significance of these two examples is not obvious, but had these two meetings taken place three or more months ago, I would have acted differently. I would have kept quiet during the meetings and let my frustration increase. Later, I would have complained to someone else about how nothing ever gets done in meetings. Now I am willing to be more open and speak up. In doing this I am, hopefully, improving communications between myself and the people with whom I work. I may also be increasing my own job effectiveness by making sure I have resolved conflicts I feel exist.

This book will help the reader to understand and perhaps even to begin the developmental journey as Amy began it. We will illustrate the inquiry-in-action process with many more examples, some as humble as Amy's, some so strategic and artistic that they transformed whole lives and whole companies. Further, through exercises and guided journal writing, we will invite readers who are interested to enter into the inquiry-in-action process. We will begin with the focus on the individual manager, then expand it outward to teams, then to organisations, and, finally, to society and human living in general.

In Part One, we view the individual manager taking part in action inquiry. We offer, in Chapter 1, further evidence that organisational learning requires individual learning and mutual learning, and that the essence of action inquiry must be seen as the individual manager in action with others. Chapters 1 and 2 describe very concretely a way of acting with others that generates learning and is at the heart of personal development processes. Chapters 2 and 3 both contain exercises which offer you an opportunity to begin building your own action inquiry skills.

Part Two puts the spotlight on key personal development issues and offers a framework for understanding how personal development progresses. Chapter 4 explains through examples and exercises how adult personal development occurs in stages, or 'frames', each including a new orientation toward leadership. We show how the developing individual may move towards transformational leadership, that is, toward being an ongoing catalyst for one's own and others' development. The exercises are designed to help you recognise your own frame and learn to recognise others' frames. This is the starting point for setting a developmental course for yourself as well as for those with whom you work. In Chapter 5 we explore the first developmental frame - which we call Individualist – and which fits within a series of later frames described as 'post-conventional'. Chapter 6 focuses on one of these later developmental frames, one we call the 'Strategist' frame. We illustrate how 'Strategists' exercise transformational leadership that can generate organisation-wide action inquiry. Today, fewer than 10% of all managers measured operate from this 'Strategist' frame. But, significantly, 85% of those who are measured as acting from this frame are found in senior management positions. Through this book, we hope to encourage more managers to choose the developmental path that leads toward this and still later frames that further heighten one's awareness of what action may be timely when.

In Part Three we widen the scope, viewing action inquiry at the levels of groups and total organisations. In Chapter 7 we show how personal development relates to corresponding stages of group and organisation development. We discuss how business meetings may be managed with sensitivity to developmental process and describe two organisations that are making developmental transitions. In Chapter 8 we explore the transitions between organisational stages through a number of examples. Chapters 9 and 10 continue with a more penetrating look at one of these organisations as it makes a breakthrough to an advanced stage of development we refer to as 'Collaborative Inquiry' (which parallels the 'Strategist' stage).

In Part Four, we look beyond the experience of most people and organisations, to levels of development rarely reached, but we offer evidence that they can be. Chapter 11 explores the impact of the CEO's or MD's stage of development on the ability of organisations to transform themselves. Some tentative and powerful hypotheses are formulated. Chapter 12 continues and broadens our 'reach' toward higher quality experiences. We suggest components of 'the good life' implied by the understanding of personal and organisational transformation presented throughout the book. At the personal level Chapter 13 describes the next frame beyond 'Strategist', and offers glimpses of the kinds of action awareness and the potentials for transformational leadership that become possible at this level of development. Chapters 14 and 15 describe the ultimate stages of organisation development we call 'Foundational Community' and 'Liberating Disciplines'. Organisations operating through these 'action-logics' would integrate personal and social transformation as well as spiritual, political, and economic transformation. We picture such organisations through a look first at a real organisation that may be attaining that stage and then at a spiritual structure that may be operating at this latest stage.

Most of this book deals with increasing the effectiveness of managers and organisations. However, it should be clear from our introduction to Part Four that we believe action inquiry applies not just to a manager's work - not even primarily to work - but also to the total life experience of the person. And it applies not just to improving an organisation's quality in terms of its competitive position as an enterprise, but in terms of its co-operative enhancement of broader common goods. Understood this way, the aims of developmental action inquiry are broad, deep, and, as we have said, involve a lengthy journey. The starting point, however, is closer in and quite manageable. It is the individual's own thought and action here and now in the current moment. We invite the reader to begin examining with us this moment of action and in so doing to commence the journey.

CHAPTER 1

ACTION INQUIRY

By action inquiry we mean a kind of behaviour that is simultaneously inquiring and productive. It is behaviour that simultaneously learns about the developing situation, accomplishes whatever task appears to have priority, and invites a redefining of the task if necessary.

When truly practised, action inquiry enhances the actor's as well as the organisation's efficiency, effectiveness, and legitimacy by:

- weaving together acting and inquiring rather than separating them as does most managerial action, action inquiry can save you time and thus increase efficiency.

- making explicit and testing the appropriateness of your purposes, strategies, inferences, and outcomes, action inquiry results in correction of errors, increasing the immediate effectiveness of outcomes.

- testing and potentially redefining your own strategy, or the strategy of a group or an organisation, action inquiry generates long term effectiveness.

- making explicit and testing your own and others' purposes and visions, action inquiry develops increasingly shared corporate purposes and visions.

- redefining when current strategies are shown to contradict the vision, action inquiry increases the legitimacy and integrity of the enterprise to its members and clients. In this way, you also guard against being seduced into illegitimate enterprises, since a good test of legitimacy is whether you can make your vision or purpose explicit to other participants without hurting the chance to achieve it.

This kind of behaviour is not merely a set of technical tools, though we will treat it that way in the next chapter to provide guidelines so you can begin experimenting on your own. Instead, when used effectively, this approach generates a reframing of your entire foundation for, and aim when, working with others. The aims of work become not attaining preconceived objectives through unilateral manipulation, but rather:

1. Increasing your own and others' awareness of a shared mission

2. Increasing mutuality and internal commitment among the players both to specifically prioritised goals and to the continuing process of marrying action and inquiry

3. Increasing communication about *lack* of alignment of individual, group and corporate objectives and actions and about *lack* of validity of individual, group, organisational, and societal assumptions

4. Increasing action toward alignment between personal aims and actions and organisational mission and operations.

Thus action inquiry heightens your awareness of your own purposes and assumptions, of the quality of your conversation moment by moment with the other person or persons with whom you are meeting, and of how your action in the moment relates to group and corporate quality. The power of action inquiry is in its potential for linking personal quality improvement and quality improvement in the immediate conversation with quality improvement longer term in the work group and the wider organisation.

We feel the best way to begin to gain an appreciation of the potential of action inquiry is to see it in operation in the modest ways any of us might at first try. We will conclude this chapter with two examples, the first among many appearing throughout this book. Both represent 'first tries' at action inquiry by evening MBA students taking a course that invites them into an action inquiry process at work and in the course itself. In the first example Jennifer, whom we met earlier, takes action that breathes life into the quality improvement programme within her own small department - the programme which had fallen dormant because people could not understand why management wasn't 'telling them what to do'. In the second, Anthony, a staff member in a consulting firm, employs action inquiry in a way that sparks change across the entire top management of his organisation.

Jennifer's Experiment

Jennifer's department consists of four women. In addition to herself, Louise and Margaret report to the department manager, Donna. All four comprise the department's quality team, with Jennifer having been appointed by Donna as its 'team leader'. Jennifer gives her initial view of the quality project, dubbed the 'We Can Do It' project by her company:

> I will admit that I initially felt some resentment since I had no desire to be responsible for this project. Anyway, as team leader I had done a miserable job if you judged my performance by what actually got done, which was nothing. There are many reasons (excuses?) why nothing was accomplished: 1) Louise was out on short term disability, 2) our department is very busy, 3) it is very hard for us all to get together (Donna is out at least one day a week), 4) our department does not work well together at all (there are personality conflicts), 5) it is difficult to think of a process to improve which affects all of us in the department, and 6) I have no managerial responsibility. But it became extremely important to me to do something with this failure. Before I began to study action inquiry, I had just given up because I didn't know how to handle the conflicts that arose whenever I tried to make progress on the 'We Can Do It' project. It was easier to do nothing. I

was accustomed to doing individual projects I could have complete control over. But this project would force me to work on a 'team' and to take others' points of view into account.

Jennifer shows a willingness to jump in and try action inquiry in a situation that is not an easy one. She also shows an explicit desire not only to restart the quality programme but also to break out of her shell and develop her own teamwork capabilities. Thus she links her personal developmental effort to her departmental group's quality improvement effort, which is in turn a part of the total company's effort. She goes on to give her views of some further features of the situation she saw as important as well as her goals for her effort at action inquiry:

> Although my company has always been managed from the top down and change has been minimal, things could be starting to change. The fact that the company is trying to formulate alternatives to the current health insurance situation, given the government's attention to national healthcare, shows the company is trying to work with, instead of react to, the government in this major reform.

> I joined the department less than a year ago. Donna, who was also new, told me she had decided to change the way the department operated. She wanted to shift responsibilities around so that the other two members of the department could learn new things. The previous manager had never done this. Thus, not only was there a new member - myself - but everyone in the department ended up with new responsibilities. These facts led me to believe the department is assuming an experimental bent - starting to search for new ways of doing things...

> Donna treats each of us very individualistically. There is no real 'team' atmosphere in our department. Although none of our projects require that we work with other people in the department, I believe we would produce higher quality work if we knew what everyone was doing. I usually have no idea what anyone else is working on. I have also felt that Donna 'witholds' or does not share information with the rest of us. My hopes have been that with time this tendency would fade if she were shown an alternative method of managing the department...

> I knew this was the situation I wanted to deal with for my action inquiry project. It is a situation that encompasses the organisation, the department, all of my associates, and myself individually. It was a project that would help me with some of my current professional goals:
>
> 1. Increased 'visibility' to my supervisor, which includes taking initiative to go above and beyond the responsibilities of my job.
>
> 2. A better working relationship with both Louise and Margaret
>
> 3. Somehow getting Donna to share information she has about our sector of the company with the rest of the department.

We can see that Jennifer begins her action inquiry attempt with several foundation pieces in place. First, she views her situation as having several nested layers: the organisation's incipient struggle to become less bureaucratic, her department's need for teamwork, her manager Donna's start at trying to build the department's flexibility and versatility (juxtaposed with Donna's tendency to withhold information), and Jennifer's own professional objectives of visibility, upward influence, effectiveness as a team member, and her desire to rescue the quality improvement program along with her record as its leader. Secondly, Jennifer makes explicit, written statements of several of her objectives. Finally, she implicitly assumes that it is worthwhile to try changing patterns of behaviour even though they may be ones that are well established (her manager's and colleagues' reluctance to share information, her own reclusiveness, etc.). Building on these foundation elements, Jennifer begins her action inquiry experiment by going to talk with her manager, Donna.

> I went into her office and began by saying, "Remember that 'We Can Do It' project"? She kind of laughed and said she did. I went on to explain why I thought it had failed at first, but how I thought it would be a good idea for our department if we got together to discuss it. It would bring us together and get us working on something in a 'team' manner instead of how we usually did our work which is in a very 'individualistic' manner. I said I thought we could learn from each other working in this manner. I was taking a risk at this point because I didn't want to come across as criticising her management style, I just wanted to offer an additional way for our department to work. She didn't really show any reaction at this point.

> I went on to say I knew Louise would be very resistant to the idea. (She has a serious personality conflict with Margaret, which Donna is aware of.) I asked for her support in this project and to help me out if I came across serious conflict between Louise and Margaret. She assured me she would. I told Donna I planned to go to Louise and Margaret separately and remind them about this project and say I would really like to start it up again. I asked for her advice at this point - did she think it was a good idea? She thought it was. I went on and said I would ask them to think about it for a few days to see if they could come up with any ideas for a 'quality initiative', my thoughts being that if ideas came from them they would be more willing to work on them. I then asked her to do the same thing, except I prefaced this with the fact that I knew she was very busy on some task forces and if she knew of anything our department could help her with, this would be a great opportunity to do so. I felt it was important to frame this part of the conversation in this way. Working on her own is something Donna was and is very used to doing. She thought for a moment and said, "That's a good idea, I'll think about it". I left her office feeling as though I had accomplished some small feats - I got her support, encouragement, and also got her thinking about the possibility of sharing with the rest of the department what she is working on.

In this conversation, Jennifer makes conscious use of four specific elements of action inquiry. She *frames* the conversation at the start by referring to the 'We

Can Do It' project and her current view of it, making her agenda clear to Donna. She *advocates* by saying what her recommendations are. She *illustrates* by telling how she plans to proceed (e.g., go to Louise and Margaret separately). Finally, she *inquires* by asking Donna for her advice. In the next chapter, we will explain framing, advocating, illustrating and inquiring in more detail. Suffice it to say at this point that Jennifer's artful use of the technical tools of action inquiry in her conversation with Donna gets her effort off to a running start.

Next she goes to Louise and then to Margaret. She encounters the resistance she has expected from Louise, who doesn't want anything to do with Margaret. Jennifer persists, however, reminding Louise of their friendship, admitting she has failed with the quality improvement program up to now, and saying how much she wants it to be different this time. She continues that this would be a good way to get Donna to share information about what is going on. She finds that "this comeback worked, because she is very interested (as we all are) in what is happening in the company outside our department." In response to a request by Jennifer that she think of projects the group could work on, Louise agrees to do so. Then, over the next two days, Jennifer returns to remind Louise to think of things they can suggest at a meeting of the team. Louise comes up with the possibility of conducting a survey of field personnel, an idea Jennifer strongly supports and suggests that Louise bring up at the meeting.

Jennifer's meeting with Margaret goes smoothly. Jennifer begins the conversation with a few friendly pleasantries and then moves rather quickly to the business at hand, an approach she knows from past experience that Margaret finds comfortable. Margaret responds with enthusiasm to the idea of reviving the 'We Can Do It' team and agrees to be of help.

When Jennifer convenes the first meeting of the team she momentarily feels panic. She recalls how she has never really taken charge in previous meetings and they have not gone well. Things 'just happened'. Now she actually takes charge, but in a very special way that invites others to take charge as well:

> The day of the meeting finally came. This time I took a leadership role and reiterated the fact that I really wanted to do something on this project this time. I stated I was committed to this since senior management endorses the quality movement. I asked if anyone had ideas they wanted to share.
>
> Donna said she had been thinking about a variety of projects, but there was one in particular we would all be able to work on. She said we needed to look at our survey process. We all agreed this was certainly a good project to begin with. I then suggested we could split it up: Louise and I could look at the in-house process costs since Louise had dealt primarily with internal people, while Margaret and I could look at the outside vendor costs, since we were the ones who usually dealt with vendors. I made this suggestion because I knew Louise was not going to work with Margaret on anything. The reasons I suggested I work on both parts were because I was team leader and because this

would be a good way to work on my goals of creating more effective working relationships with Louise and Margaret.

I asked if anyone had other ideas. Louise made the suggestion she and I had discussed about conducting a survey of our field people. Both Donna and Margaret agreed this was a good idea. Donna suggested Louise and I make a draft of the survey, since we had never done a questionnaire ourselves, and then she and Louise would look at it and make comments, presenting an opportunity for us to become trained in survey design.

After this was decided, Donna said one of the task forces she was working on would need a monthly newsletter about managed care and other issues dealing with the healthcare question in Washington. She said she would talk to Louise later about her ideas. Margaret asked about the task force, noting that she produces a monthly newsletter for the field personnel and wondered how it might be affected. After I followed with some questions of my own about the task force, I think Donna realised we were all interested in these outside-the-department task forces she works on. To end the meeting, I suggested that we meet again when we had made definite progress on our separate projects so we could share with each other. I thanked them all for coming and for their commitment to the project.

I felt great about what had just taken place. By preparing everyone individually a few days before, I think people spent time thinking about what could be done. What I felt most optimistic about was Donna's sharing of information with us. This was really something new.

In the days that follow, Jennifer begins working collaboratively with both Louise and Margaret. Good progress is made in both cases. She finds working with Louise stressful at times, but she actively inquires into the stress in a way that leads to a still more profound learning:

One of the most difficult things to deal with is her unpredictable nature. I can never tell whether she will be willing to do something or not or what sets her off. I have noticed that she tends to have outbursts when she is unsure of herself. This realisation has helped me. I take a few seconds to think about how I will reply to an outburst. At another time, I might have yelled back, or just cut her out of a project and finished it myself. But now, it has also become clear to me that I cannot always be prepared in dealing with her and have to perfect my actions on a moment-by-moment basis.

The project continues to enable Jennifer to fulfill her goals of having more contact with Donna and increasing overall information sharing within the department:

Just keeping her up to date on our progress on each project gave me more opportunities, and I was more candid than I had been before in telling her about problems my associates and I were running into. I told her how I appreciated working with each of them because I was finding out what they were working on and learning new things. Donna said she was glad about this. I also told her I was glad she was telling us more about the things she was working on. Again she said that was good.

As an aside, although Louise and Margaret's interaction had not increased, they were both aware of what each other were working on because I had shared that information with them.

Jennifer comments in her report on her action inquiry project that she sees her efforts as having 'only just begun'. In writing this, she shows an understanding of something that is basic to action inquiry, namely that it is continual. They are processes, not monuments that once completed, keep sitting there. In this and other ways her description shows she is not just practising action inquiry as an external behaviour, but is experiencing it implicitly and internally as well. She marshals the inner courage to act on a previous failure. She thinks hard about her colleagues' internal, individual points of view, realising the importance of making her thinking clear to them and strengthening her personal relationships with them as a foundation on which to conduct the team meeting. She pays close attention to what she knows about their idiosyncrasies and adapts her approaches accordingly. She has her specific personal goals in mind while in action, as when she sets up the task assignments in a way that confirms her role as team leader while simultaneously developing her relationships with Louise and Margaret. She is beginning to experience one of the ultimate destinations of action inquiry, moment-to-moment awareness and experimental actions in the midst of ongoing situations. In addition, Jennifer helps others to realise internally the significance of incidents by summarising and explaining events to them, as when, at the end of the meeting, she thanks her team members for their commitment to the project, and when she ends her conversation with Donna by saying she is glad Donna is "telling us more about the things she was working on." Thus, in several ways, Jennifer illustrates what we mean when we say that action inquiry requires a special kind of 'on-line' awareness by the individual. Action inquiry has to happen from the inside out.

Jennifer's engagement in action inquiry has reinvigorated a quality improvement program within her department. Our second experimenter in action inquiry, Anthony, has an impact across the top management of his organisation.

Anthony's Experiment

Anthony sees his action inquiry project as an opportunity to try breaking out of a cocoon. As a benefits consultant in the Wheeling office of an international human resources consulting firm, he has for the past two years immersed himself in the narrowly specialised world of a very complex method for comparing company benefit programs for large corporate clients. He becomes one of the firm's few experts in this method, which fulfills his personal ambition to:

Do something unique to differentiate myself. There were very few people who worked with this system, so I was on my own much of the time. I enjoyed knowing that every new barrier I was crossing was separating me further and further from other young associates. However, at times my perfectionist nature would cause me physical and mental stress. I would find myself obsessing in minutiae in an effort to rationalise every last variation in my results.

The opportunity to break out presents itself in two ways. First, the organisation of the Wheeling office is a non-hierarchical one, with the office divided into 12 teams, each headed by a team coordinator, who report to the office manager. It allows Anthony ready access to the office manager and the team coordinators, who are the office's strategic management team. Second, Anthony sees a quality improvement opportunity. The team coordinators are plagued by a problem he feels he can help them address:

As an employee, I encounter shortcomings in a myriad of administrative functions such as billing, training, hiring and new employee initiation, career tracking, work allocation and performance review. Our team coordinators are supposed to oversee all this while simultaneously bringing in new clients and working with ongoing clients. The coordinators are constantly forced to juggle priorities amid tight time constraints. Clients, employees, and the coordinators themselves suffer severe consequences. I developed a plan to help ameliorate some of the team coordinators' problems.

In much the same way that Jennifer strategised and planned before talking with anyone about her project, Anthony develops a detailed set of steps he proposes to take with the team coordinators. First, he will meet with the office manager to discuss the project, and then meet briefly with each team coordinator to explain his proposed approach. Next, he will prepare questions for interviews and for a survey instrument and will administer both. After analysing the data, he will present feedback to the team coordinators at one of their monthly meetings. A collaboratively determined action plan will then be developed and implemented.

With this plan in mind, Anthony meets with Don, the office manager. Scheduled for half an hour, this meeting, as Anthony puts it, "blossomed into two hours of discussion about our team coordinator problems and how this project could help address them". An important clarification occurs in this meeting. Don suggests that Anthony should make recommendations to the team coordinators after collecting his data, but Anthony responds that he does not intend to recommend solutions, "but rather to facilitate a collaborative effort involving all of the team coordinators". A framework and timetable are established for the project. Anthony is pleasantly surprised with the success of this meeting.

Even with this initial meeting, I began to achieve several of my objectives. After overcoming my initial nervousness I settled into a productive give-and-take discussion with the highest-ranking person in our office. Comments and observations from each of us were given equal weighting. Several times I provided insights that enlightened Don about the perspectives of lower-level staff members. Throughout the course of this meeting, I realised that several of my objectives were beginning to take shape:

1. To differentiate myself from the average staff member
2. To increase my exposure to senior management
3. To purposely place myself in a high-risk situation
4. To force myself out of my own consulting specialty and into other service lines within our company
5. To improve my presentation and public speaking skills.

Anthony proceeds with the survey and interviews. After several further discussions with Don, he decides to survey the team coordinators explicitly on their responsibilities - which they should retain, which should be delegated to their team members, and which should be handled through a centralised office administration. As was the case with his earlier meeting with Don, Anthony is stimulated by these meetings, both in terms of the work accomplished and in terms of progress he is able to make in developing his action inquiry skills.

My follow-up discussions with the team coordinators were fantastic opportunities to experiment with my behaviour on a one-to-one basis. They were very willing to open up and discuss sensitive subjects and were also appreciative of my efforts to make their lives easier.

Each coordinator directs a given consulting specialty. I had to constantly be aware of how to frame questions, which areas to hone in on, which to tactfully sidestep. For instance, on several occasions, I drew a chart with 'market growth' and 'market penetration' on the two axes (the old star/dog/cash cow diagram). While talking with the coordinator of a health care team, I marked his team in the star category, and a defined benefit team in the dog category. Should the leaders of these two teams have the same set of responsibilities? Perhaps the health care coordinator should let expenses rise to permit getting more revenue, while the defined benefit coordinator should work on cutting costs to increase profit.

In any event, the chart proved to be a perfect arena for using my framing/advocating/illustrating/inquiring skills. You can't just tell a senior manager and expert who's been in the business 25 years that he should change his behaviour. But the components of action inquiry verbal behaviour came right out of me. "Let's talk about revenues and expenses for the next few minutes" (framing). "I don't think that two separate team coordinators should necessarily share the same focus regarding profit generation" (advocating). "Look here on this chart. See how the pension team is at the opposite end of the spectrum from the health care team" (illustrating)? "Would you have them focus on the same issues (inquiring)"? It was an opportunity to increase the team coordinators' awareness.

After completing this round of interviews and tabulating the survey results, Anthony arrives at the time for his presentation to the monthly meeting. When the day arrives, he is hit with an attack of stage fright.

> I was to wait at my desk and they would call me when it was time for my presentation. The minutes ticked by, I paced a while, read memos in my in-box, listened to my phone messages, and paced a little more. Finally, they called me in.
>
> I broke the ice a bit by saying I felt like a bachelor who had been waiting backstage on the Dating Game. I then began the meeting by framing what I intended to accomplish (following the standard public speaking guidelines – 'tell them what you're going to tell them, tell them, then tell them what you told them'). We then entered a lengthy and somewhat spirited discussion of a chart showing results of the team coordinator and team member surveys. I sensed that several coordinators interpreted the chart as saying that they weren't doing their jobs well. I quickly thought how I could rephrase my lead-in and then announced, "The shaded responsibilities are areas which stand to gain the most through refocused attention and delegation to other team members". They were more comfortable with this way of looking at it.
>
> The meeting lasted for over an hour and produced encouraging results. In terms of practising and enhancing my action inquiry skills, I could not have asked for a better forum. I was surrounded by every member of our senior management team, they all had a vested interest in the subject matter, there was a constant interchange of ideas and opinions, and I was leading the meeting. Add to that that each team coordinator represented a different service line and years of ingrained behaviour. We ultimately decided to pilot test a delegation of certain coordinator responsibilities to three teams. I am continuing to work with the office manager and the various teams as we move forward with this initiative.

Anthony's case shows that action inquiry at the senior management level shares certain features with action inquiry in a lower level work group like Jennifer's. Anthony's effort is one in which he sees malfunctions in the work setting and develops specific plans for bringing them to light. Then he sets the stage, testing and revising plans for improvement with the key people involved, building their support and at the same time developing personal rapport with them, much the same as Jennifer did with her department manager and her two associates.

Summary

Both Anthony and Jennifer begin a process of organisational transformation that depends not just on programmatic planning, but on putting into action a venture in personal development. Both decide to 'break out' of roles where they have acted more as individuals than as team members, and to 'break into' roles which require more on-line learning and more leadership of themselves and also influence better performance by others. Both are willing to take risks, cope with initial nervousness, and move into unfamiliar territory. Conversations embodying inquiry, mutual influence, and learning are at the heart of both of these successful efforts.

Jennifer and Anthony's cases show in practice the link between action inquiry, individual transformation, and organisational transformation. Through inquiry in action, both establish reciprocity between themselves and their organisation. Jennifer's actions (to help her associates gain more information about what is going on, and to help her boss to have a reduced workload) require a developmental 'break-out' by Jennifer. It promises as well to make her department a place that will keep her functioning at a higher level of personal effectiveness in the future. The same is probably true for Anthony, whose personal developmental surge shows others he is a person who can move the organisation.

You may have noticed an additional aspect of how both Jennifer and Anthony act. Neither of them has formal organisational authority to do what they do, and neither of them tries to force their proposals or opinions on others. Instead they gain authority through their way of working in the actual situation and their way of working is to exercise the power of disciplined vulnerability - the power of actively seeking through disciplined inquiry with others what is timely action now and what is best for the larger situation over the longer term. We will talk more about this power of disciplined vulnerability that characterises action inquiry as we continue.

We hope you, like Jennifer and Anthony are beginning to think about the possibility of 'breaking out'. Or, you may be looking for more evidence that it is worth the risk, or perhaps more specifics on how to begin the process. In the next chapter we will address these concerns by describing in a more complete, step by step manner than we have done thus far, the action process Jennifer and Anthony adopted that helped them increase their effectiveness. In short, we will provide you more fully with the tools of action inquiry. While doing so, we will also add more evidence that if you take the challenge of inquiring at the personal level, you will find the effort to be worthwhile.

CHAPTER 2

FUNDAMENTALS OF ACTION INQUIRY

In the first chapter Jennifer and Anthony made clear headway towards increasing their own effectiveness and that of their organisations by taking the risk of experimenting with what was for them a new way of engaging with other people in the course of their work: action inquiry. We hope these examples serve as encouragement to you to begin your own action inquiry in a tentative and testing fashion or in a bold headlong dive into new ways of thinking and taking action. The examples suggest that even if only one or a few persons in an organisation practice developmental action inquiry with regard to themselves and their immediate group, a process leading to organisational improvement may begin. Widespread commitment to and participation in personal and organisational development through action inquiry may be the eventual outcome, but it is not the necessary starting point.

Our point is that encouraging individuals to engage in constructive inquiry, awareness stretching, and self-initiated behaviour changes in the midst of on-going work is ultimately the key to personal and organisational improvement. It is, however, a difficult process to begin and to sustain, and one that can only be convincing if it begins, again and again, with one's own actions.

Why is developmental action inquiry so difficult to start up in oneself and to prompt in others? It is difficult to start up because the vast majority of people who are under the stress of having to perform in managerial or professional positions in organisations simplify their lives by encasing their awareness and thought within assumptions they do not test. Even those who operate in stress free environments follow habits of behaviour and thinking. In this chapter we will introduce you to the three fundamentals of developmental action inquiry that enable people to radically change their assumptions and habits. These are:

1. Widening our awareness
2. Personal systems inquiry
3. Improving the quality and effectiveness of our use of language

1. Widening our Awareness

In 1981, Kathleen Kenefick, a young lender for Continental Illinois Bank, wrote a memo to her superiors saying, "The status of the Oklahoma accounts (particularly Penn Square) is a cause for concern, and corrective action should be instigated quickly". In fact, corrective action was never instigated.

Kenefick's message was explained away in upper echelons as a personality conflict with her boss, and Kenefick left the company. A year later, regulators closed Penn Square, and Continental was left holding $1 billion in bad loans. Continental itself underwent a federally supported re-organisation in 1984.

Continental's upper management assumed that since Kenefick did not get along with her boss, her report was invalid. (Whether her conflict with her boss was fact or assumption, we don't know.) Higher management also assumed that a young staff member could not be correct in saying that such important loans, overseen by much more senior and experienced officers of the bank, were in danger when nobody else was saying so. Though her warning was factually true, it did not penetrate these assumptions.

Kenefick's communication to her superiors was by memo. But simplistic assumptions can prove impenetrable in face-to-face communication as well. In their book *Managing for Excellence*, David Bradford and Alan Cohen offer the following prototypical conversation between a manager and a subordinate. The manager is a good example of someone who is sealed within assumptions:

> Subordinate: We're having trouble delivering disposable widgets to Techcorp.
>
> Manager: But they're our most important customer. Have you talked with Dan in Production?
>
> Subordinate: Yes, but he says that yields are off because of poor material.
>
> Manager: He always uses that as an excuse. Have you checked the materials report?
>
> Subordinate: Yes, I've got it right here. I thought we ought to check.
>
> Manager: [interrupting] Look at that. The material quality is within 1.5% of our usual standard. That can't be the problem. Anyway, yields can be increased by reprocessing material on overtime shifts.
>
> Subordinate: That's right. We could use overtime.
>
> Manager: OK, here's what to do: Get Alice to go over and tell Dan to increase the percentage of alloy by 7% and decrease the time in the second-batch processing. In fact, never mind - I'll call Dan myself and explain that, along with how he can shift extra materials over to widget making. Then he won't have any excuse.

But material 1.5% below a minimum standard may be unsatisfactory to the client. And the other technical factors the manager addresses may have nothing to do with the real issue. Indeed, if the manager routinely deals with Dan as he proposes to do here - dismissively, distrustfully, leaving him without 'any excuse' - then the working relationship between the manager and Dan may itself be the larger problem. Preventing the manager from exploring these possibilities are assumptions such as: 'technical factors are the only ones worth considering', 'my own experience and current state of knowledge should be sufficient to solve this problem', 'peoples' options should be circumscribed so that they cannot give excuses', and 'this subordinate's options in particular, right now, should be circumscribed totally by me'. On the basis of these assumptions, the manager takes over the problem from the subordinate, diagnoses it personally and acts on it personally. The manager's assumptions are not tested in order to learn whether they are right or wrong; nor does the manager create an opportunity for the subordinate to learn. The way the manager speaks reinforces an attention narrowed within a single interpretation of the situation, and his certainty that he is simply dealing with reality itself prevents the assumptions on which that interpretation is based from being tested and modified.

The example of Kathleen Kenefick's superiors at Continental Bank may seem a bit extreme and obviously wrong (though they did not have our major advantage of hindsight).   But we expect that many readers may not immediately have noticed what was 'wrong' with the responses of the manager in the case of the widget delivery problem. This manager's response seem quite normal or typical, indeed it seems vigilant and responsible on first hearing. Most of us don't see how many assumptions we make and how much learning we inhibit by our typical responses.

But even if you, our reader, are willing to admit in a hypothetical way that you may be making assumptions of which you are unaware, you can argue that there is no way and no time for anybody to become aware of all their assumptions. "Things must be done", you say. "The market will not wait for us to become wise. Thus we cannot help but act on our assumptions at times".

You are right, of course. In fact, one way we learn about our false assumptions is to act on them without being aware that they are only assumptions until they prove themselves to be so through our inescapable failures. The later in life you wait to learn about your false assumptions, the bigger and more painful are these ultimate failures likely to be. They can result in lost jobs, injured organisations, divorce, or alienated children, to name just a few of life's tragedies when we learn too late.

It is true that we cannot become aware of all our assumptions and that we cannot help but act on assumptions at times. But it is also true that it is profoundly important to learn how to test assumptions in the midst of everyday actions. By doing so, we create a climate where others in the organisation become more aware that they too are making assumptions - where others become more willing to help us test our own assumptions (sometimes even before we are aware we are making them) - and where others gradually become more willing to test their own assumptions as well.

Not all assumptions will be tested, and not all those that are will be tested well. But many assumptions will be tested - will be tested quickly - and will generate learning, subsequent success and higher morale, rather than failure (and lower morale, without a subsequent chance to learn).

With sustained risk taking and ingenuity, an organisation can generate a culture in which not only high quality products and services are valued, but also high quality awareness that tests assumptions early. This would be a true learning organisation. No organisation can test every assumption and thereby altogether avoid the risk of failing to test problematic assumptions. But an organisation that cultivates courageous, intelligent, competent testing of assumptions will have an enormous competitive advantage over those in the same field that do not.

In the meantime, however, the more immediate question is how you, the reader, as an individual manager (and you do manage at least your own time and actions) can become more aware of, and less bound within, your implicit untested assumptions. The first step is to begin to recognise how limited our ordinary attention and awareness is and therefore how inadequate even our factual knowledge is of what is occurring at any moment in our lives - within us, around us, and beyond us. There are four reasons why this is true.

First, our attention simply does not register a great deal of what occurs. Reading this book, for example, you are likely to become oblivious for periods of time to sounds and other events in your environment, oblivious too to your own body position and breathing, oblivious even to the fact that this book is a physical object with size, weight, and texture as distinct from the cognitive meaning of the words and sentences. Being reminded of these facts now may momentarily jolt you into a widened awareness. But, you may simply shift your attention to the outside world territory from the cognitive territory, becoming transfixed, perhaps, with the view from the window, rather than widening it to include both.

A second limit to our attention on what is occurring at any moment is the very narrow cognitive-emotional interpretive net we apply to our perceptions. For example, most of us think in only one language and one mood at a time, without feeling how these patterns limit our awareness of what is occurring. Those of you who speak a second or third language quite well can try thinking about the same human issue - for example, a disagreement with a colleague or a member of your family - in each language. You will see that you think different thoughts and even discover different feelings as you talk to yourself about the issue in each different language. Others of you may be accustomed to imagining how a mentor you deeply respect might feel and act in the situation you are in, or even how the person you are facing feels. And you know that feeling the situation from these other points of view influences your own feeling about it.

A third limit of our attention is that, although our own actions generate much of the knowledge we receive from others and from the environment, we are rarely aware how our actions skew what we know. Let us say, for example, that in a bright and cheerful manner you regularly pop into co-workers' offices briefly to find out things you need to know, always careful not to bother them long.

You may not learn for years that they view you as constantly interrupting them and putting your agenda first, with the effect that they withhold significant information and oppose you much more than they otherwise might.

The simple fact is that we are rarely aware of our own behaviour and others' reactions as we act. Seeing and hearing yourself on videotape for the first time is often shocking. You had no idea of the gestures you were making in public, of the facial expressions, the tones of voice, the run-on sentences, and so forth. But seeing oneself on videotape is not at all the same as direct awareness of oneself as one acts. First efforts toward this awareness typically generate paralysing self-consciousness. How to cultivate an ongoing awareness of how one is acting is key to development, both personally and organisationally, and is itself an inquiry and a practice for a lifetime.

A fourth limit on our attention to what is occurring at any given moment in our lives is that the data we have about the outside world is ordinarily about the past, not the present, is drastically unsystematic and incomplete, and is rarely tested for validity on the spot. Even the best of scientific studies can never prove that a proposition is unequivocally and invariably true (that is, true for all moments, and thus true for the present moment as well). At best, scientific methods can unequivocally *dis*confirm a proposition. Again, because our knowledge in the moment is less than we need it to be, we rely on simplifying assumptions, as the executives at Continental Bank did and as the manager in the widget case did. Once rigidly formed, these assumptions can blind our awareness and inhibit the very inquiry that would reveal the assumptions.

The fact that our assumptions often veil us from what is going on means we need to test them frequently whenever our best intuition in the midst of an ongoing business situation suggests the need. Doing this testing means you begin to behave in a way that reveals the unknown, enabling you to make your actions more consistent with your intentions, exemplifying a pattern that helps others to improve, and inviting others by example to join in such testing. Even if you yourself are deeply engaged in a personal development process, you may well fail at encouraging others to engage in such a process. But you most certainly cannot successfully encourage improvement in anyone else unless you are deeply engaged in self-testing-and-improving yourself.

Once you increase your credibility as a practitioner of developmental action inquiry, you are more likely to be effective at inviting your immediate work associates to participate in a way that helps each of them to find his or her own motivation. And still later, with more practice, you can enter the rougher seas of inviting a wider sector of the organisation to participate in inquiring collaboratively. This practice is the subject of this chapter and the next three chapters.

2. Personal Systems Inquiry

In our lives, both personal and professional, we are involved in more or less continual mental and physical efforts to bring about a range of occurrences, events or situations. These may be described in a number of ways: intentions, goals, objectives, wants and desires are just a few. Today, for example, I have had many goals; to write more for this chapter, to exercise for a while, to spend time with my children, to book a dental appointment, to talk to a friend about something that recently has seemed off-beam in our friendship, and so on (there have been many such goals, just today, too many to list exhaustively). I may also describe myself as being involved in seeking to accomplish some things greater than the individual sum of my goals. These might be described as my purposes or life missions; for example, writing this book with my colleagues is part of my mission to reduce violence in the world. I believe the adoption of inquiring approaches will help to do just that. Spending time with my children feeds a deep desire to create a loving family environment. This in turn also feeds my mission of helping to create a non-violent world.

We have been describing a distinct territory of both human endeavour and awareness - that of intentionality, of consciously wishing and wanting to create or mould a particular circumstance or range of circumstances.   Although we can clothe intuitions of purpose in words, the intention itself is in a realm beyond words and is never completely captured by a particular set of words.

This trans-cognitive territory of intention is the first of four territories of experience. These territories are arenas in which we 'operate' in all aspects our daily lives. Everything we do can be identified as belonging to one or more of these territories. Table 2-1 identifies all four territories.

Table 2-1   Four Territories of Experience

First territory	Intentionality: purposes, aims, intuitions, attention, vision
Second territory	Planning: strategies, schemes, ploys, game plans
Third territory	Action: behaviour, skills, pattern of activity, deeds, performance
Fourth territory	Outcomes: assessments, results, events, observed behavioural consequences, environmental effects

The second territory includes both the explicit, cognitive strategies we develop to achieve desired ends and the implicit, emotional strategies we also exhibit, even though we may not be aware of them or be able to describe them. From one viewpoint, this second territory (of planning) can be seen to derive from the first (of intending) - first decide what you want, then plan how best to get it. But in fact, we often fail to exercise the quiet, meditative inquiry necessary to come to a clear and single-pointed sense of intent and we consequently hatch a plan of mixed intent. Returning to an earlier example; in order to raise the possibly tricky issue with my friend I need some strategies to make sure it goes well. I may plan how to set up an informal meeting (for example, I may choose to make the meeting 'accidental'). I may consider a range of possibilities for starting the conversation and choose one of these. But in what sense do I intend for this meeting to go well? Do I mean that my intent is to explore the apparent incongruity in our friendship from both our perspectives and try to resolve it? Or do I mean I want to assure that we avoid any further conflict (which may lead me not to be clear about the dilemma I am experiencing). You will notice that these first two territories (intentionality and planning) are 'armchair' territories. They require no physical movement at all - they can be conducted entirely by mental and intuitive activities (although certain activities, such as a conversation about my intent or plan with a friend whom I trust to confront any incongruities he or she hears can be enormously helpful).

The third and fourth territories, in contrast, are physical and visible. The third territory is that of action, activity and behaviour (e.g. the actual way I speak in a conversation). This is where the strategy or plan (however hastily conceived, perhaps only milliseconds before action) is turned into concrete behaviour. This is where we actually engage with the friend, write the memo, make the sale, pause to talk with a colleague, pluck up courage to challenge the boss, open the door for another person, push to the front of the queue, cook dinner, and so on. The action is in the action!

And all action (even inaction) has consequences! This is the fourth territory, the outside world where results, consequences, impacts and outcomes occur. Sometimes these are just as we'd imagined and hoped they might be. We cook a meal for a loved one to create an intimate atmosphere. It tastes and looks wonderful; she or he is delighted and it is a great evening. Other times it just doesn't flow - the soup is too salty, the vegetables overdone and the atmosphere prickly! Or perhaps you start that difficult conversation with a friend, hoping to be both supportive and inquiring. At your first word the friend explodes, telling you that you are so inconsiderate and insensitive, and expressing the desire to 'never-speak-to-you-again'! If your mode remains inquiring, a new round of action inquiry may open: How do I face this moment when my assumption that a quiet chat is in order is shattered? What do I do next?

The very essence of developmental action inquiry is to seek to heighten our own awareness, understanding and skillfulness in each of these four territories:

- Inquiry may lead us to understand more deeply our intentions and to be engaged in a continual refinement of these.

- Inquiry may help us to develop our capacity to make plans and strategies that both reflect our aspirations and the ever-changing circumstances in which these aspirations are framed.

- Inquiry may enable us to see the skillfulness and unskillfulness of our actions and enable us to develop ever more skilful behaviour

- Inquiry may enable us to raise our awareness about the impact of our actions and other subtle and non-subtle changes around us from other sources

- Inquiry may enable us to witness the interplay among all four territories of experience, eventually enabling us to refine any territory in the very moment of action.

Figure 2.1 shows the four territories and three types of inquiry (single-loop, double-loop and triple-loop reflection) which link the four territories. The framework is illustrated by the case of Peter, a Chief Accountant, and his engagement with improving aspects of his relationship with his boss, the Finance Director.

Figure 2.1 Peter's Single-loop, Double-loop, and Triple-loop Inquiry Across Four Territories of Experience

Peter is not enjoying a good relationship with his manager, and determines to improve it. He imagines a relationship without the overly critical tensions between himself and his manager.

VISIONING

He formulates a plan to be less critical of his manger and to be more open in the work he is doing for her.

STRATEGISING

Each day he reminds himself of the need to be less critical of her and restrains himself. He makes every effort to keep her up to date on his work (he books time with her each week).

PERFORMING

After a few weeks of persisting with this behaviour and keeping his vision in mind he notices, sadly, that nothing has changed in the way she treats him. The tension continues and to make things worse Peter now feels badly treated.

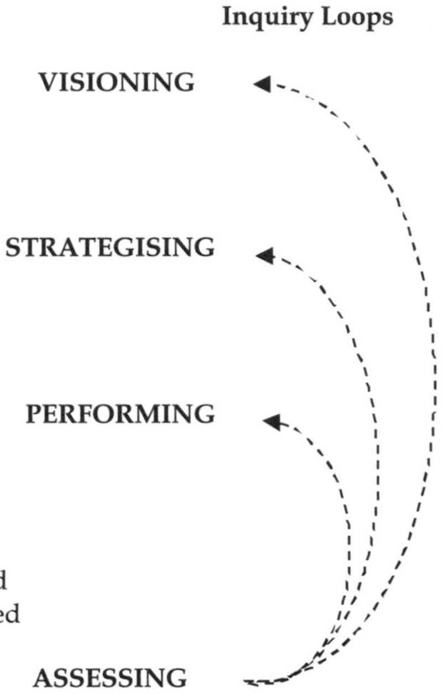

ASSESSING

Inquiry Loops

Peter's vision (an improved relationship with his boss) was not achieved through his strategy and actions. In the example the situation continued to deteriorate despite his efforts. This happens! To be uninquiring would be to give up on the vision without further thought or to keep plugging away at it. So he reflected, using the three loops which connect the territories. Was his vision of an improved relationship appropriate and attainable? How might he wish to change his vision, if at all? Were his strategies of being less critical and more open about his work sound? How might he wish to change these (if at all)? Were his actions of self-disciplined restraint and openness appropriately timed and skillfully executed? With increased attention to himself and the situation, could his efforts have been more adept? What subtle or brash change in behaviour might have created a different impact?

If Peter inquired in an open and vulnerable way he may have decided to change the content of any territory, that is, he may have changed one or more of his visions, his strategies or his actions. Any change would lead to different behaviour with the high likelihood of different outcomes. His inquiry would be deeply developmental if he were able to penetrate his assumptions, fixed patterns of belief and habits so that he would not only learn about improving the relationship with his boss, but also about himself.   He would be truly practising developmental action inquiry if were able to enter these inquiring loops not only as an after-the-fact reflection but in the very moments of intuiting the vision, thinking about the strategy, and taking the action. One of Peter's developmental challenges is to be able, moment to moment, to move between the four territories of experience, among his visions, strategies, actions and outcomes so as to continually modify and align them - leading to more effective action and greater self knowledge.

A stretching, but not impossible intent. Could one of your own intents be to increasingly practice developmental action inquiry in your life? If so what would your strategies be?

An Exercise in Improving The Quality of Your Own Action

Think of some situation at work that has been bothering you, or that you have been actively involved in trying to change or develop. Choose something where you have yet to achieve your goals, where your efforts seem to be frustrated. Choose something discreet such as improving a relationship, trying to get a new process introduced or an old one dropped, trying to create a new product or marketing approach. Avoid something large like 'improving the culture here'. Make this something of some significance for you - a situation that matters enough to you to make it well worth your while to figure out how you can get a better outcome. Now, jot down the details of what has happened so far.

The incident:

1.   Briefly describe the circumstances surrounding the situation you are thinking of:

2.   What are your goals or intentions in this situation?

3.   What strategies have you been pursuing?

4.   What actions have you taken? Describe these in some detail. What results, if any, have arisen?

Quite possibly your story to yourself about the incident is that the unsatisfactory outcome was someone else's fault, or the result of cumbersome or inappropriate organisational procedures, such as a meeting format that doesn't allow people to get at the real issues. And you may be perfectly correct in the culprit you have chosen.

However, this way of telling the story gives you no direct control over improving the quality of the outcome. The only way you can directly improve the quality of outcomes in any situation is for you to act more effectively than you did in the incident you are remembering. This does not mean, of course, that you were solely or even mainly responsible for the original unsatisfactory outcome. You may indeed have been the most constructive actor present. And it may be that the way you can act even more effectively is to learn how to speak in a way that gets 'the culprit' to change.

In other words, you can either wring your hands and blame the culprits in any negative situation, or you can ask yourself what you can do to improve it. To do this thoroughly, you must inquire into each of the four territories illustrated in Table 2-1. This will be a disciplined, vulnerable inquiry into your own intentions, plans and actions. And this inquiry may lead you to see differently what part you have played in the situation being as it is today.

First inquiry loop - your actions and behaviours
How skillful were your actions and behaviours? Can you identify the critical points at which you have intervened in the situation - could you be more skillful? If so, just how would you change your behaviour?

Second Inquiry Loop - your plans and strategies
In hindsight do your plans and strategies make sense - if skillfully carried out did they have a chance of success? Could you change them in either a minor or profound way to get a better outcome?

Third inquiry loop - your intentions and purposes
Given what happened (the outcome), how do your original intentions now look? Were they realistic, do you want to clarify, adapt, give up on, or continue to pursue them?

As you engage in inquiry about your actions, strategies and intentions you may come to a clear realisation about what you need to change. This may be within any territory. For example you may identify that you behaved unskillfully in a meeting, perhaps being rather dogmatic; simply changing this behaviour may be enough to bring a different, more agreeable outcome. On the other hand you may now consider that your original intention was not grounded in reality or was so limited to your own perspective that it did not include a sense of why others would also benefit. If your sense of your own intent changes, then your strategies and actions will also need to change.

This inquiring engagement in the four territories of experience is the very core of developmental action inquiry. By inquiring in this way you may come to understand yourself better and to improve the quality of your goals, plans and behaviour. You may improve your effectiveness. We come to see more clearly the interplay between these territories as we operate them - to see ourselves more holistically. Over time and with practice this inquiry becomes not just a reflective, after-the-event process but becomes a silent listening in the very moments of planning and action. But more on this 'moment-to-moment' awareness later.

3. Improving the Quality and Effectiveness of Our Use of Language

Speaking is the primary and most influential medium of action in the human universe - in business, in school, among parents and children, and between lovers. Our claim is that speaking based on silent listening into the four territories is the secret of conscious social life. The four parts of speech, which we will shortly introduce, represent the very atoms of human action. If we can cultivate an awareness that penetrates our own actions, allowing us to arrange and rearrange the interweaving of these atoms as we speak, we will have peacefully harnessed the human equivalent of nuclear power.

During this industrial age, we have become technically powerful, but have not cultivated our powers of speech. People who speak of moving from talk to action are apparently blind to the fact that talk is the essence of action (and they probably talk relatively ineffectively). We are in fact deeply influenced by how one another talks. The very best managers often have an intuitive appreciation for much of what we are now saying and have semi-intentionally cultivated an art of speaking. However, most of us are rarely aware of how much we are influenced by the nuclear dynamics of conversational action. Instead of attending to the dynamic process of conversation, we focus all of our deliberate attention on the passive content of the conversation.

Now, let us suggest four simple categories related to each of the four territories of experience, into which all speech acts can be divided. You can apply these categories to what each person in the conversation is saying, but particularly to your own speaking. Our claim is that your speaking will be increasingly effective as you increasingly balance and integrate these four 'parts of speech' by listening more actively into the four territories. In other words, if you find that one or two of these types of speech dominate your speaking, the recommendation is to try adding more of the other types. You can then test these claims by your own conversational experiments.

The four 'parts of speech' are called **framing, advocating, illustrating,** and **inquiring**.

Framing refers to explicitly stating what the purpose is for the present occasion, what the dilemma is that you are trying to resolve, what assumptions you think are shared or not shared (but need to be tested out loud to be sure). This is the element of speaking most often missing from conversations and meetings. The leader or initiator assumes the others know and share the overall objective. Explicit framing (or reframing, if the conversation appears off-track) is useful precisely because the assumption of a shared frame is frequently untrue. When people have to guess at the frame, they frequently guess wrong and they often impute negative, manipulative motives ('What's he getting at'?)

For example, instead of starting out right away with the first item of the meeting, the leader can provide and test an explicit frame: "We're about halfway through to our final deadline and we've gathered a lot of information and shared different approaches, but we haven't yet made a single decision. To me, the most important thing we can do today is agree on something, make at least one decision we can feel good about. I think XYZ is our best chance, so I want to start with that. Do you all agree with this assessment, or do you have other candidates for what it's most important to do today"?

Advocating refers to explicitly asserting an option, perception, feeling, or proposal for action in relatively abstract terms (e.g., 'We've got to get shipments out faster'). Some people speak almost entirely in terms of advocacy; others rarely advocate at all. Either extreme - only advocating or never advocating - is likely to be relatively ineffective. For example, 'Do you have an extra pen?' is not an explicit advocacy, but an inquiry. The person you are asking may truthfully say, 'No' and turn away. On the other hand, if you say 'I need a pen (advocacy). Do you have an extra one (inquiry)?' the other is more likely to say something like, 'No, but there's a whole box in the secretary's office'.

The most difficult type of advocacy for most people to make effectively is an advocacy about how we feel - especially how we feel about what is occurring right now. This is difficult partly because we ourselves are often only partially aware of how we feel; also, we are reluctant to become vulnerable; furthermore, social norms against generating potential embarrassment can make current feelings seem undiscussable. For all these reasons, feelings usually enter conversations only when they have become so strong that they burst in, and then they are likely to be offered in a way that harshly evaluates others ('Damn it, will you loudmouths shut up!'). This way of advocating feelings is usually very ineffective, however, because it invites defensiveness. By contrast, a vulnerable description is more likely to invite honest sharing by others ('I'm feeling frustrated and shut out by the machine-gun pace of this conversation and I don't see it getting us to agreement'.)

Illustrating involves telling a bit of a concrete story that puts meat on the bones of the advocacy and thereby orients and motivates others more clearly. (E.g., 'We've got to get shipments out faster (advocacy). Jake Tarn, our biggest client, has got a rush order of his own, and he needs our parts before the end of the week (illustration)'. The illustration suggests an entirely different mission and strategy than might have been inferred from the advocacy alone. The advocacy alone may be taken as a criticism of the subordinate or another department and may unleash a yearlong system-wide change, when the real target was intended to be much more specific and near-term. However, an illustration without an advocacy has no directionality to it at all.

You may be convinced that your advocacy contains one and only one implication for action, and that your subordinate or peer is at fault for misunderstanding. But in this case, it is your conviction that is a colossal metaphysical mistake. Implications are by their very nature inexhaustible. There is never one and only one implication or interpretation of an action. That is why it is so important to be explicit about each of the four parts of speech and to interweave them sequentially, if we wish to increase our reliability in achieving shared purposes.

Inquiring, obviously, involves questioning others, in order to learn something from them. In principle, the simplest thing in the world; in practice, one of the most difficult things to do effectively. Why? One reason is that we often inquire rhetorically, as we just did. We don't give the other the opportunity to respond; or we suggest by our tone that we don't really want a TRUE answer. 'How are you?' we say dozens of times each day, not wanting, really, to know. 'You agree, don't you?' we say, making it clear what answer we want.

A second reason why it is difficult to inquire effectively is that an inquiry is much less likely to be effective if it is not preceded by framing, advocacy, and illustration. Naked inquiry often causes the other to wonder what frame, advocacy, and illustration are implied and to respond carefully and defensively (e.g., 'How much inventory do we have on hand?' 'Hmm, he's trying to build a case for reducing our manpower').

Inquiring into your own speech patterns

This section is aimed at helping you to understand how you have used the four parts of speech in a recent conversation, or how you may use them in a conversation that you anticipate may be difficult. You may wish to continue working with the situation you reflected on earlier in this chapter, or you may wish to choose a diffe rent one.

Step I
Describe a situation in which you engaged in a difficult conversation with someone or some group. Perhaps you were trying to secure a particular outcome and they were resisting or perhaps you were jointly trying to make a decision and the process just wasn't working:

Step II
Secondly, we suggest you make some brief notes reconstructing the conversation(s) at what you take to be the critical moment(s) of the incident you just outlined. You probably won't be able to remember word for word what you and the other(s) said, but come as close as you can.

I said: (S)he or they said:

And so on.

Step III

Now, look back at your four conversational actions and try to categorise which of the four parts of speech you used and in what sequence. Are there one or two parts of speech that you regularly omitted from your statements? Do each of your comments interweave two or more parts of speech, or does a given comment usually only represent one of speech?

Step IV

Are you beginning to see ways you might have acted differently and more effectively? Can you think of ways of speaking what for you are in fact the central issues, but in a gently assertive and inquiring way rather than in an accusatory, evaluative, self-righteous way? What about those things you would 'really like' to have said, but would never actually dare say? What about the last thing in the world you would ever say (stated in a revealing, descriptive way, rather than a blaming, evaluative way)?

Does this entire exercise seem incredibly trivial to you? Does the whole issue of how you sculpt comments seem like a super-psycho-analytical academic game that no one in management could possibly take time to attend to on a daily basis? The four parts of speech may seem trivial to you because they provide virtually no unilateral, technical power to get results. Indeed, using them to tell the truth and make ourselves vulnerable is deeply threatening to whatever momentum we have developed (or imagine we have developed) in manipulating situations unilaterally. A large part of each of us does not want our momentum interrupted. Therefore, we are hesitant to try a true framing, advocacy, illustration, and inquiry approach because speaking like that may call forth true responses that interrupt our momentum and disconfirm our happy dreams.

We will not succeed in framing, advocating, illustrating, and inquiring effectively until we strongly and sincerely want to be aware of ourselves in action in the present - what our true frame/advocacy/illustration/inquiry is right now. Nor will we succeed in framing, advocating, illustrating, and inquiring effectively until we strongly and sincerely want to know the true response, *especially* when it *dis*confirms our current frame, advocacy, and illustration - until we truly value mutual influence in the service of timely action for a common good. We have to feel in our bones that only actions based on truth are good for us, for others, and for our organisations. Developing that feeling is a lifetime journey in its own right.

Not only must we really wish to know the truth, but also we need to act/inquire in a way that also convinces the other person(s) that we wish to be disconfirmed. Why? Because people generally are reluctant to disconfirm another person's frame, advocacy or illustration. To do so directly is often thought of as rude - as making the other 'lose face'. The more sensitive the question, the more important it is to go so far as to illustrate why it is important to you to hear a disconfirming response if that is in fact the true response.

Transforming a Conversation

To illustrate how the awareness/mutuality/alignment 'game' can be played in a risky situation, we offer an example from an actual business situation. The risk is very real to Jane, the key player in the example, who is a new member of one of her bank's lending groups. Like Jennifer and Anthony in the previous chapter, Jane has been schooled in the concepts of action inquiry and is seeking opportunities to experiment with it.

Having emerged from her bank's training programme, Jane is invited to join one of the bank's commercial lending groups. As is common, Jane is initially assigned to visit ten small companies where there is little business potential. In this way, the neophyte lender can practice her presentation skills and begin to learn what questions to ask, at virtually no risk to the bank's business. This procedure also permits the bank to test the new lender's ability to persevere through a string of frustratingly ambiguous and unrewarding experiences.

Jane aggressively calls all ten potential accounts the first day. From the very first instant, she finds herself faced with a choice between giving up on a potential account, persevering unimaginatively, or inventing some ingenious way of gathering information about, and better access to, any given company.

Because self-study exercises have shown her that she too easily gives up on relationships when she hears the first hint of a no, and because she has also learned that simple doggedness frequently courts further rejection, Jane now makes use of a variety of resources (such as customers of the companies and other officers of the bank) to seek access to her potential clients.

Most bank training programmes advocate creative selling of this kind. However, the lesson often does not take because the training programme has not helped individual trainees to see what blocks them from creative selling (for example, their assumptions about the adequacy of their own current knowledge and their assumptions about the extent of commitments that must be made to obtain useful new knowledge).

Ultimately, Jane visits nine of the ten companies, and eight are 'dry wells'. But to her surprise, the ninth is considering borrowing a million dollars for a major expansion. However, the company is already negotiating with another bank and expects to hear its terms within a week. Undaunted, Jane uses her bank's latest financial database (with the enthusiastic support of the MIS staff because she is the first lender to approach rather than avoid them after their offer to show lenders how to use it). Her first victory is to deliver her analysis, proposal and terms to the company on the same day as her competitor.

She calls the next day and learns both banks have offered exactly the same terms on the loan, leaving the company president in a quandary. He explains that he feels a commitment to the other bank, but is impressed by her turn-around time and the implications that may have for the future quality of her service. On the other hand, he is not so naive that he cannot imagine a change in her motivation once the sale is made. Jane asks whether the president would like to meet to discuss these issues, but he says he must make up his own mind. Two days later, Jane calls again to learn the president's final decision. He says he remains uncertain about the various legal implications of the loan. At this point, she strongly urges him to meet with her at the bank, where she can call in one of the bank's lawyers to help them if necessary.

The meeting at the bank is a prolonged one. The president anxiously asks for clarification of each legal term in the bank's standard agreement. After consulting with the lawyer for some time without achieving any sense of resolution, Jane begins to doubt whether the president will take either loan. The increasing frustration of circling and re-circling through the morass of technicalities reminds her of similar situations in previous group projects when she learned that someone can sometimes break the vicious circle by disclosing one's perception of what is happening, in a non-accusatory, inquiring way.

At this point, action inquiry ceases to be an exercise done on paper or with a supportive mentor and becomes, suddenly, a risk she can choose to take now. Heart very much in mouth, Jane interrupts the flow of conversation to say, "Can we stop and change tracks for just a minute? I'm feeling increasingly frustrated by our conversation because I sense it's not resolving your real concerns. Instead, we both seem to be growing increasingly anxious. This is the bank's standard agreement form. It's important for our ongoing relationships with our clients, as well as our general reputation in the community, that we write the agreement in a way that maximally protects both parties. It is in my interest to make sure that you are satisfied and not deceived, so that we feel that we are working together and can possibly develop an ongoing business relationship. But it seems to me that you don't believe any of that right now, or don't trust me. Is this true? Am I doing something that blocks your confidence in me? Or, if not, can you tell me what you are seeing as the real issue right now?"

With this, the president confesses that he has never before taken a major bank loan, and that the legal language highlights his fear that he will lose the business he has founded and nurtured to forces that are beyond his capacity to control.

The two discuss the dangers, difficulties, and opportunities that always attend the moment when an enterprise grows beyond the single-handed control of the founder. They also explicitly discuss their shared purpose for the first time - how doing the loan benefits both of them.

If you, the reader, are assessing Jane's performance in this meeting with an eye to the concepts we have been discussing in this chapter, you are very likely concluding that it exemplifies action inquiry, and we strongly agree. She uses all four of the 'parts of speech' and frequently interweaves two or more of them. She very carefully and clearly expresses that she wants to reframe the conversation ("Can we stop and change tracks for a minute?"), and she continues her framing of the situation by stating the dilemma: her view that the conversation is not satisfying the president's real concerns. She further frames while weaving in advocacy by adding that she wants to satisfy him and work together, but that the bank's standard agreement form nevertheless is important to discuss. She advocates (and illustrates) by expressing her increasing feeling of frustration. By referring to the bank's standard agreement form and by stating her 'interest', as a representative of the bank, in developing an ongoing business relationship, she uses the bank's practices and her role as bank representative as illustrations to legitimise the line of effort she is pursuing in the conversation. Next, Jane advocates an inference she is making ("... it seems to me you don't believe any of that right now, or don't trust me..."), and immediately tests her inference with an inquiry, asking the president to say whether he trusts her and/or what he sees as the real issue. Because she makes herself vulnerable to whatever his answer may be, rather than guiding him toward an answer, her inquiry is likely to elicit a genuine response, not just a particular answer that Jane may want to hear.

Jane takes the risk of exposing an assumption in order to test it. It could have offended the president to be told that he appeared untrusting. Furthermore, she takes the risk of possibly heightening tensions when she interrupts the flow of the meeting as she did. She also takes the risk of hearing something unpleasant about herself. However, her willingness to take these risks yields important learning as the president tells her about his fear of losing control of his business. Her willingness to test her assumption serves to invite the president into the learning process as well, and he responds by participating in a discussion that produces new information of value to him as well as to Jane.

Or are these risks so obvious? From one perspective, they can all be written off as training in this case - a cost, to be sure, but a necessary one rather than an avoidable one. Furthermore, the risk Jane takes in interrupting may in fact be smaller than the risk of continuing the conversation without interruption. Most managers who go very far in self-study find that they systematically overestimate the risks of acting differently in situations, computing all the possible costs but not the benefits. Conversely, they systematically underestimate the risks of acting habitually, computing all the possible benefits and blaming others for any costs.

Another less visible cost in this case - but one which seems too high for many managers and prevents them from emulating Jane - is that she had to give up some basic assumptions she held in order to interrupt the legal conversation with the president as she does. In a letter to her former instructor on the MBA course where she was trained in action inquiry, Jane describes her most basic assumption as having been that "the deal hinges on reason alone". From this assumption flows a series of corollaries, such as 'trust is irrelevant', 'the legalese will be accepted as soon as it's explained', and 'negotiating an agreement is a deductive process of finding the correct path to a desired solution'. Jane found in retrospect that these underlying assumptions all appear to have been illusions.

So much for the costs. How about the benefits? The president decided to do business with Jane the next day. She thereby gained the visibility of having made a large commercial loan even before being appointed a company officer. Eighteen months later, one of the eight 'dry wells' took an initiative to contact her and shortly transformed into a 'gusher'. Another six months later, she became the first member of the group of commercial lenders who had joined the bank at the same time to receive a major promotion.

In this case, we see a manager seeking to act efficiently, effectively, and legitimately all at once, ultimately employing action inquiry to restructure a degenerating situation and achieve her aims. At the outset, her use of computer software along with plain hard work enables Jane to produce an analysis and loan proposal in less time than her competitor. Her recognition that she is marketing a service to a client, not merely a logically correct financial analysis, results next in an effective series of initiatives toward the client after submission of the proposal.

Finally, we see in Jane's comments to the company president, in the midst of their meeting about the legal implications of the loan agreement, how deeply she is attuned to generating long-term success and legitimacy. In the first place, she defines her own and the bank's entire interest in terms of establishing mutually beneficial, long term, trusting relationships with clients. In the second place, she convincingly demonstrates that this is not mere rhetoric by interrupting her own attempt to persuade the president that the legal language is technically appropriate, in order to ask him whether in fact he has doubts about the ultimate legitimacy or wisdom of the loan. By engaging in a shared inquiry into the purpose and possible effects of the loan, Jane and the president create the very sense of mutual learning, mutual trust, and mutual benefit that was missing earlier. In general, a business negotiation becomes increasingly legitimate to all the parties involved as the negotiation itself is shown to be open to inspection, controllable, and aimed at benefiting all, the parties. We submit that quality management in any organisation aims too low if it does not aim at increased legitimacy.

Obviously, not every business transaction requires such a fundamental and explicit exploration of legitimacy. The manager must sense when the issue of legitimacy is really at stake and must learn how to address it when it does arise so that the very actions taken in addressing it themselves generate legitimacy. The problem is that too few managers today appreciate the practical importance of the issue of legitimacy, and too few schools of management and organisations generate the kinds of rehearsals that teach aspiring managers and practising managers how to address the issue of legitimacy effectively in everyday business transactions.

Action Inquiry, Rehearsal, and Personal Development

In your own responses to the action inquiry exercise earlier in this chapter, you 'rehearsed' an incident after the fact. The case of Jane implicitly involved numerous rehearsals before the crucial meeting with the company president. Rehearsals in an atmosphere of inquiry, both before and after significant incidents at work, are essential to a lifelong professional commitment to action leading to quality improvement.

But the unique and essential feature of action inquiry is that 'rehearsal' and 'performance' blend into one another until they become simultaneous. The right kind of rehearsal does not replace questioning and uncertainty with answers and certainty. The ultimate performance at the conclusion of all one's rehearsals is not a polished answer but a more appropriate and penetrating inquiry.

Rehearsal and performance blend into each other at the other end of the spectrum as well. Not even the earliest rehearsals can be entirely safe. Not even the earliest rehearsals can be entirely protected from real-life consequences. For at each rehearsal that is at all effectual, one's self-image is at stake. Illusions of which one was not even aware may be exposed.

Thus, there is a performance aspect even to your own after-the-fact reflections as you wrote, or even thought about writing, the exercise earlier in this chapter. Your reflection can be viewed as a performance. You had to decide what incident to write about. You took the risk of learning something less than complimentary about yourself either from the writing itself or from the inevitable comparison you knew you would be making between what you wrote and what you would then find in the remainder of this chapter. You took the risk of deciding how you could experiment with new ways of speaking in the incident you chose. Perhaps you chose a relatively 'safe' incident - one where you had already used some of the action inquiry 'parts of speech'. Or perhaps you chose an incident in which your written experiment with action inquiry necessarily produced speech that strongly disconfirmed the speech you actually used in the original situation, realising that if you chose a 'safe' incident, your learning would almost certainly prove less effectual, less potent, and less meaningful.

Next, you may choose to take the risk of trying to interweave framing, advocacy, illustration, and inquiry in new ways in an on-the-job conversation.

Ultimately, the sense of simultaneous rehearsal and performance in action inquiry introduces the manager to a new quality of awareness - to a continuous, silent, impartial observing of your own performance amidst others.

CHAPTER 3

PRACTISING ACTION INQUIRY AT WORK

Reading about action inquiry is not doing action inquiry. You have read about action inquiry in the previous chapters. In this chapter, we invite you to begin practising action inquiry.

Let us be clear, first, that the exercises in the previous chapter were not full action inquiry exercises. They were reflective inquiry exercises about action inquiry. We invited you to reflect about how you and others speak and to categorise statements as some one or combination of 'framing', 'advocating', 'illustrating' and 'inquiring'. Only if you have, since reading Chapter 2, taken those ideas into action with you at work or at home; and only if you have remembered them as you were speaking and listening to others; and only if, after observing the conversation, as it was occurring *through* these ideas, you have changed how you were speaking during the ongoing conversation; only if you have done all this, have you already begun to engage in action inquiry.

Indeed, if you have continued reading right on from Chapter 2, we recommend you stop here. Turn off your bedside or office light for five minutes while you meditate on an occasion when you can try these ideas. Sketch out on a piece of paper how you can frame, advocate, illustrate, and inquire before you continue into this chapter. Commit to a time to enact an experiment somewhat as you have sketched it. Everything we say from here on in will gain a much richer meaning for you if it enters a conversation not just with your mind as you read, but also with your mind, your feelings, and your body as you act.

If you have already begun to practice action inquiry, you have almost certainly noticed one of its primary attributes - that it initially seems scary. One's heart has a disturbing tendency to jump into one's mouth as one approaches the moment of actually experimenting in a real-time situation with intentionally-and-awaredly-different action. For example, you may imagine all the worst possible outcomes of speaking in this new way. Or you may feel that your face is flushing and that others must be able to sense your self-consciousness and discomfort.

Once you have spoken differently in an experimental way, you may become unusually self-critical: "Oh no! That didn't sound right. Not what I meant to say - and my voice cracked". Moreover, others may respond in a totally unanticipated way, leaving you confused and depressed about what to say next. (It takes quite a lot of practice before one becomes adept at responding with action inquiry to whatever is said).

Why does practising action inquiry generate fear and all these other negative feelings? Practising action inquiry brings us into contact with our fear because action inquiry is never entirely safe. Action inquiry is inherently risky because it is played in real time with real relationships. It is risky because it is played in relation to one's own awareness and to the unknown; it therefore introduces us - sometimes gradually, sometimes suddenly - to alien experiences. (If we think about horror films such as *Alien* or about ethnic wars, we can become aware just how much fear we project onto the alien).

Action inquiry is also risky because it usually sacrifices unilateral control over outcomes in favour of openness to the influence of others, as well as decisions to which the parties are mutually and internally committed. Still another reason why action inquiry is risky is that, in the interest of achieving a wider and better balance - between (for example) initiating influence and being receptive to influence - action inquiry takes us to the very frontier of our current way of balancing. It may even take us beyond our current way of balancing - out of that balance, perhaps temporarily altogether off balance - as our very way of balancing transforms.

Now: let's re-swallow our hearts and get on with some early action inquiry exercises - ones that will not send us totally out of balance. We can wait for such thrills until we are far more familiar with, adept at, and committed to, action inquiry.

In the meantime, we can protect ourselves from our worst fears of what may occur in several different ways as we start. One way is literally to take one or more deep breaths, breathing new energy in through our fear when we feel it, and then exhaling the fear. Sometimes the fear will evaporate when treated so, or at least cease gripping us in the same way, because we are brought back in touch with the reasons and feelings that urge us to act differently.

A second way to make the moment of exercising action inquiry less fearful is to experiment in a situation of relatively high overall trust. Where trust is high, risks are lower than they otherwise would be, and honest failure costs less. A third way to reduce fear is to choose an issue around which your previous, more habitual ways of acting have clearly failed; hence, you have nothing more to lose from trying in a new way than in your old way and a much better chance of 'winning'. A fourth way to reduce risk and fear is to choose new ways of acting that are in and of themselves so ordinary that no one else may even notice that you are 'acting differently'. Whenever you sense that an action inquiry experiment you are considering is too risky, you may wish to return to these guidelines in order to invent a less risky alternative.

One last, but crucial, point before we offer you a series of action inquiry exercises which you are free to amend and embroider upon as you wish. The very word 'exercise' no doubt makes some of you tired, just as the word 'experiment' may make some of you think of a cold, inhumane, manipulative science. But the idea in action inquiry is to take risks that are fun because they energise you and raise your awareness, risks that are rewarding because they increase the efficacy of your colleagues as well as yourself, risks that highlight your own and others' capacity for initiative and mutuality. Consequently, be sure to find your own pleasurable pace in working with these exercises.

Exercise I

Let's start, very gradually, to try some action inquiry experimenting in your work environment.

Try taking a 20 minute 'office holiday'. This exercise is an adaptation of the well-known-and-often-scoffed-at advice to try managing-by-walking-around. But the exercise will be more fun for you if you think of it as planning and taking a half-hour vacation while you are at work every day. One of the reasons this is a good first exercise is that it isn't high risk. It doesn't require you to talk differently to a specific person with whom you are already uncomfortable.

You can disguise your overall lack of goal orientation during this time by carrying with you several memos that you will deliver to people around the office, but don't forget that your purpose is to allow yourself to be surprised by people and things that you usually neglect or consider meaningless. Perhaps you will pay more attention to the architecture one day during your 'vacation' than you ever have before, or perhaps to the different ways that people decorate their office spaces, or to the different pace and tone of different work areas. On other days, you may start two or three conversations with co-workers you hardly know. Perhaps you go sightseeing to a part of the plant you've never visited before. Or maybe you enter a small conference room, close the door, lie down on the floor, relax (or notice your fear that someone will walk in on you, or your difficulty changing pace in the middle of the day). Feel the sensation in your feet and then follow the sensation all the way up your body.

By now, you may well be inwardly screaming: "Why do these crazy things? Isn't this irresponsible? Who has time at work for a daily vacation anyway?" This is the tone of voice in which many of the executives who try management-by-walking-around talk to themselves after their first two or three tries, and why they stop doing it. Hopefully, though, the first exercise has begun to provide you with tastes of what spending time in this way can do for you. First of all, it can re-energise you for the rest of the day. Second, you will find that the changed pace causes creative solutions to occur to you for problems that have been nagging you. Third, you will run into people that you need to check progress on little things with, but weren't getting around to calling (and the serendipity of your meeting them in the hall is likely to generate a quicker, less defensive exchange). Fourth, others are likely to experience you as more open and accessible, simply because they see you moving around at a more relaxed pace than usual. Fifth, you will gradually begin to learn about all sorts of currents within the organisation of which you were previously unaware and which influence how work gets done.

So, there are many potentially productive outcomes to this goal-less exercise, but they must be welcomed as by-products rather than sought out directly, if the exercise is to succeed in jogging your awareness. Again, the point is that a widening, dynamic awareness needs to surround our goal-oriented efforts in order for us to learn how to improve our quality from moment-to-moment. But we are constantly sacrificing the dignity and long-term efficacy of such an embracing awareness for the short-term return we imagine we'll get (our thirty pieces of silver) by totally subordinating ourselves to a particular goal.

We spoke at the end of the previous chapter about how action inquiry comes to feel like simultaneous rehearsal and performance. The performance is the goal-oriented outer action. The sense of rehearsal comes from the dynamic, widening awareness. This exercise emphasises cultivating the atmosphere of rehearsal in oneself. The next one, too, emphasises inquiry more than action, rehearsal more than performance.

Exercise II

Next, let's bring the sense of conducting action inquiry exercises to business meetings you attend, but for which you are not the formal leader. In order to enhance your sense of initiative and awareness at these meetings, try periodically unfocusing your eyes slightly. Gaze around at the group as a whole while listening more intently to the rhythm of speaking. Intentionally unfocusing (or 'soft' focusing) your eyes can generate a marvellous kaleidoscope of feelings of self-consciousness, embarrassment and vulnerability; and it may take a while to convince yourself that no one else is aware of this change that initially feels major and awkward to you.

The idea is to pay attention, not only to the content of what is said, but also, and even more closely, to the way in which people are speaking and gesturing. It is useful to keep some notes, dividing your page down the middle, with content notes on the left, and 'process' notes on the right. (Indeed, if you haven't done so already in relation to the first two exercises, you may wish to start an ongoing journal so that you can later review the pattern over time of your experiences, conjectures, insights, confusions, and questions.)

Some questions that can get you going with regard to observing the meeting include: Is the meeting well framed at the outset? Do people offer apt illustrations for their advocacies and can you see evidence that when they do so they have more influence with others? Are inquiries used as weapons, or as genuine ways of generating clarity or including more colleagues' perspectives?

As (probably over several meetings) you begin to get the 'taste' for following the conversation in this additional, more active way, you will also be developing convictions, based on real evidence, about group patterns that are inhibiting effectiveness (e.g., no one ever summarises what was decided and makes sure someone is taking responsibility for implementation). Now, you may be ready for the fourth exercise.

But before we move to that, notice that, again, as in the previous exercise, the emphasis of this action inquiry exercise has been on actions that increase your awareness. This is always the first and the primary objective when beginning to practice action inquiry: to enhance one's own awareness.

Exercise III

The previous two exercises are hopefully beginning to establish a new atmosphere of widened awareness and rehearsal while you are at work. Now, we can try taking some specific actions while we simultaneously engage in this type of awareness-jogging that you are cultivating a taste for.

Take one or two initiatives per meeting that have nothing to do with your own agenda and nothing to do with the content of the discussions, but rather attempt to help the group as a whole manage its time well, manage conflicts well, or reach decisions. Often even the formal leader of the meeting takes very few of these group-focused initiatives, and everyone else may simply blame this leader for the boredom and the meandering, or for the stressful and jagged atmosphere.

Relatively low risk, constructive actions - often inquiries - can be both very visible and very much appreciated. "The two of you obviously disagree on this. Can each of you offer us your strongest illustration on behalf of your view, as well as an illustration of the dangers in taking the other course of action?" "If we continue discussing this item, we're not going to get to the rest of the agenda. Is that OK with the rest of you, or do you think we should check on how people would vote on this one and go on?"

The examples throughout this book provide many potential 'recipes' for how to interweave framing, advocacy, illustration, and inquiry into more constructive and effective ways of speaking. It is so hard to control our own speaking that it is best to practice just one type of speech at a time at the outset. Keeping brief journals of your efforts can be very important to seeing how quickly you can begin to make changes. At the same time, the effort to practice never ends. The three of us have been practising for years. Certainly, this exercise alone is worthy of six months to a year of deliberate practice. Of course, in practising these skills, you are welcome to go beyond meetings where you are not the leader to your daily interactions with peers, superiors, and subordinates. Indeed, you are welcome to go beyond work settings altogether, as the next exercise suggests.

Exercise IV

Now let's try an exercise outside of work, in part to emphasise that all these exercises are voluntary, essentially leisurely endeavours motivated by our own intrinsic (but not always apparent) wish to become more aware.

OK. Ready? Think of jogging around a long wooded path for daily, physical exercise (feeling tired yet?). But rather than imagining dragging yourself out there for the run, pushing yourself fiercely, then not going back out for a week or two because the prospect of repeating the performance is too daunting... and rather than imagining that this is something simple and habitual that you already do... rather than imagining jogging in either of these ways, imagine this jogging as an awareness-jogging-adventure. Start, perhaps, at a walk. Then, perhaps, walk backward slowly for ten paces, just to see how your balance/agility/alertness is and how you feel about others seeing you do this 'strange' thing. Perhaps you leave the path altogether, crouch in a small bower, and emit a few animal sounds. Next, you dash into a short uphill sprint, and so on... listening for impulses within yourself that you do not usually hear, sniffing the environment for clues of... you do not know what at the outset.

Can you give yourself the time (we suggest allowing a whole hour), at least every other day for a couple of weeks, to take such an adventure? Can you enjoy the process of finding the right place (or places) if you don't already have a favourite trail? If you are balking at this whole idea, can you see what feelings are blocking you? (If you think 'facts' are blocking you [no time; no trail] look again more deeply [you are in charge of your time; any path can become your trail].) The action inquiry exercise has already begun as you read this, for you are already framing and advocating and illustrating and inquiring within yourself about it (or are you just advocating and developing a fixed attitude about the exercise?).

The fact that you do this exercise essentially alone and not at work helps to reduce the initial risk. It also helps to emphasise that these action inquiry exercises are entirely for you, not something you 'have' to do for work. Even more important, this exercise highlights the fact that action inquiry is, first and last, about generating a more vivid, embracing, non-verbal awareness that simultaneously senses its own limits. Whatever technical, verbal, or organisational skills you eventually improve, the source of continual quality improvement, in this action inquiry approach, is a more vivid awareness of what is at stake in each new moment and the courage to take an appropriate risk to enhance quality.

Conclusion

Ultimately, the sense of simultaneous rehearsal and performance that these action inquiry exercises introduce you to represents a new quality of awareness - a continual, silent, impartial observing of your own performance amidst others. The manager experimenting with action inquiry treats each performance as a rehearsal, primarily dedicated to cultivating this ongoing, impartial observing. Each on-the-job dilemma comes to sound more and more like a call both to performance and to rehearsal, both to effectiveness and to inquiry.

The silent, inquiring observing that is at the core of action inquiry determines when the time is right for what type of explicit inquiry. But your choice to make one or more explicit inquiries does not foreclose the making of further inquiries. The essential characteristic of action inquiry is that it invites and welcomes true information relevant to an ongoing situation, even if that information seems to violate your preferences or assumptions about the situation. Some people initially imagine that the openness of action inquiry implies never coming to conclusions and acting. But this represents a misunderstanding of what we are advocating. Action inquiry occurs in the midst of action and is a search for timely action; it is not an academic kind of 'eternal' inquiry that occurs before or after or instead of action.

Action inquiry is a revolutionary process - so revolutionary that it revolutionises revolution itself. In the past, revolutionaries have revolted against what they saw as institutionalised inefficiency, ineffectiveness, or illegitimacy, with the assumption that they themselves were 'on the right side'. Then they have typically established managerial styles and regimes just as closed and authoritarian as their predecessors, if not more so (think about the aftermath of the French and Russian revolutions or the aftermath of many a corporate acquisition).

Action inquiry revolutionises revolution by opening the 'revolutionary' himself or herself to the possibility of transformation. Maybe the inquiry will reveal that what needs changing is something about the actor, not about the rest of the situation. For example, the actor may need to change underlying assumptions, may need to begin inquiring into the other parties' assumptions and frames of reference, and/or may need to undertake a quest for legitimacy, all of which he or she may have habitually avoided previously.

It is this self-overcoming, self-transforming quality of action inquiry that accounts for both its costs and its benefits. Action inquiry requires the risk and often the pain of personal developmental change. But on the positive side, action inquiry provides the operational 'handle' for shifting one's thought and action away from a pattern where underlying assumptions go unrecognised and unchallenged, where one's own frame of reference is a limiting, confining boundary, and where self-interest and mistrust prevent any effort to attain legitimacy.

Because action inquiry aims at no narrow self-protection and is ever alert to incongruities among purposes, strategies, actions, and outcomes, it can restructure situations for long-term quality improvement. Personal development by the individual manager or family member can spark transformation in others. In the next chapter we examine more closely what personal development means and the part it plays in the leadership of organisational transformation.

CHAPTER 4

FRAMES AND STAGES OF PERSONAL DEVELOPMENT

So far in this book, we have introduced action inquiry as though it occurs in particular moments in time. For example, in introducing the notion of 'framing' we have focused on the importance of making clear the overall 'game' you would like to play with others at a meeting or in a one-to-one conversation, and then testing through an inquiry whether you are all in fact in the same game together. This explicit framing can improve the effectiveness of even the briefest exchange. Here is a company president speaking by phone to her special assistant: "I'm assuming you are handling the Jones contract. Let me know if you need assistance". The president makes her frame (her assumption) explicit and advocates that the special assistant seek her support, if necessary, to assure the job gets done. If the president's assumption is wrong, or if the assistant has been stymied by the project but has so far just pushed it to the back burner, it is in the assistant's interest to respond, now or in the near future, "What? I've never heard of the Jones contract". Or, "I thought Paul was taking care of that". Or whatever the truth is, if it is incongruent with the president's explicitly stated assumptions. Many of the day-to-day frustrations of work life can be avoided by such brief frame -and-assumption testing comments.

Now, in this chapter, we want to illustrate the other extreme of the framing spectrum. We wish to discuss the central and usually implicit frame that each of us is bound by during any given period of our lives. It is this implicit frame that most severely limits our effectiveness. We will make the greatest leaps in quality improvement in our own actions when we become aware of these limits and begin to experiment beyond them. If we can become aware of these overarching frames in others and in ourselves, we can reduce unintentional conflict and misunderstanding and can even help ourselves and others to transform beyond the limits of our present assumptions.

As the chapter proceeds, we will describe four different frames, the *Opportunist frame*, the *Diplomat frame*, the *Expert frame*, and the *Achiever frame*, any one of which may characterise your overall approach to managing for a whole decade or even your entire career to the present. Developing a hypothesis about your own overall frame and those of your colleagues can help you to relate more effectively to them and to challenge yourself to experiment with thinking and acting outside your current 'box'. Each successive frame we describe is 'larger' than the prior frame in that it includes all the possibilities of the prior frame and a whole new set of alternatives as well. Moreover, whereas the four frames don't recognise themselves as constructed frames and don't recognise that different people operate out of different frames, persons working from fifth and sixth frames, the *Individualist frame*, and the *Strategist frame* which we will describe very briefly at the end of this chapter and in more detail in the next chapters, become increasingly aware of the omnipresence of different frames when people interact. They therefore become more and more committed to the explicit testing of framing assumptions during particular encounters, such as the very brief exchange between the president and her assistant cited above. Later in the book (Chapter 13) we will describe still another frame, representing further development beyond the *Strategist frame*. This whole book is intended to help you move developmentally toward these latter frames, if you choose to undertake such a journey.

We think you are most likely to enjoy learning about the first four frames by listening in as business colleagues tell stories about diagnosing their colleagues and themselves. Of course, as you read these stories, you can also begin diagnosing the colleagues with whom you interact most often in order to get your work done. And, by the time you reach the end of this chapter, perhaps you will have an initial diagnosis of your own current developmental frame.

We suggest that on separate sheets of paper you list the three to seven work associates with whom it would be to your greatest advantage to work more effectively. Write your own name at the top of a whole page as well. Then, as you read the chapter, note which characteristics from each frame you associate with each person, reminding yourself with a few words of a particular occasion when he or she displayed that characteristic. You should find that each person displays one particular frame predominantly. Although that person will occasionally act in ways characteristic of the earlier frames, he or she should rarely show signs of the next frame (unless he/she happens to be in developmental transition toward that stage) and will almost never exhibit characteristics of the frame two beyond. But remember, you are not making a scientific judgment here, only an estimate; and the point of your estimate is not to be right or to pigeonhole yourself or your colleagues, but rather to help you to test whether your developmental hypotheses lead you to choose more effective actions as you work with them.

Table 41 offers you a sense of how one's world grows larger and more complicated at each succeeding frame. Table 42 offers a summary of the attitudinal and behavioural characteristics associated with each of the first six successive frames. You can refer back and forth from the stories to Table 4-2 as you read. Our storytellers are managers or professionals who were learning about frames and developmental theory at the time they wrote their diagnostic stories.

To help you recognise the frame that applies to each of the associates you listed and to yourself, we continue now with the colleague stories. We accompany the stories with further comments to clarify the nature of the frames.

Table 4-1 Key Meaning-Making Frames

Frame Name	*Percentage Found**	*Focus of Awareness*
Opportunist	1%	Own needs and self-interest. Self-protection. Acting on impulses.
Diplomat	5%	Acceptance and belonging. Socially expected behaviour.
Expert	33%	Internal craft logic rules. Consistency and improvement. Rationality.
Achiever	35%	Results, goals and plans. Objective reality.
Individualist	14%	Everything is relative. Own ability to have impact.
Strategist	8%	Process and goal oriented. Systems view. Development over time.
Alchemist	4%	Interplay of awareness, thought, action and effect. Transforming self and others.

* These distributions are derived from the profiles of 1121 managers, consultants and MBA students in America (497) and the UK (624). They are consistent with a much wider study (4510 profiles) carried out by Dr Susann Cook-Greuter.

The Opportunist Frame

A worker at a large firm gradually diagnosed one difficult co-worker, Charles, as an Opportunist with the following description:

> Charles and I are both at the same job grade, although he has been with the company longer, and I have been on the current team longer. When he first joined our team, he would stop by my desk 3 or 4 times a day to ask for work-related advice and design tips. Initially, I was very flattered and found his asking for my technical expertise very ego satisfying and a boost to my self-confidence.

**Table 4-2   Managerial Style Characteristi cs Associated with Seven
             Developmental Frames**

Opportunist

Short time horizon; focuses on concrete things; manipulative; deceptive; rejects feedback; externalises blame; distrustful; fragile self-control; hostile humour; views luck as central; flouts power and sexuality; stereotypes; views rules as loss of freedom; punishes according to 'eye for an eye' ethic; treats what can get away with as legal; forcibly self interested.

Diplomat

Observes protocol; avoids inner and outer conflict; works to group standards; speaks in clichés and platitudes; conforms; feels shame if violates norms; bad to hurting others; receives disapproval as punishment; seeks membership and status; face-saving essential; loyalty to immediate group, not 'distant' organisation or principles; needs acceptance.

Expert

Interested in problem-solving; seeks causes; critical of self and others based on craft logic; chooses efficiency over effectiveness; continuous improvement and perfection; accepts feedback only from 'objective' craft masters; dogmatic; values decisions based on merit; sees contingencies, exceptions; wants to stand out, be unique; sense of obligation to wider, internally consistent moral order.

Achiever

Long-term goals; future is vivid and important; welcomes behavioural feedback; effectiveness *and* results oriented; feels like initiator, not pawn; appreciates complexity and systems; seeks generalisable reasons for action; seeks some mutuality (as well as hierarchy) in relationships; feels guilt if does not meet own standards; blind to own achieving shadow, to the subjectivity behind objectivity; energised by practical day-to-day improvements based on self-chosen (but not self-created) ethical system.

Individualist

Works independently with a high value on individuality; self-curious; freer of obligation and imposed objectives, thus finds new creativity; aware that what one sees depends upon one's world view and experiments with this; may be a maverick as they experiment with finding their own way; uses power differently; increasingly conscious of the impact of they have.

Strategist

Creative at conflict resolution; recognises importance of principle, contract, theory, and judgement - not just rules, customs, and exceptions - for making and maintaining good decisions; process oriented as well as goal oriented; aware of paradox and contradiction, unique market niches, and particular historical moments; relativistic; enjoys playing a variety of roles; witty, existential humour (as contrasted to prefabricated jokes); aware of dark side, of profundity of evil, and is tempted by its power.

Alchemist

Disintegration of ego-identity, often because of near-death experience; seeks participation in historical/spiritual transformations; creator of mythical events that reframe situations; anchoring in inclusive present, seeing light and dark, order and mess; blends opposites, creating 'positive-sum' games; exercises own attention, researches interplay of intuition, thought, action, and effects on outside world; treats time and events as symbolic, analogical, metaphorical (not merely linear, digital, literal).

After weeks and months of more frequent and lengthy stops at my desk, I felt as if he was deliberately manipulating my time. I would work through lunch or stay late to make up for the lost time, initially resenting him, then funneling my resentment towards a system that promotes people on seniority. I now realise that I was externalising blame rather than recognising my own cowardice and inability to act.

I did try some experimentation, picking up the phone when I saw him heading in my direction, or asking to see the research he had done and where he was stuck before offering help. When he sensed that I was going to make him work a little, he began asking someone else on the team for help.

Some typical comments made about him by his colleagues include, "I have got to the point where I cannot even say 'Good morning' to Charles for fear of hearing the intimate details of his personal life for close to 1/2 hour" and "Kathy, I don't know how you put up with sitting next to him. I sit three desks away from him and I still find it difficult to tune him out".

With the benefit of hindsight I now think that my spending time trying to help him did him more harm than good because he has since been transferred to another team and has been denied a promotion. He has confided to me that his manager told him he should concentrate more on his work and less on seeking help and on his personal and social life.

Before you read on, try listing on a sheet of paper what you sense to be the distinguishing features of Charles's frame. What assumptions does he seem to be making about himself, about others and how to relate to them? What does he assume about how to be effective? How does he assume an ethical person should behave? What other patterns do you see in Charles based on Kathy's description?

The themes and patterns that you see in Charles's *Opportunist* frame:
-
-
-

Based on developmental theory and research findings, people holding the Opportunist frame try to make things and people work by manipulating them unilaterally or by making the most advantageous trades possible. Charles flattered Kathy by asking her for advice in exchange for her time and technical help. The Opportunistic manager is typically a tactful manipulator, who may even use courtesy as a ploy, but who still views the world as a one-against-all jungle fight. Charles' approach to the jungle is to go to the person who will give him the most for the least cost. He drops that person as soon as the exchange proves unprofitable in the short run. He gives little regard to what others may think of him or to the damage his immediate actions may be doing to longer term relationships.

As a basis for a management style, the Opportunist frame values only very short term visible costs and benefits. It appreciates only the financial and power aspects of organisations, not the structural and spiritual aspects. It does not value helping managers and organisations to transform and develop. Studies of managers have found a range of only 0 to 4% to hold the Opportunist frame.

For the Opportunistic manager, it is axiomatic that one must 'play one's cards close to the chest' since others are doing the same. The Hobbesian equation, 'might makes right' holds, and the Golden Rule is recast as 'he who has the gold rules'. The Opportunist is severely limited by this frame. Whereas managers at later stages can choose to act opportunistically on particular occasions, a manager who is bounded by the Opportunist frame has to act opportunistically on every occasion.

The Diplomat Frame

A supervisor in the housekeeping department of a large manufacturing company gives the following description of his superior:

> In my opinion, Phil, my boss, is at the Diplomat stage of development. He seems incapable of making decisions on his own and he has even intimated to me that he feels he is a pawn or figurehead and not really in control of his areas of responsibility. Phil is very aware of protocol and observes it meticulously. He is risk averse. He avoids conflict at any expense. I think this is the major reason he feels like a pawn. He has given up so many battles that the idea of fighting doesn't even occur to him.
>
> Phil is my immedi ate superior. It is commonly held among my peers (Phil's other subordinates) that he is ineffective in his position. He seems to accept, without resistance, anything that comes from higher up in the chain of command, and this often affects our department in a negative way. Here's an example: we (the housekeeping department) are at the point of entry to the Facilities operational area, which employs over 400 people. I am the first supervisor that newcomers are exposed to. In the recent past we have had numerous hires whom I never got to meet until the night they started. Some of these people are 'political appointees', recommended by vice presidents or members of the board of directors. I realise the world is imperfect and that favouritism occurs, but I believe I should be involved in interviewing all incoming employees. I further believe that Phil could at least object to the more blatant cases where political appointees are given regular full time status (which entitles them to full benefits) while we have people who have been here for months as temps waiting to move up to full time.

Phil has shared with me on occasion things he would like to see happen in our department or has agreed with me about some recommendation I have made to him. But all too often, those discussions end with, "That will never fly", or "The senior managers won't like that". He will then try to convince me not to make waves and to accept 'the way things work here'. I have no wish to make waves, but I hope I will never become desensitised to the point where I will just accept things that seem so wrong.

Again, before reading on, try writing a brief synopsis of Phil's frame. What do his guiding assumptions appear to you to be based on his subordinate's description of him?

The themes and patterns that you see in Phil's *Diplomat* frame:

-
-
-

The Diplomat frame focuses attention on other people: family friends, work associates, the work group, the organisation, the nation. Phil's focus is clearly on his superiors. For the Diplomat, these others' values are the highest good. Their definitions of appropriate behaviour are the best guides to action. Behavioural skills - the right moves or words at the right times - are seen as critical for gaining membership, meeting others' standards, and observing the correct protocol. From this frame others define value, not oneself. Some thing or some action has value if it sells, if it influences others, or if high status persons treat it as valuable.

Like the Opportunist frame, the Diplomat frame has its bright side but also its dark side. While the Opportunist frame can illuminate paths to adventure which the Opportunist manager embarks on courageously, it can also show the way toward the shadowier realms of deception, manipulation, and unwillingness to accept responsibility.

Likewise, the Diplomat frame has a dual nature. Sometimes, calling someone a diplomat implies that he or she has the exquisite sense of tact that permits both honesty and agreement about the most difficult issues, enhancing the self esteem and dignity of all parties in the process. In this same positive vein, the diplomatic manager can provide loyalty and good will that functions as organisational glue. At other times, the implication is that the 'diplomat' avoids and smooths over all potential conflict, masking both true feelings and objective data in an effort to maintain harmony at all costs. Thus the Diplomat can become alienated from associates who, like Phil's subordinate, are put off by Phil's dismissal of their concerns and suggestions.

Diplomatic managers do not seek out negative feedback about themselves. Quite to the contrary, they attempt to deflect it. They equate negative feedback with loss of face and loss of status. To tell them that it is constructive because it can help them achieve their goals does not make sense to them. No goal is as compelling to them as the implicit rule against losing face. This aversion to feedback helps explain why the Diplomat, like the Opportunist, is 'locked into' his or her frame and blind to the possibility of other ways of behaving.

The Diplomat manager is as unable to criticise others and to question group norms as to criticise self. We see this in Phil, who will not try to correct the apparently unjust handling of 'political appointees'. An organisation led by a Diplomat will be inhibited from adapting to changing competitive realities or to discovering and creating new strategic opportunities. Subordinates will feel a sense of stagnation and disillusion. They are likely to lower their aims and effort and may even falsify information such as sales or production records in order to 'look good'.

Studies of managers have found that less than 6% of senior managers hold the Diplomat frame. By comparison, 9% of the junior managers studied, and 24% of the first-line supervisors in these studies hold the Diplomat frame. These data suggest that the Diplomatic style limits one's chances for promotion.

The Expert Frame

The same supervisor who described Phil offers this description of Larry, a fellow supervisor:

> Larry is an expert in my opinion. He has unquestioned technical expertise in his area and believes himself to be unrivalled in this as well as in administrative record keeping. He is a perfectionist, even going so far as to criticise one of his employees about his technique of decorating the office Christmas tree.

> Larry is very conscientious, has a high sense of obligation to moral standards, and feels this differentiates him from the rest of the group. He strives to outperform everyone around him and is not against pointing out the faults of others. He is almost as unforgiving of his own mistakes, so I guess that's fair. He values decisions based on merit as long as they fit within his guidelines. He would, however, prefer to make all the decisions himself. I work closely with Larry, and find that sometimes he will take over a project we are both responsible for and complete it all himself, which makes me look bad and, worse, puts me in a weaker role in the group.

> He is ambivalent about receiving feedback and at times clearly finds it irritating. He seems to be sure that he knows everything he needs he needs to know to do his job. I am impressed with his planning and organisational skills. He has been a great help to me and I do not want to sound too negative about him, but he is extremely dogmatic. His word is law and is not subject to discussion. 'My way, or no way' is Larry's credo. Even though we are peers he seems determined to maintain a position of total dominance. I have tried to be patient and wait him out, but so far he seems to be unyielding.

The themes and patterns that you see in Larry's *Expert* frame:

-
-
-

When (and if) managers develop beyond the Diplomat frame, they begin to see other people's preferences as variables in a wider situation rather than as determinants of their own actions. Studies of various groups of managers have found that between 19% and 68% hold the Expert frame. In more junior and younger populations the percentages profiled at Expert are significantly greater than in more senior and older populations. For the Expert, the guide to action becomes logic and intellectually determined objectivity, discovered and arrived at independently: the one, provable 'right answer'. This certainly seems true of Larry based on his colleague's description of him.

Experts no longer identify with what makes them the same as others in the group. They identify more with what makes them stand out from others in the group, with the unique skills that they can contribute. In Larry's case, he takes over, without any discussion, projects for which he shares responsibility with a fellow supervisor. Experts depend less on others' judgments of quality, more on their own. In fact, because they so sharply differentiate themselves from the group, they frequently defiantly and dogmatically oppose all forms of authority other than that of their chosen specialty or 'craft' and their 'craft heroes'.

Experts focus almost exclusively on the internal logic and integrity of their area of expertise, often setting perfectionistic standards. They are not usually good team players because of their dogmatic demand for perfection. Again, Larry serves as a prime example. His logic is the only logic. He appears not to place a high value on feedback. While the Diplomat seeks others' approval, the Expert subordinates the need for peer approval to the need for self-approval for a job well done.

On the bright side, the Expert's admiration for a job well done can evoke in subordinates a striving for praise earned through perfection. But this same emphasis on perfection produces the Expert's darker side. The manager holding the Expert frame, placing primacy on rational thought, will expect strict adherence to a well-defined code of professional and moral conduct. There are no degrees of excellence - only good or bad, perfect or imperfect. Such high expectations of subordinates and frequent criticism of a job poorly done can produce a culture of competition and stress.

The Expert, too, may fall victim to this self-generated stress. In chapter two we described Anthony, a young manager who for two full years dedicated his full efforts to becoming an Expert in a very complex method for comparing company benefit programs. Anthony testified to the anguish, both physical and mental of his 'perfectionist nature'. "I would find myself obsessing about minutiae in an effort to rationalise every last variation in my results".

Anthony's successful experiment with action inquiry gave evidence that he began to develop beyond the Expert frame, an accomplishment not every manager achieves.

The Achiever Frame

Joanne, the manager we meet next is new to the Achiever frame. Like Anthony, who took on the task of helping the senior managers of a consulting firm's branch office to change their roles, Joanne is breaking the constraints of the Expert frame and is beginning to understand and experience things in a new way, the way of the Achiever. The length and detail of her story as well as its fresh, up-beat tone seem to reflect that newness. Look for themes again, and make notes about them.

> My job as Market Research Manager for the magazine requires that I be a problem solver and 'perfectionist'. It is part of my daily routine to delve into why things are the way they are - digging, analysing, and presenting the results. Comments that people make about me include, "You're really good with numbers", and "I don't know how you can understand this stuff". These are comments that an Expert would love to hear. I am now finding this frame very constraining. I would prefer to be less detail conscious and be more involved with the overall picture, working towards long-term effectiveness rather than short-term efficiency.

> Steve, the Marketing Director, had confided in me that he was interviewing for a different position within the company and, if he were to accept, it would be fairly soon. It was vital that I display more of the characteristics of the Achiever stage of development in order to be seriously considered for the position of Marketing Director. I developed a plan that included a number of experiments.

> My first action upon hearing this news was to have a discussion with Steve and ask his advice on the best way to proceed. I said I was very interested in eventually becoming the Marketing Director. Steve expressed confidence that I could do the job, but his response also confirmed what I already knew - I needed to become more visible to upper management - in general, take a proactive role in increasing my communication with these people.

> The next major action that I took was to rewrite my job description. On Steve's suggestion I included responsibilities of the Marketing Director that I am interested in taking on. I clearly stated in my letter, "I'm not sure that I've adequately expressed my abilities and interest in the past and am taking this opportunity to do so". I also told him that one of my priorities was to continue to improve my written and oral communication skills. By taking this action I was letting Jim know that I was making efforts to change my behaviour. The letter itself was unprecedented for me. I also opened myself to some self-examination

and opened the floor for criticism. My hope was that Jim would realise my level of commitment and assist my development.

While there was no direct response to my letter and rewritten job description, over the past few weeks, Jim and the National Sales Manager have sent me copies of presentations that they liked and have called to solicit my opinion on other presentations. Recently, Jim has asked me to take on the development of the general presentation. I adamantly expressed interest in this project in my letter.

An ongoing action is to maintain daily contact with Jim, the Ad Director, and the National Sales Manager. While this is not always possible, I've hardly missed a day without touching base with these three people at least once. While this sounds like a small and trivial thing, it is actually one of my most effective experiments. I used to go an entire week or two without speaking to the Publisher. By taking this initiative, I've created a 'chain reaction'. My calls to them have started conversations that have prompted them to call me more often. During these conversations I've been able to convey my knowledge on different subjects - which in some cases has led to me being given responsibility for certain projects or keeping track of certain matters. Another result is that my name comes up often in discussions between these people and other upper level managers in the company.

Another effective action that I took was to volunteer for a project with which I previously had no involvement. It involved working several nights until 9 pm and on two weekends. I felt it was important for this project to go as smoothly and quickly as possible. If there had been delays and mistakes, Jim might not have entrusted it to me again. This was an area he might not have thought I could help with. If I hadn't taken the initiative, he still wouldn't.

The next major action I took was to schedule a meeting with Jim to discuss my compensation. In essence I wanted to ask for a raise, but I also wanted to convey that I was confident in my abilities and that contributions that I make and have the right amount of aggressiveness to be successful in Marketing. This meeting was my best opportunity to properly apply framing, advocating, illustrating, and inquiring. By thinking about these conversational elements, I was able to turn a potentially difficult and tense conversation into a positive and productive meeting. We discussed my reasoning and his, and were able to make each other see the other's view on a few issues. He agreed that I was not adequately compensated for my contributions.

In conclusion, I am very satisfied with the progress I've made. While no decisions have been made to promote someone to the position of Marketing Director, I feel I've made significant progress towards the goal of being that person.

My frequent contact with the Publisher and others in the company has helped me to move fully out of the Expert stage and into the Achiever stage. I receive criticism in a much more productive manner and have changed my focus from short-term satisfaction to long-term effectiveness. The most personally felt progress that I've made, however, is my ability to be an initiator and no longer a pawn.

The themes and patterns that you see in this manager's Achiever frame:

-
-
-

The Achiever is passionate about accomplishing goals. Whereas Joanne heretofore has concentrated on digging into the inner workings of things, mastering the numbers, and presenting the answer, the Achiever frame is wider. It focuses not just on how things work on the inside, but on how to be effective in one's wider surroundings and on how to help the organisation be effective in its environment. As Joanne moves from Expert to Achiever we see her attention expand beyond digging into research data. She conveys her 'knowledge on different subjects' and takes on new kinds of projects, such as recommending a new rate structure. She advocates a promotion for herself from the more technically oriented position of Market Research Manager to the more entrepreneurially and managerially oriented role of Marketing Director, typical of the Achiever's focus on functions that help the organisation carry out its established strategy.

Much more than those who hold the prior frames, the Achiever pays attention to differences between own and others' points of view, and places a value on teamwork and on agreements reached through consensus as aids in carrying out pre-established goals. The Achiever welcomes personal feedback and seeks mutuality in relationships with coworkers. In Joanne's case, her associations with other managers are on the rise as she assumes the Achiever frame. She observes the sharp increase in her frequency of contacts with other managers, noting that her initiative in this area is even beginning to cause 'chain reactions'. She exchanges 'reasonings' with her boss on the subject of her salary emphasising not just that she got her way, but that mutuality was achieved. Increasingly, she appears to be seeking and valuing feedback.

There can be a flip side, a darker side, to the Achiever's way of handling feedback, however. Bluntly, the feedback had better fit within the Achiever's already established scheme of things (his or her frame), or it will be rejected. You have probably encountered examples similar to the two below:

> The project manager asks you along with managers from several other departments to attend a meeting in order to give your department's inputs and comments about how the project is being run. Many changes are suggested, but the project manager accepts only those that are consistent with the basic approach she is already using.

> A friend phones you one evening excited about a new business venture he hopes to launch. He tells you his plans and asks your advice. He asks, in addition, that you invest money in the enterprise to help get it started. You think his plans are not sound. You suggest to him several key questions you feel he should explore before proceeding. You tell him further that you do not have the money to invest. He is extremely upset with both your responses. He ends the conversation by saying you and he are no longer friends.

In both these cases the Achiever seeks feedback, but when it is given it becomes clear that the Achiever's effort to achieve is made in terms of his or her own pre-established framework. The Achiever is not prepared to question the validity of the *frame itself* and possibly reframe his or her approach in the midst of action. In Joanne's case, the thing Joanne emphasises in describing her associations with others is the impact she had on the others: she 'created a chain reaction', she conveys her knowledge; she convinces her boss she is not adequately compensated.

The Achiever's orientation toward subordinates is complex. On the one hand, the manager at the Achiever stage values and encourages creativity among subordinates and is able to delegate significant responsibilities to them. On the other hand, however, the Achiever's inability to question his or her own limited conception of the organisation's larger goals prevents any serious consideration or acceptance of alternatives that deviate from the official mission.

You are undoubtedly aware of many examples of the thought and action of the Achiever. In our profiling of 1121 managers, consultants and MBA students the Achiever frame represents 35% of the total.

A Summary of Four Frames And A Look Ahead

Now we will revisit the four frames we have considered in this chapter, the Opportunist, Diplomat, Expert, and Achiever frames, with one more story. Sanjay is a manager in a business owned by his family. In his story, Sanjay describes transitions he has made through each of the four frames. This affords us a review, but also highlights in a remarkably vivid way something we glimpsed in Joanne's story: the potential people have for acquiring successively larger frames. Sanjay presents himself as having accomplished at least four such transformations, with a fifth possibly underway. The last two paragraphs of his story provide a look at three further frames, the Strategist Transition, the Strategist and the Alchemist, which are all developmentally beyond the Achiever frame. When you reach that point in Sanjay's story, you can look for new themes - post-Achiever themes. Sanjay's story:

> When I was 15, I worked in my grandfather's store and I saw in myself some Opportunistic tendencies. I would do things that made me look good at the time, but had poor future consequences.

> At 19, when I was in college, I worked for my father who had bought a large vehicle body repair franchise. My managerial behaviour was

Diplomatic: I wanted everyone to like me and I avoided confrontational situations. Due to the nature of the people who work in that industry I could not, and did not, remain a Diplomat for long. Our employees generally had alcohol, drug, emotional, behavioural, social or legal problems. Many were in and out of court and jail and could not handle their finances from one week to the next. In retrospect, this put most of them clearly as Opportunists.

I remember the turning point from a Diplomat's to an Expert's mindset, though I had no name for it at the time. The incident was the first time I had to fire someone. After that, my focus was on driving the employees to do the job right. I was very organised, methodical, and procedural, inspiring procedures in our shop that were recommended for use across the country. I hated for anyone to try to tell me that there was a different way to do something other than the 'perfect' way I was already doing it, though I often would try new ideas after work when nobody was around. I also welcomed and enjoyed people asking me about problems they could not figure out.

I came to a brick wall using this strategy when we could no longer find any new employees because of the low unemployment rate. I was not able to fire anyone for not following the rules because there was no one to replace them.

Then I saw a move towards the Achiever style. Rather than adhering to the strict procedures, I decided to have the goal be to have the jobs done right and that there could be many ways to achieve that goal. I learned quickly the value of flexibility, working with an alcoholic who would often disappear for several days or weeks, a paranoid individual who put a mirror on his tool box so he could see if anyone was watching him, a person I would call hyper who would run through the shop jumping over cars, climbing walls, swinging from pipes, coming up behind people to startle them, and an employee who, when I asked how he did such a good job, replied that he would just get high and work. Previously, I could easily have fired any one of them, but I learned that each was useful in his own way. At this time, I also sought out critiques on what I did and if there were ways that I could do better. I watched others to see what I could learn from them and found that everyone had something I could learn from.

After a while, I started doing arbitration, and I think this introduced me to the Individualist's sense of multiple frameworks and of the interaction between process and task. The first brief would seem so convincing, then the other brief would change my mind, and then the oral presentations would again change my view of the whole case. It was also interesting experimenting like a Individualist with different ways to resolve problems that leave each side feeling as if they had their say and accepting my decision as fair and reasonable. In dealing with customers and employees, I now use these same techniques strategically.

The next precipitous event, which may be a glimpse of the Alchemist/Witch/Clown stage, happened when a customer was yelling about something to do with their car. It was also during the busy season. I had 15 employees, 75 cars, hundreds of inventory items, and customer inquiries to handle. I remember that while the person was yelling I felt that I was above the situation looking down. I figured out what I should do to correct the situation and then went back down. After this incident, I could do this as needed, separating myself from the circumstances and calmly determine what I should do to control the situation. After several times, I was both amazed and scared of being able to do this.

Sanjay himself identifies some of the themes of frames beyond the Achiever when he refers to 'the Individualist's sense of multiple frameworks and of the interaction between process and task' and to the Alchemist/Witch/Clown's experiencing an interplay of detachment from, and committed action in, present circumstances. This is not our first encounter with such themes. In Chapter 1 we met Jennifer, the leader of the 'We Can Do It' project, who wanted to revive that project, but spoke with special energy about her vision of the project as a means of transforming the process by which her department members worked with each other. She also shared Sanjay's ability to detach and reflect during conversations in which a certain colleague produced an 'outburst'.

We will explore these post-Achiever frames in more detail in the chapters that follow, but in the meantime, we hope you, the reader are beginning to become as fascinated and delighted as Sanjay at the possibility of acquiring new frames yourself. If you have written on that sheet with your name at the top the frame that you think represents your own, along with a list of some of your own characteristics which typify that frame (or if you do that writing now) you will have taken the first step in the developmental process. Perhaps you will observe, like Sanjay, that your list includes characteristics of more than just one frame, suggesting you are already in a transition from one frame to the next.

By estimating where you are in the developmental sequence (or by taking the Leadership Development Profile at www.harthill.co.uk) you can proceed to begin thinking about and experimenting in action with themes that characterise the next frame beyond your present frame, as Joanne and Sanjay are doing. For now, we return to the doorway Sanjay has opened for us into a new realm, the world of the post-Achiever frames. These frames, starting with Individualist, differ from the four earlier frames we have focused on in this chapter in ways that are vital to you as a manager and to your organisation. Recent research (examined in Chapter 11) indicates that people at the Individualist stage and beyond are likely to be more effective in transforming their organisations, than those whose frames precede the Individualist. Because of the importance of this developmental move beyond the Achiever stage, we aim the spotlight in the next two chapters on the Individualist and Strategist frames to show how their themes differ from those of the Achiever and to show the kinds of performance these post-conventional frames enable.

CHAPTER 5

THE INDIVIDUALIST FRAME:
A BRIDGE TO TRANSFORMING LEADERSHIP

In Chapter 1 we said that developmental action inquiry has at its centre a process of learning. We said that this learning process is not a mechanistic feedback process producing continuous change. Instead it is a bumpy, sometimes up-ending kind of learning that brings to individuals and to organisations a widening and deepening of vision and a new capacity for learning and improved performance.

In Chapter 4 we have illustrated our sense in which 'lifetime' learning is bumpy, not continuous. Every person (and every social process as well, as we will show later) goes through several frame transformations during the first twenty-one years of our lives. The vast majority of us transform from the Impulsive frame to the Opportunist frame, a very large majority transform from Opportunist to Diplomat, and a smaller but significant proportion of us transform to the Expert frame by the time we are twenty-one. These transformations are likely to be bumpy because neither we ourselves, nor frequently, our parents and teachers know that we are going through them or are intentionally guiding us through with a developmental map, such as we are constructing here.

But even *with* a map the developmental process is likely to remain bumpy because, like the Escher painting of the artist drawing himself, we are truly redrawing ourselves and all our maps in each developmental change. In fact, linear lists of the different developmental frames or action-logics are themselves misleading in that they imply a straightforward movement, with the map itself remaining unchanged, yet that is not the reported personal experience of developmental transformation.

To bring about this not-always-pretty, but truly transformational learning, a special form of leadership is required. We have already seen several examples, all from persons who began taking leadership without being labelled as a leader by anyone else. In Chapter 2 we saw Jennifer using action inquiry to make her department more collaborative and to revitalise its quality improvement program, Anthony breaking out of his technical specialist role to spearhead a redefining of roles in his organisation, and Jane interrupting a company president's habitual way of thinking (and her own) to form a new lending relationship for her bank.

These examples reveal a form of leadership that we describe as *post-conventional*. Post-conventional leadership is no longer entirely bound by current conventions, but rather participates in sometimes seeking to transform them, whilst simultaneously seeking to learn and prompting others to engage in learning. Such leadership also aspires to generate individual and organisational learning concurrently. This frame values learning, in the moment, through action inquiry. The Diplomat, Expert and Achiever frames of meaning-making show a progression through what are identified as the *conventional* frames. The conventional frames take the already-objectified social categories, norms, and power-structures for granted as constituting the very nature of reality, and persons operating within those frames typically do not recognise themselves as seeing themselves, others, and the world through a frame. In a mixed population of 1121 managers, consultants and students a full 73% profiled at these conventional stages. In this research only 26% profiled at post-conventional frames of Individualist, Strategist, and Alchemist. (The other 1% profiled at the pre-conventional frames.)

People who have constructed post-conventional frames increasingly appreciate themselves and others as operating with different worldviews and increasingly appreciate that these may indeed transform. Furthermore, they increasingly appreciate that they are exercising forms of power with others in each social interaction. They increasingly recognise that they are either reinforcing or transforming existing structures of power as they do so. And they increasingly appreciate that new shared frames can be generated in the *present* situation. Indeed, they appreciate shared frames often *must* be generated if co-operative solutions are to emerge. Because of the new capacities that they bring, these rarer later stages are of particular significance in the development of leadership capability that can successfully support organisational transformation.

The Individualist Frame

As we have seen, the Achiever represents a certain peak in effectiveness and productivity. It is a powerhouse stage. It drives the economies of the West and Asia. Many very successful entrepreneurs and senior executives are to be found making meaning and taking action solidly and unquestioningly within this stage.

From a personal economic point of view one could argue that development beyond this stage is unnecessary. This may be true. We know many successful executives and several millionaires who are Achievers. Many feel themselves to have 'arrived'. But human development is not shaped to serve only the god of financial gain, and even the challenges of our times are not purely economic, as the unresolved world issues of conflict, poverty and ecological crisis are currently demonstrating.

Either through necessity, curiosity, boredom or hap-chance, a small percentage of people find themselves beginning to experience the limits of the Achiever frame, or are drawn to the logic of the post-conventional frames. The movement beyond the Achiever frame toward the post-conventional frames is a movement toward recognising that none of these earlier frames sees the whole emergent truth. Allowing for frame transformation and seeking to develop shared frames may be activities critical to personal and organisational success. Individualists, for example, come to realise that theirs is just one viewpoint among many and that how events are viewed and understood depends upon one's own perception. In other words, 'reality' is relative to where you stand. Ideas such as truth or justice become increasingly elusive. The rock of certainty upon which the Achiever so confidently stands shakes.

Other changes occur - the principles by which one aspires to live become a stronger influence; the rules of others become less determining and are increasingly felt as a restriction of questionable legitimacy. At the same time, the question of whether oneself or an institution of which one is a member is acting consistently with espoused principles becomes more important. Questions of how to overcome incongruities and avoid hypocrisy become important and relevant.

As with all transitions from frame to frame, there are losses and gains. The reliable certainties of the conventional stages (Diplomat, Expert and Achiever) are swept away and the world becomes altogether more fluid and uncertain. The very questions that to the Individualist and later frames become essential will often strike persons making meaning in conventional frames as untimely, unnecessary, and even unrealistic. To become effectively transformative such questions must be advanced artfully, with dramatic illustration of the potential benefits in taking them seriously. And such skills only begin developing as the Individualist further transforms into the Strategist frame, to be described in the next chapter.

During their journey into the post-conventional frames, people develop the capacity to think systemically in action about the different frames at play and how they mutually influence one another. No longer is the world seen as a place of discrete objects, like billiard balls on a table, in which events are linear and sequential and in which plans and strategies may lead directly to outcomes. Instead, causation is recognised as circular, relational and systemic. Now, for the first time, the notions of *framing*, *advocating*, *illustrating* and *inquiring* that we introduced in Chapter 2 become principles of discourse as well as skills. This manner of discourse brings people's assumptions and effects on one another to the surface, revealing in real time the system they are constructing.

This dawning of awareness of post-conventional meaning making may be a confusing time. Yet it is also likely to be a time of dramatic new insight into the uniqueness of the self and of others, of forging relationships that seem to reach new levels of intimacy, and of pursuing new interests in the world. Excitement alternates with doubt in unfamiliar ways. If this sounds like a contradictory jumble, then this is a fair representation of the Individualist's experience. There is no stopping point for the Individualist, he or she is engaged in a uniquely long journey of re-evaluation of one's prior life and action-logics.

Two Examples of the Individualist Frame in Action

It is now time for us to introduce the Individualist frame in some detail. We will start with story of a manager with whom we had the privilege of working over a number of years, whom we shall call Mark. This story illustrates the transition from the Achiever frame and the consolidation into Individualist that Mark made. This is followed by a short comment by an internal organisational consultant at a leading university. Both people have been scored at the Individualist stage using the Leadership Development Profile. (See Endnotes for information on the Sentence Completion Form and the Profiling process)

Mark – Transition To and Consolidation Of the Individualist Frame

Mark worked for a British utility company with considerable international operations. When we first met him he had risen to a senior management grade quickly - at 32 years of age he was in charge of a large budget and over 900 staff. His staff respected him for his prodigious appetite for work, his boldness in pushing ideas and projects forward, his knowledge of the industry and his positive attitude. The main concern that staff had was his 'pace setting' style and his lack of care for those who seemed unable or unwilling to contribute at the right level.

From the organisation's perspective Mark's star was rising – an external company had rated him as 'alpha / world class', putting him in the top 3% of all managers on a basket of aptitude and intelligence tests. Mark completed the Leadership Development Profile when we first met him and then again three years later. His initial profile was scored as strongly Achiever, and this score was validated both by his own perceptions and by those of the consultant who interviewed him.

Towards the end of the year in which we first met him, Mark was given responsibility for managing the integration of a major acquisition. This was a politically sensitive acquisition and the Chief Executive made it clear to Mark that he was responsible for managing a smooth take-over. Several months in, Mark knew he needed to make hard decisions about the closure of several large sites. He met with his Chief Executive, raised his concerns about the dangers, presented his strategy and received approval.

Mark began crucial meetings at the sites concerned, working hard to cover all of the angles. Before they were ready to go public a press leak occurred, pillorying Mark's organisation for making 'fat-cat pay-offs' to the senior staff and miserly redundancy packages for the blue-collar workers. In what seemed like nanoseconds the national press, already engaged in a season of fat-cat stories, grabbed hold of it and ran the story for all it was worth.

Mark's Chief Executive came under heavy criticism from the Board. As a result he called Mark into his office, relieved him of the acquisition role, and put an official disciplinary note on his file. Mark's rising star had taken a nosedive. Of course one may pursue some interesting questions about the frame and behaviour of the Chief Executive, but here our interest is with Mark. He felt the injustice very keenly and looked to move to another company. Nothing emerged and he stayed - entering a period of feeling bruised and somewhat depressed. Tortoise-like, he withdrew into his shell and stayed there until a new Chief Executive was appointed some 18 months later. By this time the organisation no longer saw Mark as high potential.

Surprisingly this was not a stagnant period for Mark. It was a period in which many changes in how Mark made sense of the world were occurring. In fact, Mark was transitioning from the Achiever frame and into the Individualist. It was the up-ending experience of the strongly felt injustice that created the impetus for this developmental step, though other experiences that he initiated became the main factors in consolidating his new worldview, as we will see.

Mark's unexpected and, from his perspective, unjust fall from grace was causing him to re-think some of his taken for granted views of himself and life in general. Up to this point Mark had a robust ego and a sense of personal invulnerability, built on an unbroken run of success from school, through university to his current position. He believed it was through his own energies, abilities and achievements that he would be judged – and he had great faith in all of these. After a good early career and a very sound handling of the acquisition, he felt he was being used as a scapegoat by the Chief Executive, who was clearly using his greater power to protect his own position. The business world was not fully the meritocracy it advertised itself as being and that an Achiever wants to believe it is. Perhaps for the first time in his successful life, Mark felt the pangs of injustice and a questioning of the overall shape of the organisational system. And, because he had no ready-made strategy to deal with this injustice, he felt cynicism and moments of hopelessness. Importantly, and helpfully, this led to some core re-evaluations.

If working hard and playing the game fairly resulted in unjust punishment, then what exactly were the rules by which one played? He had served the Chief Executive with allegiance based on trust and loyalty until the disciplining episode – and it seemed that he had been wrong. Certainly Mark was demotivated. He stopped working the same long hours and found he had creative energies for other activities. He took up writing and started his first novel, based broadly on his great-grandfather's experiences in the Boer War. In the process of writing, he joined a writers' group and became friends with half a dozen people from outside the corporate world, some of whom had chosen a 'free' life style and its associated relative poverty in preference to a large salary.

For Mark there was not one single moment of revelation, yet over the period of the next two years he experienced a rolling diverse kind of an expansion within him. At times he felt a release, like a great exhalation of breath, and at others he felt aware, alive, even potent in a way that was new to him.

He also felt perplexed, as if the reason for 'it all' had been mysteriously stolen. In a range of ways he gave up on *the* truth, a single reliable perspective. Rather, he saw that many perspectives co-existed and often clashed, each one arising from the particular and unique experience and psychology of each individual human being, set in their history culture and history. And not only were other people different from him in so many ways – what came to fascinate him was his discovery of the differences *within* himself. For the first time in his life Mark began to be a keen observer of the different characters within himself, as well as deeply reflective about them. He also began to see inconsistencies between his entry intentions in many situations and his actual behaviour.

At work these changes manifested in many ways. Most obvious was the change in his drive to achieve. People said that he'd 'lost his edge' or simply that he'd 'lost his appetite for success'. From inside it felt different from this. After the initial period of feeling betrayed and disenchanted, he began to reflect on what had happened and what it meant for him. There were some unanswered questions. Why had the Chief Executive not simply sacked him? How could he do this and live with himself? Why had other colleagues not stood up for him? And why was his own reaction not a resolve to 'show them what I'm made of', as he would certainly have done years before, but a slower introspection?

After being relieved of the acquisition role he returned to his previous role and found it satisfying enough. He did feel a change in commitment – now he was more interested in supporting his people and to understanding how he might help them, and he realised that he could deliver all that was expected of him, and more, without working at full tilt. Without planning to, he improved both his delegation and coaching skills, which in turn changed how he related to his reports.

A subtle shift occurred in his life beyond work during these years. During his 'rising star' years work had dominated his life – he enjoyed it, felt good about himself in it and had many friendships in which he worked and played hard. After the 'fat-cats' debacle he felt a sense of a vacuum in his non- working life. He reflected on the nature of his relationship to work, and he understood how much he, as a human being, identified himself with what he delivered. His novel about the Boer War was not the result of a grand plan or an intention to write himself out of depression – he was simply pulled into writing by the vacuum his shifting relationship to work had created.

Mark's story so far, and there is more to tell, describes his transformation from a solidly conventional achieving view of the world to the more complex and less focused perspective of the Individualist. Mark did not seek this change; unwelcome and distasteful events led to it. *Even so, developmental transformation was not an inevitable consequence of external events.* Other people, or even Mark at a different time, may have responded differently in developmental terms. For example, we recall Samara, an HR professional with an explicit interest in developmental transformation who first measured at the Expert frame by the Leadership Development Profile. Dissatisfied with her work and life she took a sabbatical from her job, intent upon finding a new key to life. Six months later she took up a new job in the same profession that lasted for three years. At this point Samara profiled again, and despite her experiences was disappointed to find that she still measured at the Expert frame. There had been no developmental transformation.

Later she found herself attending silent Quaker meetings, engaged in a new relationship with a partner who had a disabled son, and started her own small company. Eighteen months later she measured as an Individualist, having moved rapidly through the Achiever frame. Samara's engagement with these experiences at this particular time in her life had led to developmental transitions.

Some developmental movement must already have been occurring in Mark before the acquisition debacle jolted his cohesive world. This movement may have been a tantalising foretaste of the world as seen and lived in from beyond the Achiever's conventional perspective. Or it may have been a sense of growing dissatisfaction with the Achiever's drive. Mark may have wondered unconsciously what would follow in the coming years, having achieved so much at the tender age of 32. Or he may have glimpsed in a book, a film, or the actions of someone near to him a way of living in a different tempo. Whatever the cause, Mark was ready to use his disappointments to learn and to transform how he made meaning.

We do not want to suggest that all transitions come from unhappy experiences. This is not the case. Humans learn in a range of ways and these include building on successes and modelling ourselves on the admired characteristics and capabilities of others. The developmental journey can be a joyful dance. It will, however, always be built upon change and challenge as existing certainties are replaced by the uncertainties of the unknown. In fact, at the latest stages, the unfamiliar and the unknown themselves become attractive rather than frightening.

We have described Mark's transition from his Achiever centre of gravity into that of the Individualist. A developmental journey has begun, but it is incomplete. Mark has still to consolidate in this stage. The rest of his story describes the consolidation:

As chance would have it, and chance plays a key role in developmental journeys, Mark's new Chief Executive was a natural coach and developer of people - she recognised the hurt that Mark still carried and saw tremendous potential in him. In an early action, she moved him to a new department and gave him extended responsibilities for a troubled Italian operation. She supported him with regular coaching sessions in which she was authentically appreciative of him and his work and was direct in her challenges. For example, she found his humour to be surprisingly cynical; her challenges led him to reflect (rather than reject it as irrelevant or soft as he may have done several years before). Without defensiveness, he asked his reports and peers for comments. To his surprise, and some dismay, he discovered that despite his 'misfortune' many still saw him as arrogant.

This did not fit with a set of evolving personal values about how he aspired to lead and he began to act differently. What bemused him was how to continue to act powerfully and yet not come across as arrogant. He still cared passionately about performance - he was determined to create a turn-around in Italy measured in cold financial terms – but how to do this without seeming authoritative or arrogant?

Mark had generally disregarded his physical well-being. Over the years he had become accustomed to working long hours, eating badly and taking almost no exercise. He had seen little or no connection between his physical, emotional and spiritual well-being. During this transformative period he rediscovered a strong liking for walking. He discovered a meditative quality on long walks and enjoyed the wonderful sense that well-earned physical tiredness can give. Several colleagues commented that he looked healthier and more relaxed.

Not everything was rosy though – those who had known him before the acquisition now saw him as indecisive. It seemed he could always see many sides of an argument and where he had once been free in giving advice and orders, he now more often asked questions, listened, and then asked more questions. Some staff felt he really didn't show commitment because he now worked only 45 hours a week (much less than his peers), and he had started to take all of his annual holidays. Others found him unpredictable – sometimes seeming to want to drive ahead and other times to consider the picture as fully as possible. He had, most agreed, become prone to moods where previously he had been consistently upbeat.

Two years after Mark had been removed from heading up the acquisition we had reason to profile him again using the Leadership Development Framework. This time he scored solidly at Individualist, a full stage later than three years earlier. In discussion Mark confirmed this felt right. He described his world from the inside – subjectively – thus emphasising the core shift from Achiever to Individualist. He described the sense of ill-ease he felt, of not knowing quite what to rely on in his former view of the world, and yet also of a sense of curiosity pervading his life and work. He expressed intolerance of the constraints imposed upon him by the drive and goal orientation of the Achiever's frame.

What interested us greatly was his relationship to the novel he had been writing and had finished. He submitted it to a number of publishers and it had been rejected, in only one case receiving some extensive recommendations about how to improve it. He realised it would take major re-working. He didn't plan to do this – instead he celebrated the part the novel had played in connecting him to his long dead great-grandfather across the generations of his lineage. He now felt a strong sense of trans-generational family identity as one of the distinctive fabrics interwoven into his identity as an individual. "It was worth it for that" he said.

Comments from an Individualist consultant

When one of the authors told a consultant colleague that we were working on this chapter, she raised questions about whether the title 'Individualist' conveyed enough of the feel of this frame. She first suggested 'Perspectivist', but agreed that almost no one would have any idea what that meant. Then she suggested 'Subjectivist' because that title may convey the primacy of personal experience at this stage, as opposed to any ideology. The next day she sent an e-mail proposing the title 'Participant-Observer'. She wrote, "I know I have nerve prolonging this part of the conversation given you are at deadline, but I am intrigued by the notion of naming this stage since I did score at it the last time I did the Sentence Completion Form! There is something about seeing multiple frames, knowing you are embedded in just one of them, knowing they are 'context-and-perspective-specific' and not necessarily knowing what to do with the insight". It is a particularly appropriate illustration of this subjectivist frame that a person scored at it should author-ise her own voice, as this consultant does, to participate in defining it!

Individualist Overview

These two stories give us some insights into how meaning is made by people with the Individualist frame as their centre of gravity and the transitions that accompany movement to this frame. The key features of this action-logic are:

- the understanding that objectivity is itself a social construction and that what one sees is conditioned both by one's own particular subjective standpoint and historical conditioning and by the particular context of the current situation

- that each variable, be that people, organisations, or the natural world are whole in their own right and embedded within more widely embracing systems; and thus

- a growing sense of curiosity, even absorption, about oneself and the power one has to play different roles in meetings, relationships, and social processes of creation and destruction

- an increasing clarity about the principles that he or she aspires to have inform one's own living and a parallel conscious awareness of the rules of others and of one's own conscious choice about whether to be constrained by them

- a willingness to be seen as different – to be seen by others as unorthodox

- a willingness to inquire and experiment with many of the hither-to taken-for-granted aspects of life.

With Mark's and the consultant's help we have encountered the first of the post-conventional frames. In some development models this frame is not viewed as a complete frame in its own right – but rather as a transition to the Strategist stage. There are certain qualities of impermanence in the

Individualist frame that lead it to be best viewed as a continual journey. For example, there is often a keen sense of what is being given up or rejected from the Achiever's worldview, but what is being adopted is often confused and contradictory. There is a dark side to every frame and this is particularly so for the Individualist. Within this frame there is often a more troubled sense of something needing resolving or unravelling than is present in any other frame. Paradoxically, there is often a strong sense of an ongoing journey with new experiences around each corner. The Individualist is likely to feel a much stronger sense than the Expert or Achiever of living in the moment rather than strung out on a timeline, blown back and forth by deadlines imposed by others.

In our work, we see an increasing number of managers profiling at this stage. We frequently find that managers who have left roles in large organisations to take a position in small consulting firms or to set up their own both feel and score as Individualists. This trend may be influenced by the decreasing job security in firms worldwide. It may derive from the increased interest in one's own psychology, which in turn may be influenced by the post-modern, expressive trends in popular culture and technology. Or, are more and more of us responding to the dramatic 'signs' we are receiving that the environmental, political, business, and spiritual worlds are a systemic whole/mess that requires a different kind of awareness and action?

Whether this is a separate or a transitional frame, the Individualist clearly bridges between the pre-constituted, relatively stable and hierarchical meaning-making systems that we grow into as children, learning how to function as members of a pre-constituted culture, and the emergent, relatively fluid and mutual meaning-making systems that highlight the power of responsible adults to lead their children, their subordinates, and their peers in transforming change.

The Strategist frame, to which we turn next, is the first general response to the question of how to lead transforming change in a mutual way that invites and even sometimes challenges others to join in the leadership process.

CHAPTER 6

STRATEGISTS IN ACTION - MANAGERIAL AND ORGANISATIONAL LEARNING

The Strategist frame is rare because it not only recognises other frames but also sees them as valid, vital, usable, and potentially open to transformation. Growing out of the acknowledgement of individual differences and of complexities of circumstances of the Individualist stage comes a greater appreciation that all personal and social systems are at different points in transformation. Timely action by others can support such transformation. But each individual can only increase his or her freedom and individuality by participating in the choice to transform. Hence, the little known and rarely practiced power to transform is a mutual, vulnerable power, disciplined by careful attention to the timing of each interacting person, group, organisation, or nation.

The new step the Strategist has taken is to not only accept individuality, but to welcome evolving individuality in the context of mutual relationships. The Strategist is attuned, implicitly if not explicitly, to the developmental process, recognising that other persons have developed as a result of their past experiences and that they need the opportunity to develop autonomously. Accompanying this recognition is a willingness to let others (such as one's subordinates or one's children) make their own mistakes. However, the Strategist is also conscious of the limits to autonomy, realising that emotional interdependence is inevitable. Paradoxically, Strategists value the personal ties between increasingly autonomous friends as deeply important. In Chapter 12, 'Seeking the Good Life', we explore this further.

Unlike the Achiever frame, the Strategist's is open to the possibility of 'reframing' his or her viewpoint and purposes and helping others to 'reframe' theirs. The Strategist consciously seeks and chooses new frames that accommodate the disparities, paradoxes and fluidity of multiple possibilities. Moreover, the Strategist senses that such frame changes cannot be generated unilaterally either by external command or by internal effort. Instead, the exercise of transforming power is a mutual process in which all the participants are initiators and in which all participants make themselves vulnerable to transformation in the service of greater organisational legitimacy and effectiveness.

A distinctive mark of the Strategist is the ability to acknowledge and deal with inner conflicts, such as conflicting needs and duties. It is not that this person has more conflicts than others, but rather has the qualities and the will to acknowledge and deal with conflicts rather than ignoring them or blaming them on forces beyond his or her control. The Strategist seeks ways to unite and integrate ideas that appear as irreconcilable polarities to those at prior stages.

The manager at the Strategist level focuses attention on developing a concept of how mission, strategy, operations and outcome may be in conflict with one another and can be aligned coherently. The Strategist will develop ways to detect disparities between mission and strategy, strategy and operations, and operations and outcome so that ineffective and unethical processes can be corrected. The Strategist's sensitivity to systemic disparities includes a keen awareness of inequities in race, ethnicity, class, gender, and development among colleagues and subordinates. This perspective demands that the Strategist make every effort to redress social inequities and is engaged with a global rather than ethnocentric vision.

This person has the capacity for developing mutually satisfying relationships. The Strategist sees the circularity of social interaction. A person does not simply 'cause' another's behaviour. Instead, behaviour - its causes and its outcomes - is viewed in an interactive context. For the Strategist, the self is embedded in social relationships.

The Strategist's expressions are spontaneous, combining genuineness and intensity. Feelings are expressed vividly and convincingly, including sensual experiences, poignant sorrows, joy, and delight. Expressions often have a light touch, including fantasy and a sensitivity to life's paradoxes. The Strategist and the later post-conventional frames become increasingly sensitive, not just to how the past influences the present, but also to how one's current actions, including one's speaking, affect the present and the future.

People with the Strategist's worldview see purpose in life beyond meeting one's own needs. Continuing self-development and self-actualisation are primary concerns. They seek to discover what they can do uniquely well. They may well be involved in a personal quest - a life work - with a sense of vocation. This quest may be focused within the workplace, outside it, or both. The question of identity for the Strategist includes the question of one's social and spiritual vocation.

The Strategist frame is not without potential shadows and turmoil. The ability to see multiple frames in conflict can lead to suffering. The ability to choose a new frame, to create new meanings, may leave the person feeling virtually paralysed at moments by the weight of the implied responsibility. However, it is this very ability to see many meanings simultaneously that enables the Strategist to develop an encompassing frame that makes order out of chaos and creates a motivating shared vision that leads beyond debilitating conflict.

The Strategist's subordinates, who may be unable to see from so wide a perspective, may feel out of touch with their manager and with the organisation. But the manager with the Strategist frame, having keen awareness of multiple frames, is well equipped to act to maintain institutional and personal connections to subordinates.

Research that is summarised in Chapter 11 has shown that the Strategist's ability to accommodate diverse frames, to adopt new frames, and to collaborate with others in reframing is an essential element in leading organisational transformation. This is particularly true of transformation to the later organisational stages when the organisation institutionalises the ongoing inquiry processes that generate sustained organisational learning. Chapters 8 to 12 introduce the stages of organisational development.

Single-Loop and Double-Loop Learning

The great victory of the Achiever frame is that it reliably digests single-loop feedback and learning. As discussed in Chapter 2, single-loop feedback is feedback through which one learns that one's actions are not achieving a pre-established goal, and then 'proves' one's learning by adjusting one's actions to increase the likelihood of achieving the goal. According to adult developmental theory, single-loop learning does not occur consistently for persons who have not reached the Achiever stage of development. This means that single-loop feedback does not always register on every person to whom it is directed and therefore does not always generate single-loop learning and more effective action.

The great victory of development to the Strategist frame is that it begins to explicitly seek out and digest double-loop feedback and learning. With double-loop feedback one learns that the structure of one's strategic, goal-seeking, status-maintaining system is problematic. Double-loop feedback enables individuals and organisations to learn through examining alternative policies and objectives from new perspectives rather than to simply improve ways of functioning within present perspectives. According to developmental theory again, each stage change is a double-loop learning process, but the fact and the process of such double-loop changes remain implicit before the Strategist stage. Only persons who reach the Strategist stage explicitly seek out and act on double-loop feedback that highlights incongruities and incompletenesses within one's meaning-making system. Adult developmental theory suggests that it is at the Strategist stage that a person begins to develop the capacity for integrative awareness needed to work with people holding different frames, to redefine presented problems, to seek underlying issues, and to foster a manager's or an organisation's transformation. To persons at the earlier stages, ambiguity, paradox, and exploration of implied, underlying meanings are likely to seem vague and a waste of time rather than being seen as clues to innovative agendas, genuine collaboration, and new stages of development.

In this chapter we will illustrate leadership as practised by post-Achievers. We will introduce you to several managers we met through our research who illustrate sharply the difference between the learning disposition of the Strategist frame and the relative 'disability' of the earlier frames to generate transformational leadership. We hope these illustrations will help you, the reader, to explore the later frames - perhaps to rehearse Strategist thoughts and actions as they apply to your own circumstances.

A Research-Based Look at The Strategist

Research confirms that later stage leaders (Strategists and beyond) have a greater capacity to successfully lead organisations, where the context of the organisation is complex. Our own research specifically points to a link between the post-Achiever frames and the manager's tendencies to redefine problems and to propose collaborative rather than unilateral action in responding to problems.

In one of our studies, we placed 49 MBA graduates in a simulated management setting called an 'in-basket' exercise. We were able to apply statistical tests to show that people at later developmental stages redefined problems in response to more of the in-basket items and made more collaborative action proposals than people holding the Achiever, Expert or other earlier frames.

We were excited when we obtained such clear research confirmation that two particular types of managerial behaviour, redefining of problems and undertaking collaborative action, were indeed more characteristic of managers holding the post-Achiever frames than of those holding developmentally earlier frames. But we wanted to know more. The results of our in-basket study whetted our appetite for learning how post-Achievers performed, not just in an exercise setting, but also in their everyday at-work situations.

To find out more about Strategists in action, we did a follow-on study, interviewing nine men and eight women who held a range of positions in service and manufacturing organisations. All held advanced degrees, mostly MBAs. Nine held managerial positions, including one Chief Operating Officer and three functional Area Heads. Four were in specialist or individual contributor positions (such as Financial Planner or Loan Officer), and four were consultants. Fifteen of the 17 were in their 30s, with the median age being 36, and the median length of work experience was 10 years.

Nine of these individuals were profiled at the Individualist or the Strategist stage, with one measuring at a later stage called Ironist. The other seven held the developmentally earlier frames of Expert (two) and Achiever (five). We separated the transcribed interviews into two groups, Strategists and pre-Strategists. Because our primary focus was on how those who have attained the post-Achiever frames differ from those who have not yet reached those stages, we referred for simplicity to all seven of the pre-Individualists as Achievers, and to all of the other ten as Strategists.

We discovered that there were indeed important differences in the ways the Achievers and Strategists thought, spoke, and acted at work. We found the differences to be particularly striking in three major arenas:
    1. their ways of exercising leadership
    2. their relationships with their superiors
    3. their ways of initiating action when proposing ideas or progammes.
We will examine each of these arenas.

As you read each of the stories these managers told us, you might wish to try recalling how you yourself thought and acted in a similar situation. Was your approach that of the Strategist? If not, see if you can 'try on' the Strategist frame and make some notes about how you might think and act in that situation, or one like it, were you to engage it from the Strategist perspective.

1. The Exercise of Leadership

When Achievers and Strategists spoke about leading, their contrasting frames showed clearly. Achievers saw leadership as being able to cultivate and mould subordinates to their own way of thinking. In some cases they acted as mentor, in others as law enforcer or watchdog representing their own bosses.

Bill, an Achiever, shows this way of thinking as he describes his relationship with a low performing member of his staff who, according to Bill, 'did not do a lot of work, tried to coast, and this was obvious to everybody in the group'.

> It was a series of specific conversations where I'd tell him, "You're missing the boat here. You've got a job to do and I want to make sure you get the job done . . . I don't think it's fair to the others, who are working very hard and aren't being rewarded any more than you are".

> At various times we would come head to head and I'd threaten to fire him. Then he would buckle down and get it done for a little while. I would give him specific objectives and certain reward systems for him.

> He had a good relationship with my boss. I made it clear to him I thought he was taking advantage of that, and I told my boss the same thing. My boss agreed. He said, "I'm out of it", but he never really was. This went on for six months, and that guy is now in my position. That was a very disappointing situation. I think I could have taken greater control; just fired him.

Bill says his problem lay in not taking a stronger stand and, in retrospect, this may be true. But at the time he could only have known this to be true if he could have taken a wider perspective, as a Strategist would be likely to do, encompassing the points of view of all three actors. Only if he had understood that his boss was not really going to act and that the subordinate did not really share the productivity objectives would 'a stronger stand' have made sense.

And what would the stronger stand have been? To the Achiever the stronger stand would have been to fire the subordinate at some point prior to the time that the subordinate took over the Achiever's position. To a Strategist... well you, our reader, are the person who wishes to practice the Strategist frame, so... what would have been a Strategist's approach to this situation, from the outset? We invite you to take a piece of paper and outline your approach, if you wish, prior to reading the following examples of Strategist approaches to subordinates.

By contrast, the Strategists' interviews provide several examples of much more patient efforts to work with a subordinate's frame, questioning it rather than dismissing it. Susan, a hospital marketing manager, describes a conversation with a subordinate whose performance had recently slipped:

> I wanted to crack her shell, because she is really tough. You can see the strain behind Francine's eyes, but she says, "I'm fine". I attempted to approach her by really sharing my feelings about the situation, not so much demanding that she open up, but saying I'm feeling concerned, I'm concerned about you. And I said, "I need you to know that a lot of people are wondering what's wrong. Is something wrong?" That kind of conversation. It wasn't the first time we had had it.

> She finally said in a very matter-of-fact way, "It really upsets me that everyone came to you to tell you they were bothered by my behaviour, and not to me". So I said, "In the future, I promise you, if people come to me I will tell them to go to you. She said "Thank you". Her behaviour has changed drastically".

Susan describes Francine's perspective ('I'm fine') and the incongruity between her perspective on herself and how she enacts herself ('You can see the strain behind her eyes'). Susan engaged Francine not by trying to enforce or mould her, but by offering her own and others' points of view ('a lot of people are wondering what's wrong') as points of departure for inquiry. In Argyris and Schön's terms, Susan undertakes double loop learning by designing a situation where the other person can be the origin of causation, in which the task is controlled jointly and where the other has room to make choices and take risks. She sees her subordinate's frame as worth exploring and is willing to change a characteristic of her own frame (namely, her implicit belief that it was appropriate for others to come to her to discuss issues relating to her subordinate) when that aspect of her frame became problematic.

The Strategists expressed a fascination with varied, potentially opposing frames (their own, their subordinates', other managers', their clients'). Rather than choosing one among these perspectives as authoritative, they strove to find a way to operate effectively amidst this variety. In this integrative awareness, the Strategists differed from the Achievers, who spoke more as though they had opted for a choice among dichotomies, for example by taking the role of law enforcer or watchdog, or by undertaking to 'mould' a subordinate.

2. Relationships with Superiors

The data on relationships of both Achievers and Strategists with their superiors was perhaps the most unexpected and counter-intuitive of our study. The conventional view is that the boss has the power so you've got to do what your boss says. In fact, however, neither Achievers nor Strategists in our study accept this frame or operate from it. Both assume that it is possible, legitimate, and even necessary to influence what the superior believes, wants, and does. Frank, a consultant, shows the strength of the Achiever's urge to bring his 'superior' (in this case a potential client who was a corporate CEO) to see his framework. Frank believes he succeeded in getting the CEO to see his point:

> The CEO opened his mouth and let one of the vice presidents have it. He said, "Surely you don't mean so-and-so". He said, "That's absurd; you can't run a business that way". I said, "Let's explore it. How do we know we can't run a business that way"? The CEO and I had a 15-minute dialogue, and by the time that ended he began to see what I was talking about. The other people present told me they saw that I wasn't going to be intimidated ... nor would I get into his hip pocket.

Frank and the other Achievers saw clearly the difference between their own view and that of the superiors. Like Frank, the other Achievers were not afraid to advocate their views to their superiors. At the same time, like Frank, they implicitly held the rationality and efficacy of their own view to be beyond question. The end of Frank's story is that the CEO did not hire him to consult, an outcome that Frank attributes, not to any possible learning he may be able to do, but rather to his not having had enough time with the CEO.

In contrast to the Achievers, Strategists were more likely than the others to speak in terms of their perceptions rather than in terms of unquestionable realities. The Strategists would frequently discuss how they had revised and sharpened their definitions of themselves by juxtaposing their perceptions of self against their perceptions of their superiors. Sharon, a team leader in a consulting firm, provides a striking example as she discussed her differences with her boss, who was not, Sharon explained, the type who is accustomed to candid discussions of differences with his subordinates:

> I was working with a manager that I knew had a style very, very different from mine. I knew if I was going to make manager this year, it was crucial that I get this guy on my side, that I make him see I was ready to be manager.
>
> He was called the assassin. He was known for picking people off in that critical year. I figured the only way I know how to approach this is to talk to him about it - be honest and get things out on the table that no one talks about. So I said, "Steve, I am scared to death of working for you this year because I know you don't promote people. I know you think I'm screwing up because it's different from the way you do things, but trust me. It will work. I know it".
>
> He was very task oriented. He wanted to look at budget analyses and all this sort of junk, and I keep telling him, "Steve, there are six people on this project. I don't need to look at a written report to tell you what's going on". I think that was the pivotal point for me in changing because I realised we had two different styles. His had worked for him for many years. I could learn from him, but I could never be that way. And that's when I realised my style was no less valid. My way was not the wrong way. I don't need to continue looking for *the* answer.

I had several conversations with him about our differences. I don't think any staff person ever confronted him on his evaluations of them or his approach. I just kept pointing out to him, "Steve, we're different but trust me. I have delivered everything on time, haven't I?" And he would have to say, "Yes". "My project team is happy?" He said, "Yes". I said, "See, it's not that I do it worse, it's that we're different, and it's not that I can't learn from you". And I think he got a lot from me. And everyone told me, "Sharon, what did you do to Steve? He gave you an 'outstanding'. He stood up and supported you".

Significant here is the way Sharon addresses the differences between her boss's frame and her own in conversations with him. In action inquiry terms, she combines assertion and illustration of her views with explicit recognition of the differences in frames and with inquiry in the process of testing and building her commitment to a style of working. She does this even with a subject previously considered unmentionable in her organisation, her boss's evaluation of her. She does not refrain from discussing this subject when her principles demand that she discuss it.

According to developmental theory, the Strategist will recognise the importance of principle over accepted conventions and rules in deciding how to act. Thus principle becomes an integrating force providing central meaning among diverse views of reality. Principled choice can sometimes mean explicitly violating rules, even ones established by one's superior. The story of Roger, the newly appointed Director of Operations for a manufacturing firm, illustrates this. Operations was to be a new unit, formed by consolidating two existing departments. Roger felt he had to call his new staff together and begin working with them despite the fact that his boss had said to wait and not tell the new staff members that they had been selected:

> While I knew these people were going to be on my staff, my boss's process and the process defined by the company was 'don't tell an individual for sure, for definite that they're going to be here'. So I had to play games. In reality, what I did was to violate rules all over the place. I couldn't handle it. I had to lie to my boss and the Human Resources Manager and say to them that I didn't inform people when really I did. I couldn't do it any other way.

We will see how this situation evolved in the next section, as we discuss the different ways in which Achievers and Strategists were effective in taking action.

3. Action Initiatives: Proposing and Implementing Ideas and Programmes

In general all of our interviewees were effective. The Achievers as well as the Strategists got things done, met objectives and were making career progress. They came up with new ideas and moved them forward. As our earlier examples have already suggested, however, there were differences.

When Strategists described how they took action, they conveyed a sense of the simultaneous validity of others' ways of looking at things and a sense of the uniqueness of the situation. The process of action was not generalisable, meaning that one often could not go according to the book. Let us return to Roger's story as he describes his work in forming his new management team:

> I got everyone together off site and said, "You're going to be on my staff". My boss didn't like that. He found out afterward that I had talked to these people. I was going to fail one way or the other. I was going to fail if I didn't talk to them, so I figured I'd be able to deal with my boss.

> I had a team building meeting two days ago, all of these people in a meeting with a facilitator, again off site. I made an opening statement. I said, "OK, you're the consultants. I've just hired you. I want you, as consultants, to satisfy your needs for information so that you can recommend to me a future business strategy".

> What that did was it opened the floodgates. I got asked every question. We got every issue exposed. I said at the end of this, "I do not want any hidden agendas between me and you". So Im finding things out. They told me they thought my boss or my boss's boss told me what to do. I said, "No, they don't. It is my decision and I am expecting you to push back on me". They said that they hadn't because they felt if they had pushed back it wasn't going to do any good.

Roger goes well beyond the task as defined by the organisation in order to achieve his own goal of forming an effective team. He shows the acceptance of paradox and contradiction by his deliberate choice between 'failing' with his boss and 'failing' with his team (while really intending to fail with neither). He does not limit himself to a single process. He makes himself vulnerable by 'opening the floodgates'. His remarks make it clear he sees his effectiveness as relating to stage setting - developing a new type of frame for an interaction or process to take place in which his own aims can be expressed, but which can also accommodate those of others.

Sarinda, a Market Analysis Manager at a major computer manufacturer, provides the contrasting perspective of the Achievers with regard to action initiatives. Sarinda describes her efforts, which she views as quite successful, at bringing together and leading a cross-functional team to design and market a new software package.

> It involved at least half a dozen organisations' representatives who sat around the table on a weekly basis designing this progamme and coming up with something that both they and the customer who was piloting it were very happy with. I felt very good about that because none of those people reported to me, but they all saw the advantages of doing business this way. The customer benefited, their goals were met. We channelled it from a lot of people to a single organisation and the single organisation dealt with our point of contact for support and

service. Administratively it just became a much cleaner and tighter way of doing business for us. It was one of the major achievements I've accomplished inside the corporation. It had a lot of impact inside and a lot of impact competitively on the industry. As in Roger's case, Sarinda is effective in putting together a team, but she sees it differently. While Roger stressed the importance of 'opening the floodgates' to learn things he hadn't known, Sarinda emphasises that the team members 'all saw the advantages and benefits of doing business this way'. What Sarinda sees as important is that it is her solution, her way of doing business that gains acceptance. She sets up and monitors 'a clean, tight way of doing business'. Roger, on the other hand, relies on principles of fairness and valid information since 'the rules', as defined by his boss and his subordinates, are in conflict. Sarinda's effectiveness, like Roger's, involves coordinating the efforts of many different individuals, but do not, as she described it, involve double loop learning - looking at or questioning, her own frame of reference, process or ideology.

How Strategists Think and Act

Our interviews provide a basis for several summarising statements about the managerial practice of persons who have moved beyond the Achiever frame to the Strategist frame. These statements may be grouped in the three areas illuminated by the interviews: leadership practice, relationships with superiors and the taking of action initiatives.

Leadership Practice

1. Strategists are more likely than Achievers to undertake double loop learning, designing situations where others can be the origin of causation, where tasks are controlled jointly, and where others may make choices and take risks.

2. Strategists make more frequent and more conscientious efforts than Achievers: a) to understand subordinates' frames, inquiring about them rather than dismissing them; b) to form an integrative awareness of these frames, including discrepant frames; and c) to use them as a basis for synthesising new shared meanings.

3. Strategists are more likely than Achievers to test the limits of their organisations' and their superiors' constraints and to create new spheres of action for their subordinates and for themselves.

Relationships with Superiors

4. Both Strategists and Achievers see it as appropriate to influence their superiors' beliefs, goals and actions.

5. Strategists, in influencing superiors, are more likely than Achievers to undertake a negotiation among initially diverse frames to create a new shared frame, while Achievers are more likely to assert their own view as beyond question.

6. Strategists are more likely than Achievers to identify their perceptions as perceptions, rather than as immutable realities, and to discuss differences in perceptions explicitly with their superiors.

7. Strategists, more than Achievers, base their actions on principles rather than rules, even when those principles are at odds with rules established by their superiors.

Action Initiatives

8. When their actions are inconsistent with their own principles, Strategists are more likely than Achievers to notice the discrepancy and act to reduce it.

9. Strategists are more likely than Achievers to view their action processes as unique rather than generalisable and rule governed.

10. Strategists are more likely than Achievers to define their effectiveness as consisting in setting a context in which their own as well as others' aims can be expressed, rather than in getting their own solutions and processes adopted.

11. Achievers use their awareness of others' points of view to design ways of gaining acceptance by others of their own goals. They see implementation as a linear move toward the goal. Strategists, however, use their awareness of others' points of view to question and revise their goals. They see implementation as an iterative process involving creation of new shared meanings, leading to the reframing of problems.

Taken as a whole, these statements argue strongly that the capacities that managers need in order to create settings in which they themselves, their colleagues, and their organisation as a whole can transform, require a developmental shift of perspective beyond the Achiever frame to the Strategist frame.

The cases and exercises we present in this book suggest what is involved in making that shift. It is a shift that involves an unusual kind of learning. Most management development teaches managers new knowledge and skills that enable them to function better within their existing frame (single-loop learning). However, the developmental shift from Achiever to Strategist requires understanding and questioning what has been taken for granted (double-loop learning), as Roger did when he 'opened the floodgates' to let his team members' hidden agendas come forth. Roger's inquiry led him to discover that he had held two implicit assumptions that were invalid: that his team members knew he was free from autocratic control by his boss and that they would 'push back' on him if they disagreed with him. Making this developmental shift also requires experimenting in action with new frames (assumptions about oneself, others, and one's situation as Sharon did when she confronted her boss about the 'undiscussable' topics of his style and how he evaluated his people.

We are convinced that this exposing of implicit assumptions and this experimenting with a new frame is crucial not only in helping individuals become leaders, but also in the process of continual quality improvement in organisations. Jean Bartunek and Michael Moch describe in detail a 'quality of work life' (QWL) intervention in a manufacturing organisation where it was vividly clear that successes during the project, where they occurred, were due to the ability of people to replace an old frame with a new frame. The old frame, widely shared in the organisation, assumed management should be paternalistic. People who developed a new frame assumed the relationship between employees and management should be collaborative. Ultimately, the progamme failed because the new, shared frame never took hold sufficiently and the organisation slipped back into the old frame.

These cases support our contention that the manager's frame is central to his or her effectiveness. It offers further evidence that it is the leader whose frame has developed to the Strategist stage who brings to the arena of action a realisation that people and organisations differ from one another in the frames through which they interpret events, an ability to examine his or her own, as well as others' frames, and a willingness to set a stage where new shared ways of making-meaning can develop.

Conclusion

Research continues to show that managers who hold the Strategist frame are more effective than those holding earlier frames in leading organisational transformation and supporting personal development. You as a manager, or as one who develops and mentors managers, are afforded a compelling new perspective, which we believe you ignore at great cost.

If the Strategist perspective is new to you, as it is to a great many people, we hope the reflections and notes you made while reading this chapter have helped you to begin anticipating the Strategist frame and rehearsing Strategist actions. By exercising in this way, you can begin to develop the wider vision that enables personal autonomy as well as the kind of collaboration with others that produces a self-renewing organisation. Shifting your frame is vital to your own effectiveness. Moreover, your nurturing of later stage frames in others is vital to your role as a catalyst in the process of transforming other individuals and your organisation. It is to this role of catalysing transformation that we invite your attention in the next chapters.

CHAPTER 7

DEVELOPING LEARNING ORGANISATIONS

When individuals within an organisation practise action inquiry they engage, possibly alone, in a double loop process of learning. If by chance or design those individuals come to share their inquiry with other colleagues, either formally or informally, then their organisation is exposed to a vital opportunity to become more learningful and move towards what is described as a learning organisation. Learning organisations, like the Strategist at the individual level, intentionally and explicitly seek out single-loop and double-loop and eventually, triple-loop feedback and change.

In learning organisations openness to questioning exists, assumptions are tested, seeming mistakes are rarely punished but are a basis for further learning, new knowledge is shared and new knowledge is collaboratively co-created. In short, inquiry, and specifically developmental action inquiry becomes an activity of the organisation. The word 'organisation' may be a little overblown for a small group or small groups of inquirers, but we have found many 'cells' of learning operating within larger organisations which are not initially characterised by this open ended learning process, and we have seen how these learning cells have come in time to influence the larger organisation.

One of the largest organisations in the world began from just such humble beginnings. We are referring to Alcoholics Anonymous and all the other 12-step groups that the AA approach has since spawned. Alcoholics Anonymous began as a conversation between two persons who wished to change their practice.

Alcoholics Anonymous is a learning organisation in the sense that it supports individual persons in reforming their lives when they are down and out. Alcoholics Anonymous is a good example of a learning organisation, in that it demonstrates how eager the individual member must be for transformation in order for transformational, developmental change to occur. Granted, we cannot directly generalise from Alcoholics Anonymous to the organisational situations most of us inhabit at work and in our leisure. We rarely inhabit organisations where everyone shares the same intense motivation to transform in a particular direction, and where there is no other order of business but personal transformation.

We also recognise that Alcoholics Anonymous is not focused on organisational learning and transformation - on creating a learning organisation - but rather on individual learning and transformation. But, for our present purposes, the example of Alcoholics Anonymous is very useful as a pointer in the direction of a kind of organising that encourages both personal and organisational transformations along the path toward personal development and a learning organisation. Indeed, Alcoholics Anonymous exemplifies the Social Network type of organisation that parallels the Individualist frame at the personal scale (see Table 7-1 below). Like a large international conglomerate that allows its subsidiaries to retain their corporate identities and individual strategies, Alcoholics Anonymous allows its thousands upon thousands of separate meeting places wide autonomy.

The Parallels between Personal and Organisational Development

As we explored action inquiry at the personal level, we examined the transformational learning that can occur as people move through developmental stages toward action inquiry that is increasingly all encompassing. Paralleling that movement, we present in this chapter an analogous way of understanding organisational development as a sequence of stages. A given stage may characterise a given meeting or project, or a whole organisation over many years. Thus you can become as subtle as you wish in analysing overlapping and mutually influencing developmental processes in your organisation. Within the organisation's overall frame, particular projects or divisions may represent leading or lagging developmental tendencies. Similarly, your own department or team or task force on which you serve may transform from one stage of development to another during a single meeting or over several meetings.

As a group or organisation evolves toward the later stages it increasingly approaches the true character of a learning organisation. We illustrate organisational transformations from one stage to another in this chapter and the following we will show that the more the transformational process from one stage to another is itself structured like a temporary learning organisation, and the more it encourages the brief recapitulation of the early stages of development as sub-stages within that transformation, the more likely it becomes that a genuine and successful frame-change will occur for the organisation.

Table 7-1 indicates how the two stage theories of development at the individual and the organisational scale are directly analogous to one another. (You will note that we show an early childhood stage - the Impulsive stage - and a late adulthood stage - the Ironist stage. We did not mention these stages in earlier chapters, since we found no managers in our large samples at either of these stages.)

Table 7-2 describes the unique characteristics of the first seven stages of organisational development in a little more detail. (We will defer discussion of stages eight and nine until Chapters 13 to 15.) We will offer a few comments on each stage, to highlight the personal-organisational parallels in Table 7-1. Then, we give some concrete illustrations of particular meetings and of whole organisations moving from one stage to another. Organisations very often halt along the path to becoming learning organisations when they reach what could be frame-changing opportunities and challenges. Instead of transforming, they defend their current culture and structure and tend to rigidify. Hence, it is important to get a feel for the sorts of leaderly initiatives that can generate organisational transformation.

Table 7-1   Parallels between Personal and Organisational Stages of Development

Stage	Personal Stage	Organisational Stage
1	*Impulsive* Impulses rule reflexes	*Conception* Dreams about creating a new organisation
2	*Opportunist* Needs rule impulses	*Investments* Spiritual, social network, and financial investments
3	*Diplomat* Norms rule needs	*Incorporation* Products or services actually rendered
4	*Expert* Craft logic rules norms	*Experiments* Alternative strategies and structures tested
5	*Achiever* System effectiveness rules craft logic	*Systematic Productivity* Single structure/strategy institutionalised
6	*Individualist* Reflexive awareness rules effectiveness	*Social Network* Portfolio of distinctive organisational structures
7	*Strategist* Self-amending principle rules system	*Collaborative Inquiry* Self-amending structure rules matches dream/mission
8	*Alchemist/Witch/Clown* Process (interplay of prin-ciple/action) rules principle	*Foundational Community of Inquiry* Structure fails, spirit sustains wider community
9	*Ironist* Intersystemic develop-ment rules process	*Liberating Disciplines* Widens members' awareness of incongruities among mission/strategy/operations/ outcomes and skill at resolving them

Table 7-2   Characteristics of Each Stage of Organisational Development

Conception

Dreams, visions, informal conversations about creating something new to fill need not now adequately addressed; interplay among multiple 'parents'; working models, prototypes, related projects or business plans developed. Critical issues: timeliness and mythic proportions of vision.

Investments

'Champions' commit to creating organisation; early relationship-building among future stakeholders; peer networks and parent institutions make spiritual, structural, financial commitments to nurture. Critical issues: authenticity and reliability of commitments; financial investment appropriately subordinated to structural and spiritual investments.

Incorporation

Products or services produced; recognisable physical setting, tasks, and roles delineated; goals and operating staff chosen. Critical issues: display of persistence in the face of threat; maintaining or recreating consistency between original dream and actual organisational arrangements.

Experiments

Alternative administrative, production, selection, reward, financial, marketing, and political strategies practised, tested in operation, and reformed in rapid succession. Critical issues: truly experimenting - taking disciplined stabs in the dark - rather than merely trying one or two preconceived alternatives; finding a viable, lasting combination of strategy and structure for the following stage.

Systematic Productivity

Attention legitimately focused only on systematic procedures for accomplishing the pre-defined task; standards, structures, roles taken for granted as given; marketability or political viability of product or service, as measured in quantifiable terms the overriding criterion of success. Critical issue: whether organisation 'remembers' analogical concerns about congruity from mission through outcomes during this emphasis on deductive, pyramidal systems.

Social Network

Strategic or mission-focused alliances among portfolio of organisations, with strong value on maintaining distinctive traditions, craft-orientations, and relative financial autonomy. Critical issue: will organisation regress or progress in economically adverse conditions?

Collaborative Inquiry

Explicit, shared reflection about corporate mission; open interpersonal relations with disclosure, support, and confrontation of apparent value differences; systematic personal and corporate performance appraisal on multiple indexes; creative resolution of paradoxes -inquiry/productivity, freedom/control, quality/quantity; interactive development of unique, self-amending structures appropriate for this particular organisation at this particular historical moment.

Although Table 7-1 shows the individual stages of development as paralleling the organisational stages, it is not immediately clear how. Let us start with a brief comment on the parallels between the Impulsive stage of personal development and the Conception stage of organisational development. Just as very young children are highly imaginative and express many impulses (e.g. to become an artist, or a nurse, or a professional athlete) that they do not necessarily follow up on in their later life; so adults frequently fantasise with friends about organisations they would like to create (e.g. to market a baby buggy that can be folded up and would have made today's visit to the city easier), but then do not necessarily follow up on them. In retrospect, when one in every ten thousand or so such conversations eventually evolves into a major organisation, as Alcoholics Anonymous did, and as the idea to create a fold-up baby buggy did, the founding of the organisation can be traced back to such incidental or passionate or calculating conversations.

The parallels between the next three stages of personal and organisational development are less obvious. When we described the Opportunist, the Diplomat, and the Expert we were describing, not children in the normal process of development, but rather adults in organisations who are still motivated by relatively early stage logics. Therefore, we can see the rigidities and limitations in their effectiveness quite easily. By contrast, when we discuss organisations at these three early stages (Investments, Incorporation, Experiments) in the next chapter, we will describe them in their natural developmental process (i.e. in their 'childhood') at those stages, so the constructiveness of that stage will be more obvious than its shortcomings (see also Table 7-2).

Let us now, however, describe the similarities between persons and organisations at each stage. Both the person at the Opportunist stage and the organisation at the Investments stage seek resources from the environment and capabilities with which to manipulate the environment. At best, an 8 to 12 year old child who is at the Opportunistic stage has parents who are making inspirational and social network investments in him or her (e.g. offering the child an integrative faith of some kind and exposure to good teachers). Similarly, wise organisational founders and wise venture capitalists will be concerned with the inspirational resonance and profundity of the organisation's mission and mentors, as well as the social, professional, and business alliances that can support the organisation during its Investments stage. On the other hand, if the organisational founders are themselves still arrested at the Opportunistic stage of development, they will act as though tangible financial resources are the only significant resource needed. Such an organisation may appear very successful in terms of financial backing in the short-term, but the lack of network resources and inspiration will result in lower commitment by all stakeholders and will stunt its development in the longer term.

Given some resources and capacities to work with, a person who enters the Diplomat stage during the early teenage years and the organisation at the Incorporation stage are both learning how to operate successfully according to the rules of their social milieus (which we call 'peer groups' in the case of teenagers and 'markets' in the case of for-profit companies). In both cases, there are many difficult moments, and neither the young teenager nor the young company may have the persistence to succeed. Or, both may lose their 'honour' (sense of self-respect based on loyalty to a constructive mission) in their eagerness to conform to the demands of their milieu.

Failure to meet the demands of the larger milieu may result in a person's lifelong membership in a semi-illegitimate, dependent underclass. In the case of an organisation at this stage, failure usually means outright economic failure or else a very contingent survival in a small local niche. Success in meeting the demands of the milieu at the price of one's 'honour' also has a significant dark side: it makes development to further stages much less likely.

People who are able to 'break the mould' of their immediate social milieu begin to seek out something more consistent to subordinate themselves to than the helter-skelter, conflicting demands of the others about them. They are seeking for a more purposive, craft-like way of organising their life and a more objective way of measuring their relative success at doing so. They may experiment with various types of expertise along the way. There are countless different human activities to which one may apprentice oneself, which have craft logics, craft masters, and (relatively) objective methods of measuring success. The teenager who says, "I like track better than soccer because in track you are measured by your actual time in the event, whereas in soccer it's whether the coach likes you" is expressing her growing attraction to the Expert stage logic of doing well in terms of objectively measured standards and rejection of the Diplomat stage logic of doing well what will gain another person's approval. (Of course, her statement may also contain a significant degree of defensiveness and unfairness to the soccer coach.)

In any event, this movement from Diplomat to Expert stage logic parallels an organisation's movement from Incorporation to Experiments. The Expert's experiments toward excellence in any given craft involve a relatively narrow-gauged series of 'stabs in the dark'. An organisation transforming toward the Experiments stage at best conducts such experiments in all realms of its business, from the way in which it conducts its accounting (typically moving from the cash to the accrual method and from manual, paper records to computer systems) to the very fact of engaging in proactive marketing rather than simply servicing clients who come through the door.

These brief portraits begin to suggest the parallelism that exists between the two models of development.

Organising Business Meetings with Sensitivity to Developmental Process

Having developed a little feel for the possible parallelism of the individual and organisational scales of development, we can now get a glimpse of how the social process in which we are engaged comes into focus once we apply developmental theory to all scales of social development. In principle, we can view each new project or new product, each new team or task force, each new agenda item, meeting, or series of meetings as a developmental process. When we try to do this, we quickly realise two things: first, that there are multiple developmental processes which influence one another, either interrupting, inhibiting, or encouraging development at the scale we have originally focused on; and second, that human and social development does not proceed in the smooth path that Table 7-1 implicitly suggests. A brief look forward to the representation of chaotic development suggested in Figure 13.1 contrasts with this smooth path. These realities make the process of observing and encouraging the development of a learning organisation more difficult. But they also make the theory seem much more realistic.

For example, as this author edits this chapter for the next edition of this book, he is also wondering whether the book should now be offered to a different publisher altogether. He is also teaching in an executive program for a major German company with many international subsidiaries that appears to be operating at the Social Network stage. The company suddenly has to re-invent itself because economic austerities are destroying several markets at once, and the author must judge how heavily to engage in consulting to that process. In addition, the author has six other distinctive developmental transitions occurring in his family and work life (e.g. one son is teetering along the edge of finding fulltime employment). Every moment spent attending to one of these developmental processes involves neglecting another. How does the author choose among these mutually interrupting processes in his own life? And what about the sense of indispensability and ego inflation this paragraph hints at? Does the author engage in some ongoing form of spiritual practice that undercuts that?

As a second example, let us see how micro-spirals of development in single meetings nest within wider project, departmental, and organisational cycles. Let us listen to a top management team member of a Fortune 100 company who, without ever having thought of himself as using developmental theory, in fact manages meetings in a manner that parallels the early stages of organisational development we have just been reviewing.

This senior Vice President has an undergraduate mathematics background, with an interest in the Pythagorean theory of the octave as the organising structure for colour (the seven colours of the rainbow), for sound (the musical octave), and for human activities such as meetings. Of business meetings, he says (with our organisational stage names in parentheses):

> The first note 'doh' is the leader's vision for the whole meeting. It has to be both crisp and inspiring. It's got to surprise people just a little - jog them awake, make them reconsider what they came in prepared to do. [**Conception** - generating a surprisingly creative new vision]
>
> 'Re' is the first response, the first chorus from the group. The leader has got to allow for this if he wants a creative, committed meeting. How he choreographs that first response determines how far the meeting can go. [**Investments** - helping others to join and own the issue]
>
> 'Mi' is the first concrete decision of the meeting. If it's taken early on and makes sense to everyone, there's a general loosening up, and the

rest of the meeting is likely to fly. [**Incorporation** - something being produced; the vision becoming real]

A lot of meetings end there, but if you want to go further, you've got to realise there's a big interval between 'mi' and 'fah'. The leader can best bridge this interval with a new structure for the meeting. 'Fah' is primarily the group's note again, so the leader's structure should be something that brings out the chorus, something like breaking into subgroups on different issues. [**Experiments** - exploration and testing of many implications of the vision] (He goes on to discuss the rest of the 'meeting octave'.)

...But the actual meeting can also be viewed as the middle part of the octave 'fah, 'sol', 'la') between the two intervals. In this larger perspective, the pre-meeting preparation is the first part of the octave and the post-meeting follow-up is the final part.

This final paragraph of the executive's vision of how meetings are best conducted points to the very notion of overlapping or nested developmental processes that we mentioned above. You are welcome to compare back and forth between Table 7-2 and the executive's description of each musical note in a well-run meeting to see to what degree they parallel one another. But our point is less that there is a perfectly precise parallel and more that this illustration brings to life the general sense of how a meeting can be viewed developmentally (not to mention how much more interesting and productive business meetings in general would be if more executives were this imaginative in managing them!).

In this spirit, and to continue the exercise of imagining how to 'see' developmental theory at work on different scales of social organising, we present the following one-page guide that one senior management team uses to help its members to manage particular agenda items at their senior management meetings (each item is typically scheduled for half an hour or forty-five minutes). This guide is not explicitly modelled on developmental theory at all, and the individual stages of development are therefore not as obvious as in the previous example. But the guide does use the framing/advocating/ illustrating/inquiring language introduced in earlier chapters, and you should be able to follow a general developmental path in the sequence of handling a particular agenda item.

Can you follow the stages of development in the foregoing agenda item management process? Step 1 provides the overall Conception for the manager using the guide, and Step 2a represents the Conception stage of the given agenda item during a meeting. Step 2b addresses the question of how to gain other members' Investments. Steps 2c and 2d attempt to develop a specific solution or procedure with regard to the agenda item - the Incorporation stage. Then, Steps 3a, 3b, 3c, and 3d represent Experiments around reaching a decision. Steps 3e, 3g, and/or 3h get the job done - Systematic Productivity. And finally, Steps 3f, 4, and 5 look forward to a process of Collaborative Inquiry that may restructure the approach and the decision. The fact that Step 3f is slightly out of sequence suggests that it may function more effectively as the final step.

Having now explored some ways that the developmental stages of organising can be used in meetings, let us turn in the next three chapters to exploring how whole organisations can be helped to transform from one developmental action-logic to another.

Table 7-3   Agenda Item Management at Meetings

When you are preparing and presenting a particular agenda item at senior management meetings, consider the following steps:

1. Divide the time between a diverging, including period and a converging, concluding period.

2. The diverging period will typically include the following sub-steps:

    a) framing the overall flow of activity you intend for this period and framing what the issue is

    b) testing/inquiring whether this way of framing meets others' expectations and the demands of the issue

    c) presenting your advocacies and illustrations about what to do

    d) eliciting others' counter-advocacies and illustrations.

3. The converging period will typically include the following sub-steps:

    a) framing the kind of decision necessary and the decision-making process you propose

    b) testing/inquiring whether this sounds appropriate or anyone has an alternative procedure to suggest

    c) poll the group quickly, making clear this is not a vote, but is for information purposes

    d) test with members who are going to be critical to the implementation if they are on board or have any amendments

    e) attempt to state a consensus of the group and test whether everyone can buy in

    f) explicitly develop an assessment process that someone not in agreement can implement, in order to bring the issue back for reconsideration if the current solution is not working

    g) test for CEOs buy-in, or wish to impose his/her solution

    h) have formal vote if consensus is not forthcoming.

4. Check proposed procedure with the relevant agenda advocate.

5. Possibly seek coaching from CEO or consultant prior to meeting.

Conclusion

We have been exploring the links between the frames by which individuals make meaning and so create the context for their actions and how this process has its parallel in organisations. We have discovered that organisations, and parts of organisations, evolve through different action logics of their own which are partly derived from the stage of history of the organisation and partly derived from the frames of the people who lead the organisation. We will pursue the impact that people's frames have on their organisations and on society throughout this book

CHAPTER 8

THE EARLY STAGES OF ORGANISATIONAL TRANSFORMATION

Let us now change our focus from small meetings on single occasions and look more closely at three examples of whole organisations moving from one stage to the next. Each example is intended to illustrate how the consultant who intervenes creates a temporary learning organisation, with a great deal of feedback and creative decision-making, as a vehicle for encouraging organisational transformation and reframing. Each example is also intended to illustrate how each later developmental logic comes progressively closer to establishing a learning organisation that challenges and transforms, not only its members' assumptions, logics, and practices, but also the organisation's systems, structures, and standard operating procedures. However, since none of the transitions that we will illustrate in this chapter goes beyond Systematic Productivity, the organisations we present here will not reach the stage of explicitly and self-consciously encouraging transformation. Such explicit and self-conscious work typically begins during the transitions from the Systematic Productivity stage through the Social Network stage to the Collaborative Inquiry stage, transitions to which we devote the next two chapters.

The cases presented in these chapters are meant to help you to imagine what stage of development currently characterises your company or department or work team. They also explore the kinds of pressures, questions, and values that may make a time ripe for developmental transformation. Later, in Chapter 11, we will look at a study that compares the 'transformational adventures' of ten different companies.

Let us begin with an organisation that is, from our point of view, transitioning from Investments to Incorporation. Before you begin reading this case, take a look back at Table 7-2 to remind yourself of the characteristics of the Investments and Incorporation stages of organisational development. Then see if you recognise these elements in the case as you read it. As you reach the point in the case when you hear about the consultant's clinical diagnosis of both the organisation and of its two leading partners, remember that what is presented very briefly here represents only the tip of the consultant's perceptions of the company.

Transforming a Computer Software Company
From Investments to Incorporation

A small software company has burned through its initial round of venture financing, with net revenues for its products not yet foreseeable. The partners are seeking a second round of venture capital, and everybody at the company knows they must make a breakthrough in marketing and sales; yet, this 'bottom-line' negative feedback alone, as stark as it is, is not propelling the company into a new operating pattern.

An organisational consultant who takes a developmental action inquiry approach is invited to help the company over a two-day period. He approaches the assignment with the sense that he must discover what disharmonies among the corporate dream, the leadership's strategies, and the day-to-day operations account for the company's continuing losses. But more than this, he must discover a positive way to reframe or restructure the situation so that the leadership is motivated to correct the disharmonies.

The consultant interviews the top management (the president and the three vice-presidents for production, marketing, and sales) of the computer software company, which numbers 35 employees in all. The president is a generation older than the three vice presidents, and the company is a partnership between the president and one of the vice-presidents. Together, the two of them developed the initial product.

In the following three years, the company has produced a large number of high-quality products, but they are not selling well, and the company is nearing the end of its initial venture capital financing. The consultant discovers numerous problems that have remained unresolved for a long time. Neither mission nor markets are well defined. Pricing is a subject of acrimonious controversy. Employee morale is fragile because it is unclear whether competence or cronyism is the basis for rewards. Decisions are not driven by any internal sense of mission; they are made only when situations deteriorate into external emergencies.

The bottleneck in decision-making appears to be the relationship between the two partners. They respect one another and attempt to share responsibility as though equals. But they repeatedly fall prey to differences in age, formal role, and in managerial style. The president plays the role of optimistic, benign, absent-minded father. The vice-president plays the role of pessimistic, sharp, rebellious son.

Having interviewed the senior managers individually during the first six hours of his two-day visit, the consultant is next slated to meet with the two partners to set the agenda for the next day's problem-solving retreat. But based on what he has heard, the consultant fears that the agenda-setting session may itself fall prey to the partners' well-intentioned wrangling. In his ten minute walk around the outside of the building prior to the session, the consultant decides that the partners' pattern of behavior must change before any other productive decisions are likely.

Applying the developmental theory to his own two-day visit, the consultant interprets the initial interviews as the **Conception** stage of the intervention. In this light, the agenda-setting session with the two partners may represent the **Investments** stage. If so, the question is how to restructure his consulting style at this point from a more passive, receptive interviewing process to a more active, intervening process that highlights the new investment the partners themselves must be willing to make if they are to achieve the major changes necessary in the organisation as a whole. This reasoning convinces the consultant that he must attempt to reframe the partners' expectations and pattern of behavior from the outset of the agenda-setting session.

Applying the developmental theory to the company as a whole, the consultant sees the organisation as spread-eagled across the fluid, decentralised **Investments** and **Experiments** stages, still living off venture capital on the one hand, while on the other hand experimenting with a whole line of products. At the same time, the company is failing to 'bite the bullet' and meet the limiting, centralising, differentiating demands of the **Incorporation** stage – the demand, in short, for net revenues.

In this context, the communal and egalitarian aspects of the company's dream seem like an excuse for avoiding decisions. The communal, egalitarian ideology is evident in the partners' pattern of acting as though they are equal despite their different titles; in the fact that all four of the other top officers are invited to attend the next day's retreat, even though the vice-president of sales himself and the two partners have all mentioned the desirability of demoting him because he is over his head in the vice president role; and in the fact that both partners wish to avoid any form of favoritism toward particular employees, yet have employed one partner's daughter and the other's best friend. However important and viable an aspect of the corporate dream this egalitarianism may ultimately be the partners must show themselves capable of differentiating in an economically prudent and politically just way before their efforts to be egalitarian will become credible.

This analysis persuades the consultant that he himself must act in a decisive, differentiating manner throughout the next day and a half and encourage the two partners to do so as well. In particular, he decides to recommend at the agenda-setting session that only the partners and the consultant participate in the retreat and that whatever decisions the partners reach the next day be put in writing with definite implementation dates.

Applying the developmental theory to each of the partners as individuals, the consultant estimates that the vice-president is in transition from the **Expert** stage to the **Achiever** stage of development, both itching for and resisting the true executive responsibility that a person at the **Achiever** stage relishes. The consultant estimates that the president is in transition from the **Achiever** stage to the **Strategist** stage, ready to give up day-to-day executive responsibility in favor of an elder statesman role of mentoring his junior partner and godfathering the company's research and development function.

In their initial interviews, both partners have used the image of ballots to describe their relative power within the company. The president, referring to their equal salaries and to his style of consulting his partner on all significant decisions, spoke of the partners as holding "ballots of the same size" in company decisions. The vice-president saw the president as having the larger vote. The consultant now reasons that if the two switch their formal roles, the (erstwhile) president should still see their votes as equal, while the (erstwhile) vice-president should see his vote as having become larger. Thus, the twosome should be more powerful. Moreover, the new roles will be more developmentally appropriate to each partner.

More immediately, the mere fact of having the two officers reverse roles for the agenda-setting meeting and the day-long retreat should alter their usual dynamics and put them into a posture of simultaneous rehearsal and performance conducive to action inquiry. Of course, the consultant himself will be in a similar posture as he makes this unexpected suggestion.

The consultant begins his feedback/agenda-setting session with the two partners by proposing that the vice-president either resign or become president. This puts the vice-president in the action role right away, rather than his usual role of reacting to the president. Although quiet, the president seems ready to play this game. After considerable probing by the vice-president to explore the consultant's reasoning, the two senior officers agree.

Now the vice-president (in the role of the president) acts decisively rather than reacting combatively. He and the consultant propose various changes, with the president (in the subordinate role) making constructive suggestions and raising questions. The two partners reach written agreement on six major organisational changes the next day. The first of these is implemented at lunch that day. The vice president for sales is invited to join them. The partners discuss the major changes they are considering, and ask him to accept a demotion. He agrees, expression both his disappointment and his relief that his duties will be more circumscribed.

A month later, all the changes have been implemented. Two months later, the company completes, six months ahead of schedule, a first-of-its-kind product for a definite and large market. The company fails to get a second round of venture financing, but sales revenues begin to exceed costs for the first time in the company's history due to the new product.

In the meantime, the vice-president decides *not* to become president. The president stipulates that henceforward he will draw a higher salary than his partner and exercise the managerial authority of president and CEO on a day-to-day basis, treating the vice-president as a subordinate except at the monthly board meetings, where both of them sit in their roles as partners. Both agree on the six specific changes, along with the new clarity in roles, represent major improvements. And both agree that treating the planning meeting simultaneously as a role-playing rehearsal and as a for-real negotiation has prompted the changes.

Another three months later, the vice-presidential partner decides he wishes to become president and negotiates the change with the other partner...

In this case, the developmental theory evidently generated a convincing story about, and strategy for, the next steps that the partners and the company as a whole needed to take. But why was the developmental perspective so convincing? The mere fact that it helps to explain many of the phenomena that consultant encountered at the company is *not* why it was so convincing. Many theories that explain much never gain practitioners' attention.

The key to convincing the partners to take this theory/strategy seriously was the process of enacting the theory together rather than merely discussing it hypothetically – the process of action inquiry introduced by the consultant. Because the consultant himself acted on his developmental analysis and modeled action inquiry in his approach to the agenda-setting session, the partners saw the approach could have practical consequences. By enacting different roles rather than merely discussing them, the partners directly experienced the value of differentiated roles during the next day and a half. By sharing the new decisions with the vice-president for sales at lunch the second day, and by implementing one of the most sensitive of the decisions there and them (his demotion), the partners again directly experienced the value for the organisation as a whole of making crisp decisions and of differentiating roles.

Each of these instances involved a process of simultaneous rehearsal and performance – a process of testing strategies that may be useful for future action by using them to guide present action. On the issue of the presidency of the company, the partners continued the process of simultaneous rehearsal and performance for four months, intervening to reframe their respective roles twice during that period.

The idea of rehearsal and performance is obviously drawn from the performing acts. During rehearsals for a theatrical performance, it is legitimate for the director to 'break the frame of the play' at any moment, in order to give the actors feedback and possibly reset the scene altogether before the play continues. Such moments take 'time out' from the ongoing action of the play. From another point of view, these moments represent a 'time in' to the true perceptions of the different persons involved about what they are trying to do and what they are actually doing. Repeatedly taking these paradoxical 'time out/time ins' ultimately generates a better performance.

Some other highly predefined social settings, like American football games and courtrooms, also have 'time out' procedures that interpolate feedback, rehearsal, and reframing the right into the midst of the actual performance. Again, the purpose is to generate better performance.

Managerial settings are much more ambiguous and much less defined than football games and trials. Participants frequently bring conflicting agendas and assumptions to an occasion, yet there is no official procedure for 'time outs'. Consequently, when a manager believes that one of these paradoxical 'time-out/time-ins' will help improve performance, he or she must simultaneously 'break the frame of the play' and legitimise the break. Action inquiry is the process of appropriately interpolating inquiry, feedback, and reframing into any conversation, meeting, negotiation, or institutional procedure, whenever such a break seems to serve the purpose of generating better performance.

Ordinarily, of course, critical organisational or family events are rehearsed 'off-line', over coffee, with persons other than the main characters, before or after the event rather than 'on-line' with the main character during the event itself. The trouble with 'off-line' rehearsals for relatively unstructured real life events is that they cease to be of use as soon as the actual event begins to take an unforeseen course.

To untangle the messes that frequently result when the inadequate order of our minds meets the unfathomed order of everyday business requires the practice of simultaneously rehearsing and performing, of simultaneously interrupting and continuing the action, of simultaneously offering negative feedback and a positive reframing of the setting. To realign corporate dream, strategy, operations, and outcomes requires the practice of action inquiry.

Transforming from Incorporation to Experiments

Next, let us follow a merger of three small organisations as they each transform from their separate Incorporation stage experiences to a shared Experiments stage (see Table 8-2 to remind yourself of the characteristics of these two stages).

A small, but rapidly growing company has recently become geographically dispersed because of two acquisitions of other small companies by its president. The president asks a consultant to design a two-day quarterly retreat for the 40 managers who constitute the top three layers of management of the new multi-site organisation. "The people equation is the most difficult, recurrent, and intractable issue", says the president, "and we need our managers to have new core competencies that include recognising and taking responsibility for the impact their actions have on one another, not only in the same office but at the other sites, and for the organisational values that their actions are creating". The president proposes a lecture/ discussion of the consultant's theory of managerial and organisational development and some skill-building sessions.

The consultant interviews six members of the organisation by phone and returns to the president with a plan for the two days that interweaves managerial and organisational learning in ways which, if successful, will directly transform the organisation, rather than just talking about transformation. Instead of pure skill-building sessions, the consultant proposes (and the president agrees after some concern about the risks) that the staff meet in four cross-functional/cross-locational groups of ten to develop new ways of organising in the four areas that the interviews have indicated are of greatest concern: 1) Budget Development; 2) Recruiting and Training; 3) Internal Communications; and 4) Meeting Management. Senior management is asked to prepare to make binding decisions with regard to the proposals before the end of the retreat (and such decisions are in fact made at the actual retreat). Thus are inquiry and productive action integrated at the retreat. We can also see that this procedure will result in organisational learning and change. The meeting processes arranged for the retreat and described below show how individual, managerial learning is interwoven with organisational learning.

Each of the groups of ten is to be managed through five leadership roles, and two members will hold each leadership role. The two persons with the most influence over the ultimate implementation of any changes in that area serve in the 'Expert and Follow-Through' leadership role. The other four leadership roles are 'Meeting Leader', 'Decision Clarifier and Codifier', 'Process Facilitator', and 'Clown' (whose express function is to make 'outside the box' comments, use humour, and turn suggestions inside-out in order to see whether they are thereby improved). Members are to be assigned roles that their fellow group members judge are most developmentally provocative for them. (For example, the president later finds himself assigned a 'Clown' role and plays it so well that several extravagant stories about his performance quickly make the rounds!)

Without reproducing here any of the detailed supports provided, the schedule in outline calls for an initial presentation/discussion, led by the consultant, that connects the managerial and organisational development theory presented in this book to the history and dilemmas of the organisation. The consultant suggests that the three independent sites have each been operating at the Incorporation stage, and that the new multi-site company will require a frame-change and a lot of experimenting on everyone's part, such as this retreat as a whole involves.

Next, the conference splits into the four topic areas. In each case, one sub-group of five is to develop a set of proposals in one hour, while the other sub-group of five observes their role-mates and gives five minutes of feedback at the end of the first half hour and again at the end of the hour. After a short break, the observers and the actors switch roles, with the same feedback arrangements, and the new actors come up with a different set of proposals for the same concern (e.g. budget development). After another short break, the entire group of ten develops an agreed-upon proposal. These organising processes provide individual managers with an unusual amount of immediate feedback about their leadership choices, while at the same time increasing the likelihood that divergent views on the organisational issues are developed, considered seriously, and resolved.

The next morning, each of the four groups makes ten-minute presentations to the other 30 managers, followed by five minutes of discussion and concluded with written feedback from all 30. The groups are given half an hour to digest the feedback they have received. Then the entire group reconvenes for two-minute comments by their (senior management) 'Follow-Through' leaders on how their proposals have been influenced by the feedback and what they are committing to do as of the next day in the office. The consultant next leads a discussion debriefing the entire exercise and then leaves the room while the management group develops feedback for him.

At the end of the actual meeting, the feedback to the consultant included suggestions such as 'needed more leadership for group assignments at outset', as well as positive comments such as 'great to see branch participation without corporate interference', 'meetings in this organisation will never be the same again', and 'progression of programme was great and lack of structure strengthened learning'. On a scale of 1 to 7 (where 1 meant 'Time wasted', 4 meant 'As good as an average quarterly retreat', and 7 meant 'Best quarterly retreat ever'), the 40 participants rated this retreat 6.5 on average. Major changes followed in all four areas of concern identified.

Almost every activity at the retreat represented Experiments stage organising on the part of the participants. Everyone experimented with new meeting roles, none more so than the president in his Clown role. Everyone experimented a great deal with giving and receiving feedback, from the determination of what role each was to play, through the feedback, to the consultant at the end. Moreover, all four efforts to create new organisational structures in the four areas of concern represented disciplined stabs in the dark. The methods of rapid group decision-making were new to the organisation as well.

What may be less obvious is that the organisational characteristics of the retreat as a whole themselves represent a distinctive 'logic of practice' that is more ironic and subtle than the Experiments stage logic. You may have noted that the structure for the retreat was quite complex, yet the participants claimed at the end that "the lack of structure strengthened learning". We call this kind of paradoxical structure that widens rather than restricts participants' freedom of action 'liberating structure' or 'liberating disciplines'. You will see that Liberating Disciplines is shown at the bottom of Table 8-1 as the most advanced form of organising we can imagine. Neither it nor the prior stage of organising, Foundational Community, are described in Table 8-2 because they are so uncommon. We will not consider these uncommon stages in detail until the final two chapters. But, in this case of the two-day management retreat, you now have one small, time-limited example of an organisation that simultaneously learns and produces results and generates personal learning by its members - all at the same time. Such an organisation, and only such an organisation, truly deserves to be called a 'learning organisation'. Our example suggests that an invited consulting intervention is more likely to generate an organisational transformation to the degree that the consulting intervention itself represents a temporary, late stage learning organisation.

Organisational Transformation from the Experiments Stage to the Systematic Productivity Stage

Now let us turn to an example of an organisation transforming from the Experiments stage to the Systematic Productivity stage. Again, we will have the opportunity to glimpse as well an invited consulting intervention structured and enacted in a late stage, learning organisation manner. Before reading the case, look again at the descriptions of the stages of development in Table 8-2. Prepare yourself to look for evidence of this organisation's movement from Experiments to Systematic Productivity. But this time, be ready to watch the developmental unfolding of the transformation process, led by a consultant and an executive vice-president. Notice how this process itself became a temporary learning organisation, recapitulating the early stages of development en route toward helping the organisation change its overall frame.

The Case

This company has become quite complex in terms of legal structure during its Experiments stage, in an effort to maximise the entrepreneurial freedom and initiative of every member of its senior management. As a result, the corporate structure shows a not-for-profit parent company and an umbrella for-profit subsidiary containing seven subsidiary companies. Each of the seven vice-presidents of the for-profit company serves as president of one of the subsidiary companies. Each subsidiary president has developed his own profit-sharing formula with the umbrella company, based on whatever chips he has to work with and hard bargaining. Other members of the senior management 'team' view each such bargain as relatively illegitimate. The vice-president and chief financial officer of the umbrella for-profit company is the only woman among the ten senior managers, the only person who is widely trusted, and the only person who is not president of a separate entity.

This jerrybuilt structure that reinforces cowboy opportunism rather than developing any coordination or team spirit is outflanked, in a desperation move, by the president of the umbrella for-profit, who negotiates the 50% sale of the whole company, in order to raise new and absolutely necessary capital. The new 50% partners agree to grant the company operating freedom, but demand careful accounting of revenues and costs and a return on their investment proportionate to the net revenues of each subsidiary. This apparently minor demand, along with the new capital controlled by the president of the umbrella for-profit, gives him new forms of effective control over the presidents of the subsidiaries. But it simultaneously increases their distrust of him.

A consultant who works with the developmental theory presented in this book is hired to assist the senior team in a retreat that is explicitly intended to restructure the company internally to fit its new ownership status and capital structure. From the first luncheon with the entire senior management to determine whether every member can accept the consultant, the consultant is aware of the high level of tension and distrust. One member recommends that the consultant pay for the opportunity to work with the group, rather than being paid, since he has not worked in this industry before and will therefore be learning. The consultant earns a round of laughter by parrying with the comment that he thought the mark of a good consultant was how much he can charge to learn. After a slight pause, he continues by saying nonchalantly that at least he's learned how to talk to more than one person at a time without causing instant distrust - a trick which he understands most of them haven't picked up yet. This generates another round of laughter, and the consultant is hired.

The consultant proposes that he begin with a round of one-on-one interviews, followed by feedback from him to each individual. At the retreat, each member of senior management will be asked to discuss the feedback he or she has received and to set two goals for personal behaviour change, before restructuring of the organisation is discussed.

The interviews with, and feedback to, each individual permit the consultant to develop some trust with each member, while simultaneously letting them know how others view them and where there is collective agreement about the future of the organisation, without allowing any dysfunctional group dynamics to occur. It is during these interviews that the consultant begins to see that the chief financial officer is the person with the best relationships in the group, the one who focuses most impartially on the welfare of the organisation as a whole, and the one who seems most strategic overall. During the feedback to individuals, he explores not how willing each member is to acknowledge others' issues with him and to set significant personal change goals which they will share with the group as a whole. He also explores how willing all are to cede some of their autonomy to a more centralised organisational structure, characteristic of the Systematic Productivity stage of organising.

In particular, the consultant probes members' reactions to the suggestion that he says emerged from the initial interviews that the chief financial officer be promoted to executive vice-president of the umbrella for-profit corporation. This suggestion is widely agreed to, either because persons genuinely trust her and respect her competence, or because they see her as a buffer between themselves and the president of the umbrella corporation.

During the first day, the retreat is highlighted by astonishingly revealing comments by each member, along with commitments to change aspects of behaviour which others would never have predicted they would acknowledge, much less change. This only happens, however, after the consultant is initially challenged about why the group should start with 'touchy-feely' behavioural issues before dealing with the 'infinitely more important' structural and financial issues. The consultant responds that the group is, of course, free to redesign the retreat as it wishes and that he himself would not usually lead with such a personal activity, but that the trust in the group is so low that he is personally convinced that no lasting progress can be made of the 'objective' issues without a new kind of spiritual investment by each member. This challenge and response seems to bring the stakes into focus for everyone.

During the second day, the retreat is highlighted by a series of consensual agreements. The first is to promote the chief financial officer to executive vice-president. The second is to centralise accounting and budgeting. The third, which provokes the longest argument, is to do away with the separate stationery for each subsidiary that has highlighted that president and to substitute a single version of corporate stationery that lists all the vice-presidents on the team as, first, senior vice-presidents of the umbrella for-profit and only secondly as presidents of their own subsidiaries.

It is difficult to stress strongly enough how essential the new executive vice-president's overall style and specific actions are to the success of this day and the later success of the reformed company. As soon as she receives her mandate from the group, she proposes the importance of centralising accounting and finances. Because of her past record of trustworthiness, reasonableness, and competence, the group comes to agreement on this without undue difficulty. Then, when the stationery issue becomes divisive, she adroitly highlights what an important symbolic issue it is and says that she views the decision as a vote of confidence or no-confidence in her ability to make the newly centralised organisation work.

The consultant continues in an occasional coaching relationship to the new executive vice-president. Six months later, the consultant meets with her and the senior vice-presidents for a one-day retreat. Three months after that the senior vice-president who had been least willing to accept the leadership of the executive vice-president takes a position with another company. The executive vice-president, in turn, takes over the presidency of his subsidiary as well as continuing to serve as executive vice-president of the umbrella for-profit.

In twenty-four months, the organisation has generated enough net revenues to be able to buy itself back from its 50% partners, and the president of the umbrella for-profit and the executive vice-president have married one another.

In this case, we see that each subsidiary corporation, true to the Experiments stage, had become a distinct, almost completely decentralised experiment, with very little trust or cooperation between the parts. So little trust or cooperation, in fact, that the consultant chooses to maintain the decentralisation in the early phase of his relationship to the company, while he builds trust with individuals and discovers the one member with good enough relationships to serve as the hub of the more centralised organisation needed for the Systematic Productivity stage. So little trust and cooperation, in fact, that the consultant designs a retreat format that asks each person to offer a gift to the group (their willingness to make a difficult behaviour change) before the group tries to make any collective decisions. The consultant puts heavy emphasis on sharing the developmental theory as a new vision (recapitulating Conception) of what the next stage in this company's history ought to be about, and in particular to legitimise the notion of greater corporate centralisation which has heretofore been anathema to virtually all the members. The consultant also puts heavy emphasis on the inspirational gifts (recapitulating Investments) members need to offer (in this case, each member's commitment to a difficult behavioural change), in order to develop the trust necessary for more interdependent work. Finally, the consultant puts heavy reliance on creating a very specific structure (thereby recapitulating Incorporation as a sub-stage of the organisations transformation), along with a heavy reliance on the person with the most Strategist-like perspective. The executive vice-president's experiments over the next year represent the Experiments sub-stage of this company's transformation to the Systematic Productivity stage.

As previously mentioned, the three cases described in this chapter are meant to help you to imagine what stage of development currently characterises your company or department or work team, and what kind of sustained action commitments may be warranted to help it to transform.

Conclusion

The next two chapters continue this conversation. There, we will first discuss the environmental conditions that today lead many larger companies to the Social Network stage of organising. Then, we offer an in-depth case of an organisation transforming from the Systematic Productivity stage toward the Collaborative Inquiry stage. This transition parallels the move we examined in Chapters 5 and 6 from the Achiever through the Individualist to the Strategist frame on the personal scale. Just as few managers develop to the Strategist stage, few organisations develop to the Collaborative Inquiry stage. Yet this is the first stage at which the organisation begins to develop an explicit, ongoing learning capacity that can truly support developmental action inquiry as a way of being within the organisation.

CHAPTER 9

THE SOCIAL NETWORK
ORGANISATIONAL STAGE
AND TRANSFORMATION TOWARDS
COLLABORATIVE INQUIRY

(written in association with Barbara Davidson)

In the previous chapter, we have already followed a number of the steps through which any organising process evolves, if the objective is to create a genuine learning organisation. Ultimately, a genuine learning organisation truly encourages the practice of developmental action inquiry among all its members and is actively open to reexamining and transforming its own assumptions about its environment, its shape, and its strategies.

But, even though the previous chapter describes five steps along the path toward a learning organisation - Conception, Investments, Incorporation, Experiments, and Systematic Productivity - there is a very significant sense in which an organisation only reaches the threshold of becoming a learning organisation after these five steps. Occasionally, an organisation is shepherded through one early transformation or another by executives or consultants, as illustrated in the previous chapter. But most organisations, like most people, evolve through each of these early developmental transformations by a process of more or less traumatic trial and error that is never named, never explicitly recognised as a transformation of assumptions, and never undertaken with the intention of eventually establishing a learning organisation.

Even idealistic, mission-driven companies and not-for-profits are, during their development to the Systematic Productivity stage, typically based on the assumptions:

1. that the *mission is known*; and
2. that the *organisation's challenges are*
    a) to *find the right structure and strategy* to accomplish the mission and
    b) *to overcome external competition or external political blocks* to accomplishing the desired outcomes.

Beyond the Systematic Productivity stage, an organisation, like a person moving through the Individualist stage toward the Strategist stage, begins to recognise the multiplicity and dynamics of frames and strategies. At the Social Network stage, a holding company often mixes and matches a portfolio of operating companies through a constant process of buying, selling, and redirecting their capital assets. During the past generation, we have experienced a great deal of experimentation in the business world with a kind of portfolio approach to organising, whereby a parent holding company either more actively or more passively manages dozens or even hundreds of operating companies.

At the Social Network stage, senior managers of the holding company tend to be relativistic about the overall mission of the enterprise and about questions of 'right' strategy and structure. They aspire to be 'agile' and responsive to the market. In practice, this often means that they shift their liquid capital toward investments that in the short-term appear likely to generate the highest profits, while reducing investment in companies and projects that cannot match the 'hurdle rate', with little attention to the peculiarities of different industries, regions, or longer time horizons. This is a kind of Opportunistic Relativism characteristic of global finance capitalism.

But a Social Network stage organising process can also be based on a sense of mission and values that transcend and include financial value. Take the development over the past twenty years of Socially Responsible Investing (optimising three bottom lines: financial, social, and environmental). In the middle 1980s Joan Bavaria, the CEO of Trillium Asset Management, the first and to this day the largest company entirely dedicated to socially responsible investing, also became one of the leading co-founders of the Social Investing Forum and served as its chair for a time. In 1989 Bavaria co-authored the Valdez Environmental Principles (soon renamed the CERES Environmental Principles) and played a key role in attracting signatories such as General Motors. By 1999 CERES, which Bavaria chaired, organised 19 institutional investment groups, representing $195 billion. During this same period, through CERES, Bavaria and colleagues launched the Global Reporting Initiative, a set of global sustainability guidelines supported by both corporate and NGO partners, with a $30 million grant from the United Nations Environmental Programme. "We're moving beyond the concept stage and into the implementation stage", she said. "Our goal is simply to make environmental reporting standard procedure for public companies around the world" (quoted from the Trillium newsletter *Investing for a Better World*, 1999: 2). We will return to Joan Bavaria and Trillium in Chapter 14.

As you can appreciate, the notion of Socially Responsible Investing raises a basic question about the very purpose or mission of business. In this sense, the entire social investing sub-industry (which has been growing faster than conventional investing over the past several years) is a learning process organised in response to a question. In this sense, it begins to model the next organising stage - Collaborative Inquiry. Only in the transition to Collaborative Inquiry does the purpose and process of establishing a learning organisation typically become self-conscious.

The motivation for developing towards the Collaborative Inquiry stage comes from a dawning recognition that the organisation's mission is actually a mystery that requires continual re-searching and re-formulating if members' actions are to become truly mission-oriented. At the same time some organisational members may begin to appreciate that there are inevitably systematic gaps between the espoused mission, values, and strategies of organisational members, on the one hand, and their actual patterns of practice, on the other hand.

Therefore, there is not only *a mystery about what an organisation's mission really means*, but there is also *a mystery about how to recognise and correct the incongruities* that tend to grow between espoused directions or priorities and actual practices. In other words, what motivates organisational transformation towards Collaborative Inquiry is the growing recognition among some members who are willing to take leadership responsibility that it is not only the changing external environment that creates new problems for the organisation, but its own way of operating. Significantly, Trillium Asset Management is structurally organised as a Collaborative Inquiry in two ways: not only does it engage in collaborative inquiry with its clients, advising them about how to invest in companies whose substantive values they support; but it also engages in collaborative inquiry from top to bottom of the company hierarchy because it is a worker-owned company in which the employees are also shareholders.

Ever since the 1950s the attempt to seriously address the mystery of mission and the incongruities that arise among mission, strategy, operations, and outcomes has led to a variety of organisational and managerial education ventures - to T-groups (sensitivity training groups), to the whole field called OD (organisational development), to QWL programmes (quality of working life), to TQM (total quality management), to Process Re-engineering and most recently to the use of Whole Systems Interventions such as Real Time Strategic Change and Future Search. The developmental theory we have been discussing can help us to understand why these approaches so quickly become disappointing fads. One reason is that, in order to become marketable on a larger scale, each innovative approach to Collaborative Inquiry develops through its own distinct stages until it reaches its own Systematic Productivity strategy and structure. Because the specific innovative strategy and structure is different from the client company's strategy and structure, it may help that company to make one significant adjustment in its manner of operating. *But it does not transform the whole company into a Collaborative Inquiry stage learning organisation that continues to research its mission and correct incongruities among mission, strategy, operations, and outcomes.*

A second, related reason why these well-known managerial education ventures fade after sometimes having an initial impact on the organisation is that only organisational members who themselves transform to the Strategist stage (or beyond) fully appreciate the value and the logic of Collaborative Inquiry process (for, as shown in Table 7-1, the Strategist and Collaborative Inquiry stages are parallel action-logics). Therefore, only managers at the Strategist and later stages are able to implement Collaborative Inquiry on a continuing basis. As we have seen earlier, only about 8% of managers are found at this stage, and more than half of the managers we have measured fall two or more stages before the Strategist stage. Thus, the task in helping an organisation transform to the Collaborative Inquiry stage is not only to transform the structure of a social entity, but also to transform the consciousness of many of its members. We do not know what proportion must become Strategists before the organisation can reliably be expected to maintain itself at the Collaborative Inquiry stage. But we are convinced that the proportion of the senior management team that is operating at the Strategist stage, and whether the CEO is a Strategist, makes a disproportionate difference (and Chapter 11 offers some statistical findings in support of this proposition). Since each developmental transformation can take several years, and since the person developing must first discover the internal motivation to seek beyond his or her current frame, it would seem astonishing to us if a company could increase its proportion of Strategists from 5% to, say, 20% in less than five years.

Very few companies have the vision, the will, or the resources to evolve to the Collaborative Inquiry stage. Consequently, the training processes that are developed for the company's employees typically aim to instill Achiever/Systematic Productivity skills. These may be useful in the short run, but they will not generate transformation beyond the Achiever/Systematic Productivity stage.

One way of highlighting the radical difference between the reality of the Achiever/Systematic Productivity stage and the reality of the Strategist/Collaborative Inquiry stage is to show the following diagram (see Figure 9.1) in which the horizontal line represents the limited Achiever awareness, whereas the horizontal and vertical lines together represent the added dimension of awareness that the Strategist begins to cultivate.

Figure 9.1   Achiever Sequential Awareness vs. Later-stage Simultaneous (and Sequential) Awareness.

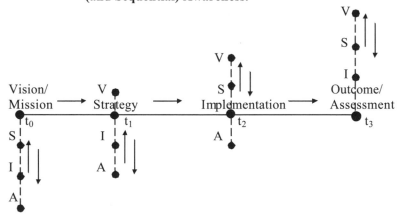

(This additional dimension of awareness, which includes single-loop, double-loop and triple-loop feedback, is fully internalised in a person during the transformation beyond Strategist to the Alchemist/Witch/Clown stage that we will introduce in Chapter 13).

The horizontal line in Figure 9.1 represents the sequential thinking of the Achiever: first a vision and mission is conceived at the organisation's founding (though it is not necessarily written down and codified); next, through a process of experimentation, the organisation evolves a workable strategy; the strategy is then implemented; and, finally, one measures the results and finds whether the organisation is successful. The Achiever may enact this sequence without conceptualising its sequential nature, much less recognising that multiple microscopic reenactments of this process occur within the larger sequence.

The Strategist begins to appreciate first that there is a nameable, systemic, historical dynamic to action and that sensitivity to timing can make one's actions more effective. The Strategist is able, in effect, to 'see' the horizontal line of history because he or she cultivates at least moments of 'vertical' experiencing during which she escapes identification with the horizontal and can take a point of view on it. Thus, the Strategist is able to systematise 'horizontal' history and also to get inklings that reality is not only sequential, but also, in an even more profound sense, 'vertical' or simultaneous.

So, at stage t for the person operating at Strategist stage there is a plan, implementation, and outcome even at the time when Visioning is the central task. The moment-to-moment awareness that spans these four simultaneous realities enables the possibility of 'seeing' when actions and effects become incongruent with mission and strategy. Only such an awareness of incongruity permits self-correcting, in real time, at the moment of incongruity. Only a person exhibiting such awareness and self-correction will be trusted over the long run to lead the process of generating a self-correcting, continual quality improvement process in an organisation.

For example, suppose you find yourself saying the following immediately after some particularly unskillful advocating behaviour on your part, to which 'Jane' is responding by walking towards the door:

> "Jane, will you forgive me? I can be so competitive at the moment when I'm struck by what I think is a brilliant idea. Maybe it's not such a brilliant idea, and there was in fact nothing wrong with yours either. But I need you and the others to help me at moments like this. Will you stay, so we can find out what does make sense and do something exciting together?"

By becoming self-critical and vulnerable, based on a non-defensive, simultaneous awareness of several different 'layers' of experience, you can self-correct in real-time. Strategists begin to have occasional glimpses of this vast region of simultaneous awareness and thus are more likely than Achievers to initiate self-corrective action. As persons evolving toward the Alchemist/Witch/Clown stage of development, Strategists are seeking ongoing contact with this 'pulse-of-life' awareness. Only at the still later Alchemist/Witch /Clown stage does simultaneous experiencing become more or less continual.

As you have probably been seeing, this whole book is attempting to help you to begin cultivating this kind of fourfold, simultaneous awareness - whether we speak of intending/planning/acting/effecting, or of framing/advocating/ illustrating/inquiring, or of visioning/strategising/implementing/assessing, or of jogging our awareness through the variety of action inquiry exercises.

From Experiments through Systematic Productivity towards Collaborative Inquiry

Now that we have suggested in general terms what the project and the difficulties of transforming toward the Collaborative Inquiry stage of organising are, let us gain a more concrete sense of what can be involved by following one company's adventure in this direction.

This company is an HMO (health management organisation) that we will call Sun Health Care, headquartered in the Southwest of the United States. Founded 18 years ago, Sun's growth really took off about ten years ago, showing first respectable and then enviable retained earnings while growing at twice the average rate of the industry as a whole. The organisation was involved in a continual quality improvement programme for four years during the early nineties, then merged with another HMO, and became the top ranked HMO in the USA in 1998. In the following pages, we will introduce you first to the recent history of the industry as a whole, next to the overall history of Sun, and finally to the internal actions within the company that generated those results. In the next chapter, we will be able to see how the personal development toward Strategist-like actions of certain key individuals interacted with the company's development to the Collaborative Inquiry stage in the early 1990's.

Brief History of the Industry and of Sun Health Care

HMOs were created in the U.S. as early as the 1930s, but their popularity soared during the early 1980s as the lower cost alternative to skyrocketing health care costs. In 1987 and 1988, the HMO industry was hit with large losses as a result of under pricing to gain market share, excessive medical and administrative costs, poor management, and under-capitalisation. Two-thirds of the U.S. HMOs lost money in 1988. In 1989, the industry began to recover. Loss margins shrank to 0.4% from 3% the year before. At the same time, an industry shakeout was beginning: although overall enrollment rose by 12% between 1988-90, the number of plans decreased by 7%, including the highly visible bankruptcy of Maxicare in Los Angeles which left thousands of enrollees without coverage.

Between 1990-92 the industry returned to profitability, increasing premiums and reducing costs. Enrolments grew at 8% and the number of plans decreased by 3%. Quality improvement initiatives gained momentum despite some poorly managed attempts and some physician resistance. Service options were widening, and new alliances emerged that turned complementary service providers into full service organisations. Consumer surveys showed mixed reactions to HMOs. Doctor revolts hit the two largest plans in Sun's state: one revolt caused the CEO to resign, partly due to a new compensation system that tied physician pay to productivity; at the other HMO, complaints about slow payments and lack of attention to physician demands forced the resignation of three top executives.

In November of 1992, Bill Clinton won the presidential election with a campaign promise to control health care costs and ensure universal access. With the anticipation of government mandated health care reform, the framework of the entire industry was put into question. It was clearly going to change in one way or another. Physicians showed an increased interest in entering into affiliations. Hospitals seemed eager to buy or form health care organisations, not only to contain costs, but also to position themselves as part of larger networks that could potentially become regional health care providers under the new national system. Employers were increasingly limiting the number of health care choices they offered, seeking out plans that showed evidence of cost reductions and high quality service.

Sun had produced a small profit even in 1988 when many HMOs suffered considerable losses. From 1989-93, Sun's enrollments grew over 20% annually on average, more than double the industry average, through increased penetration of its original service area and expansion to contiguous regions. At the same time, its net worth grew to twelve times the 1989 level. In 1993, an impartial consumer satisfaction survey showed Sun as tied for first place nationally in terms of consumer satisfaction. A national industry ranking of overall performance showed Sun as the smallest and youngest HMO among the top ten nationally. And an employee climate survey conducted by a large firm specialising in such surveys showed the most significant improvement from one year to the next ever found by that firm.

The natural question is, "What happened in Sun between 1989 and 1993 to produce the balanced and positive results just enumerated?" In 1989, the president decided that senior management should develop a formal strategic plan because the organisation's size and growth seemed to warrant it, because he wanted the senior group to act more as a team than as division directors, and because he wished to influence his two boards of directors (a corporate board and an independent physicians' board) to think more strategically.

Internal action

After interviewing a number of consultants who might help the senior management in developing its first formal strategic plan, the president engaged one who emphasised the importance of developing a mission statement that recognised the importance of clients and employees as well as of physicians and profits. This consultant also emphasised the importance of helping the senior management team evolve, not just to the point of planning together, but of implementing the plan together effectively, and of continuing to work together in a strategic manner. In other words, the consultant was advocating the simultaneous (or 'vertical') development of visioning, strategising, and implementing. It may not come as a surprise to you to learn that this consultant is measured as beyond the Strategist stage of development.

The plan that evolved included objectives related to profits, enrollment growth, cost control, expansion analysis, employee development, and quality improvement. The company also hired a new manager to create an internal training department.

Equally important, the process of developing the plan included study, feedback, and discussion of the senior team's views about one another's performance and relationships. The president learned that he could improve the levels of initiative, shared understanding, and commitment to follow through among team members by managing the team meetings in a more collaborative fashion. The team members became aware that one member whom they had somewhat isolated because of his many initiatives was not so much a self-serving rate-buster as they had inferred. In fact, the president said he wished other team members would act more like him. To a significant degree, this vice-president could be viewed as a model member of a more peer-like team where not just the president, but all team members could legitimately take initiatives. These changes in the way the president learned to lead the senior management team and in the kind of membership behaviour that was valued prepared the team to be effective in implementing the new strategic plan.

Overall, then, the company appeared to be transforming away from a more informal, decentralised form characteristic of the Experiments stage of organising. Up until the development of the strategic plan, the company had operated without an explicit mission that embraced its major stakeholders, without a strategic plan, without an organised senior management team meeting process, and with vice-presidents who saw themselves preeminently as departmental heads. Now, the company was evolving toward the Systematic Productivity stage of organising - toward a more focused form. It is important to note that, contrary to the usual experience that greater centralisation disempowers participants because their jobs become narrowly and bureau-cratically defined, this way of vertically aligning mission, strategy, and action process empowers an organisation.

Indeed, the process of developing the strategic plan, much like the interventions described in the previous chapter, itself had a Strategist/Collaborative Inquiry quality about it. When the consultant left the organisation upon completion and adoption of the plan, however, the shared leadership structure for the senior management team soon fell into disuse, with the exception of the president's ongoing efforts and successes at guiding meetings in a more collaborative manner. So, the senior management team 'settled into' a strategically directed Systematic Productivity manner of operating and the still-later-stage aspects of the consulting intervention receded from view.

After the consultant left, the quality programme initiated by the company as one of its newly adopted strategic objectives combined departmental operational studies and work redesign and based both on TQM principles. Although an external company was initially hired to support this process, the new manager of employee development led the way in taking full ownership of the process into the company, transforming the prefabricated work redesign methodology into a training process suited to this particular company and to the departmental redesign teams, as well as to the cross-functional new product and cost containment teams.

Thus, although the senior management team and the company as a whole settled into a Systematic Productivity mode of operating, the president, in his effort to manage the senior group more collaboratively, and the Manager of Employee Development, in his leadership and redesign of the quality improvement programme, both acted in more Individualist/Social Network and Strategist/Collaborative Inquiry-like ways.

At the same time, the company was offering doctors the choice of organising themselves into joint ventures, which monitored their own costs with the incentive of sharing in increased net revenues. These joint ventures were offering doctors collegial review, better returns, and lower costs. As a result, the percentage of the network organised into joint ventures grew rapidly, and those who continued as independent practitioners were faced with the ongoing question about what form of organisation served them best. From a developmental point of view, this structure is a particularly interesting Social Network approach which allows everyone a free choice about how to organise. Although management (and an increasing number of doctors) believed that the joint venture form was in fact the wave of the future, combining greater efficiency, greater profits, and peer control rather than third party control, management did not unilaterally mandate this choice for all the doctors, but instead created an ongoing choice making situation.

As each year passed, the senior management team was transforming the strategic planning process from a top-down, departmental process to a yearly, bottom-up, inter-departmental process. Each succeeding year's plan included more detailed objectives and accountabilities for interdepartmental dependencies. Performance measurements were identified and publicised throughout the company for member growth, member satisfaction, and profit. And, as already summarised in the introductory history of the company, everybody in the company could be proud of the results.

Jogging Senior Managers' Awareness

Nevertheless, the senior management team was not entirely prepared for the degree of controversy that began to develop as more and more departments undertook re-organisation. All of the re-organisation plans highlighted the critical nature of interdepartmental cooperation (Collaborative Inquiry between departments). But two of the seven vice-presidents and their departments were increasingly experienced as roadblocks to interdepartmental coordination and as less collaborative within the senior management team, even though both believed themselves to be strong proponents of the CQI programme as a whole and of interdepartmental cooperation. Their differences from the rest of the team were highlighted by the president's new, more collaborative style of running meetings.

Others saw one of the two as too frequently 'oppositional' at meetings, slowing down team decision-making to an exasperating degree. The other was seen as taking an independent, 'cowboy' attitude and not contributing sufficiently to the senior team. Both were seen as encouraging an attitude of superiority, priority, and entitlement within their departments, rather than an attitude of cooperation and service. The 'oppositional' vice-president had generated a great deal of irritation and resentment, and the president was considering firing her. The 'cowboy' vice-president stayed out of other people's way and ran his own show, so he was more tolerable, and the issues surrounding his performance were fuzzier. Also, he was a 'cheerleader' within his own department, commanding enthusiastic loyalty among many of his subordinates.

The two most probable scenarios at this point would be either:

1. for the president to continue struggling to work with both vice-presidents, perhaps strongly reprimanding and warning the 'opposer' and rapping the knuckles of the 'cowboy'; or

2. for the president to fire the 'opposer'.

At this point, however, the actual scenario departed from the probable. The president sensed that neither of those initiatives would be consistent with integrating action and inquiry, or with exercising transforming power, or with generating an opportunity for developmental transformation on the part of either vice-president (not that the president used this language). The story of what actually happened is retold in detail over the next pages. It shows the president learning more about the Strategist/Collaborative Inquiry type of awareness and action that concerns itself with the vertical alignment of mission, strategy, action, and outcome at a given moment, while dealing with senior managers who did not initially appear to share this concern. As you read, you can work on developing your own Strategist/Collaborative Inquiry awareness by observing the striking differences in thinking and action between the managers (including the president) who were acquiring this awareness and those who were not.

The president realised that the 'opposer' generated inquiry by her opposition, even if she often did not help such inquiry to reach closure in mutually agreeable action. Firing her could potentially send two negative messages to the company: (a) critical inquiry is not encouraged; and (b) persons who do not conform to the preferred managerial style will be dealt with summarily. Both these messages would directly contradict the development of a transformational continual quality improvement culture. Moreover, lower level managers were being asked to transform their managerial styles from superior/supervisory assumptions to collaborative/facilitative assumptions (supervisors' titles were literally shifting to 'team facilitator'). Thus, it would be consistent to offer vice-presidents the opportunity to transform their styles (if, upon further inquiry, they required transforming). Such an exercise would also give the senior management group as a whole the opportunity to learn how such transformation could be facilitated on an ongoing basis.

To help structure and conduct this new action/inquiry, the president recalled the consultant who had assisted the strategic planning two years before. The initial investigation indicated that the 'opposer' had indeed lost the trust and patience of all direct associates. Views of the 'cowboy,' on the other hand, were highly variable and not as raw.

What the 'Opposer' Did

The reactions of the two vice-presidents to the feedback about their performance were different from what one might have predicted. Accepting that she was not opposing effectively, even if opposition was warranted, the 'opposer' agreed to 'surrender' her customary role ('surrender' was the word actually used). With the consultant, she crafted a three-page plan of action for the next six months, which they proposed first to the president and then, incorporating his modifications, to the senior management team. Because of the frankness of the problem-assessment, the clarity of the proposed goals and coaching procedures, the commitment of the vice-president, and the explicit evaluation process (which put the burden of proof on the vice-president), the team agreed to make the necessary effort. In so doing, the senior team was embarking on a (potentially) transforming Collaborative Inquiry adventure.

The early weeks of implementation of the plan involved great efforts on the part of almost all on the senior management team and the consultant because, despite her best intentions, the vice-president repeatedly acted in ways that others' interpreted as oppositional. After about the fourth concrete instance of immediate feedback, however, the vice-president appeared to 'get' just what micro-actions worked (in the sense that other team members saw them as positive, good-faith experiments) and what micro-actions didn't work (in the sense that others saw them as more of the same old tendency to oppose). Thereafter, this issue was effectively resolved, although other aspects of the erstwhile-opposer's style still irked her peers on occasion.

What the 'Cowboy' Did

By contrast, the 'cowboy' resisted both the validity and the significance of the performance feedback about himself. People's perceptions were wrong, he felt, and his style was in fact optimal for the organisation.

If this were true, the consultant asked, would he participate in developing a process with the consultant whereby other members of senior management could come to appreciate his efficacy and perhaps amend their own approaches? No, the 'cowboy' responded, that was their problem, not his.

Could he see how this response might evoke the evaluation that he was not collaborative/facilitative in his relations with his colleagues? To this question, he responded with some anger that he was being trapped.

Before a planned meeting between this vice-president, the president, and the consultant, the vice-president met with the president on a separate matter. He intended to fire one of his managers for 'gross insubordination.' What was the evidence, asked the president. The vice-president described a pattern of behaviour, based on hearsay, supplemented by a memo by this manager to the Human Resources department questioning the justice of a corporate decision. The president said this evidence was not unambiguous enough to justify firing. In fact, it was not clear the manager had done anything inappropriate whatsoever. He added that he believed other senior managers held a significantly different interpretation of the same events.

Then and there, the president called the rest of the senior team in for an impromptu meeting, and several of them confirmed that their information from several sources made it seem like more a problem of how the vice-president had acted than of how the manager had acted. The vice-president was not able to find a constructive way of using this feedback, later describing the event, during an interview with the consultant, as a humiliation at which "I got my brains beat in". The consultant interviewed both the vice-president and the manager he had wanted to fire, and found inconsistencies within the vice-president's own story and no basis for firing the manager.

The president continued to try to work with the vice-president, but the 'cowboy' became increasingly suspicious that his job was on the line. Several weeks later, the president asked this vice-president to perform a task that the vice-president quickly asserted he could do "standing on my head". The president responded in a pleased tone that this was good because it would increase the senior management team's trust in the vice-president. To this, the vice-president responded angrily that he should have received a major bonus for his previous year's work rather than being tested in this way and that they should discuss a separation package together. At this moment, both men had to part for other meetings, so the matter was left hanging.

The president related the event to the consultant over the phone, adding "I'm sure he'll change his mind when he thinks it over". "What do you care?" the consultant responded. He argued that the president's suggested task for the vice-president, as well as his whole manner of treating the difficulty from the start, had been one that integrated action and inquiry, aligning his own strategy of acting collaboratively with his actual practice (e.g. when he called in the other senior managers for the impromptu meeting). By contrast, said the consultant, the vice-president's response was both uncollaborative and uninquiring, as had been his entire pattern of behaviour since the issue of his performance had first arisen. The president was continuing to search for convincing second-hand evidence that the vice-president was effective or ineffective (e.g. in sales figures). The consultant argued that the president now had a plethora of first-hand evidence that the vice-president did not integrate action and inquiry, did not collaborate well, and did not engage in a learning process with regard to his own performance.

Whereas second-hand evidence is always subject to alternative interpretations, this first-hand evidence struck the consultant as more unambiguous because it offered a simultaneous view of the vice-president's vision (not becoming vulnerable to inquiry), strategy (alternating between compliance and angry rejection), action (non-collaborative), and outcomes (no signs of learning). The consultant said that he did not wish to pressure the president toward agreeing with the vice-president's separation proposal if he was not comfortable with it. The question was how valid to regard, and how seriously to take, the relatively unambiguous first-hand data from the president's own interactions with the vice-president, in contrast to the relatively ambiguous second-hand data. The consultant urged the president to take 15 minutes of quiet, meditative time alone at the end of the phone call to see whether a clear conviction about the proper course of action announced itself.

Immediately following this period, the president asked the vice-president to meet again in order to work out the details of his resignation, separation agreement, and announcement to the company. Twenty-four hours later, the vice-president was no longer working at the company. After his departure, a systematic pattern of misrepresentation about senior management decisions to the 'cowboy's former subordinates was discovered and corrected.

What was the president becoming clearer about and more committed to during this experience? Perhaps that the true challenge of developmental transformation is the challenge of generating not just continuous, incremental improvement in outcomes, but also continual, simultaneous awareness of the vision, strategy, and implementation associated with outcomes. To engage in transformational improvement in real time senior management encounters requires integrating action and inquiry and exercising mutual, transforming power, as the 'oppositional' vice-president and the team had done with one another. She and the team transformed from a limited, limiting awareness of outcomes (the things she was complaining about and her status as 'opposer') to the simultaneous awareness of vision, strategy, implementation, and new outcomes needed to produce jointly the six-month plan of action. The logic of the Collaborative Inquiry stage of organising can only flower and come to be trusted within a company if it is practised in micro-encounters such as the difficult one just described.

None of the other senior executives, including the president, would have predicted at the outset of the inquiry regarding the two vice-presidents that the 'opposer' could or would transform as radically as she did, or that the 'cowboy' would resist and resign as he did. Because of the action/inquiry procedures, however, and the clear initiatives by both vice-president's (one transforming, the other resigning), the outcomes knit the senior team together more strongly. Once again, however, the team as a whole did not adopt the Collaborative Inquiry logic as its general mode of operating. Instead, as if relaxing after a difficult trauma, it returned to its Systematic Productivity mode.

The Next Challenge

The president all too soon gets a chance to test his growing appreciation for the invention of Collaborative Inquiry type procedures with another vice-president whose performance appears problematic. Astonishingly, after nine months, the new marketing vice-president, the 'cowboy's' replacement, acquired through an expensive national search, appears to be generating some of the same problematic effects as his predecessor, despite significant differences in their overt managerial styles. Whereas the predecessor was relatively loud, enthusiastic, and motivating, the new vice-president is relatively quiet and concerned with accountability. Nevertheless, the new vice-president is also similar to the "cowboy" in several ways. He speaks up relatively little in senior management meetings despite repeated invitations. He seems to under-inform his area about company-wide direction. And he generates enough discomfort among his subordinates about the ethical nature of some of his actions for the president to hear about it.

The president is very careful not to prejudge the new vice-president on the basis of limited information, and also recognises that the apparently close analogy between the predecessor and the current vice-president may point to an organisational issue rather than a personnel issue. As a result, the president invents a new Collaborative Inquiry procedure that is not merely a tactic for dealing with this problem, but also a strategy for team-wide learning and change. He proposes that the entire senior management group create an executive development process for itself. The senior management team agrees, deciding to define together: 1) standards for the 'ideal' senior management team member, 2) developmental issues that the team as a whole faces, and 3) a first-year set of developmental objectives for each member. At the same time, the president raises the specific issues he is aware of with the marketing vice-president and, together, they rehire the original consultant to work with the vice-president and the marketing managers as well as with the senior team.

Table 9-1 shows how the team came to define its 'ideal member'.

Table 9-1   Standards for 'Ideal' Senior Management Team Member at Sun Health Care

1. Leadership
- desire and ability to become a strong leader, taking executive responsibility for entire company as it grows
- seen as a leader of the company (not just own dept.) both inside and outside the company
- seen as effective manager of own area who keeps it working harmoniously with corporate-wide objectives
- wants to teach others knowledge, skills, orientation and judges own success by the ability to develop one's managers
- demonstrates creative problem-solving under pressure
- gets things done well

2. Vision/mission

- dedicated to Sun and the health care industry
- exemplifies in daily practice who we are (mission) and who we want to become (vision)
- able to motivate staff to share in our vision, philosophy

3. Creative work ethic

- strong commitment to
  - working hard
  - honesty
  - conveying energy, enthusiasm
  - quality improvement
  - customer orientation
- acts with highest integrity as well as sensitivity to the culture of the company
- prioritising skills guided by mission and strategic objectives
- manages time not just efficiently, effectively, but also creatively

4. Knowledge of what's really going on

- broad understanding of industry
- understanding of all areas of Sun Health Care
- knowledge of technical issues affecting our business
- expertise in matters concerning own department
- keeps finger on pulse, knows what's really going on

5. Implementation-focused strategic approach

- able to weigh business options objectively
  - uses effective problem solving tools
  - acts on behalf of corporation, even if not popular in own area
- demonstrates leadership in the development and execution of strategies and business plans
  - contributes innovative ideas
  - strong-willed, persuasive, and also
  - seeks out disconfirming data
- contributes to development and implementation of corporate priorities involving other departments
  - understands issues in other departments
- oriented toward cross-functional problem-solving and sharing of information

6. Artful performance in meetings

- without usurping others' leadership, assumes leadership accountability in all meetings in which he or she participates
  - gives full attention to meeting
  - prompt at start of meeting and after breaks
  - carries out all assignments in a timely manner
  - willing to ask 'dumb' questions to assure understanding
  - respects the contributions of others
  - willing to clarify/elaborate on ideas
  - willing to compromise, or craft a better third alternative
  - eases tension in the group without diverting attention from significant differences

7. Transformational interpersonal skills

- develops interpersonal skills consistent with Sun Health Care, such as
  - caring
  - down-to-earth
  - teamwork
  - ability to change
- excellent communication skills - listening, speaking, writing
- effective team player
  - actions help achieve consensus
  - supports achievement of agreed-upon goals
- negotiation skills
- recognises, manages, and transforms conflicts into energising new modes of cooperation

8. A gravity-defying learning orientation

- continual development of technical, business, managerial skills
- sees difficult challenges and stretch goals as a reason for being here
- thrives on notion that we defy gravity and will keep doing things people believe we can't achieve
- develops assessment processes for measuring own knowledge and leadership within own department
- physician executives learn business skills and business executives learn about medical thinking and the unique abilities needed to affect physician behaviour
- seeks new ways of understanding what customers want
- able to ask questions that keep you from being fooled for long

Tables 9-2 and 9-3 describe the senior team's 'ideal process', and the steps its current members can take to move toward the ideal. It may be of interest to you to think of the senior managers in your own organisation as you read through the standards for an ideal manager shown in Table 9-1. How many of them meet the first five standards, which might be termed the 'ordinary' ideals we have for persons in executive leadership roles? And how many are in contention as examples of the final three, which are more extraordinary and paradoxical ideals? Would we even recognise such subtle forms of leadership as 'assuming leadership accountability for a meeting without usurping others' leadership'? How does one 'ease tension in a group without diverting attention from significant differences'? Certainly, if such performances occur at all, they must be the manifestation of the sort of simultaneous awareness of self, group, task, and purpose that we begin to cultivate as we move toward the Strategist stage and later.

But, interesting as it may be to consider the eight ideal standards that the senior managers at Sun Health developed, perhaps it is even more important to emphasise that we are in no way suggesting that other senior managers pin these in front of themselves at their desks. What we are suggesting is that other senior management teams can gain clarity and inspiration by engaging in similar exercises. This one began by having each senior team member develop his or her own list of standards. These lists were then integrated and categorised, but without names for the categories. The subsequent discussion turned out to be both fun and touching, as members jokingly and truthfully vied to caricature how badly each other failed to keep their fingers on the organisation's pulse. A number of the members also expressed their excitement at the idea of 'defying gravity and doing things people believe we can't achieve'. The president admitted that this had been a phrase he contributed and was delighted that it had evoked such a spontaneous, positive response from others. These are the 'moments of truth' that generate shared vision and commitment within a team. At best, Table 10-1 reminds the Sun senior team of those moments. If you are interested by the result, consider creating a similar list with your current team.

In this initial sequence of events, we see how the president generates two whole sets of organisational learning processes (one for senior management, one for the marketing managers) as part of his response to the dilemma with the marketing vice-president. The president is clearly getting more of a feel for creating Collaborative Inquiry-type organisational learning opportunities.

After interviewing the vice-president and the six marketing/sales managers (see Table 9-4 for interview schedule), the consultant offers the vice-president feedback about the findings (including direct quotes, but no identification of particular speakers). The findings show, among other things, that the team meetings are viewed as unimaginatively led by the vice-president ('They are one gigantic 'to-do' list, with routine check-ins'. 'There are no discussion items at meetings, no strategy, no decision-making, no discussion of relationships within the team'.)

Table 9-2   Sun Senior Management Team Development Agenda

As agreed by the team members, the principal team development issue for this year is:

Developing a focused, overall agenda.

The team has further agreed to rotate the agenda development and meeting leadership function to a different team member every three months.   In addition, the team has defined six agenda categories, each of which requires creative and disciplined management. These are:

1. Updates
2. Open Items
3. Visioning
4. Strategising
5. Implementing
6. Assessing

The meeting leader manages the first two agenda categories, while four other team members serve as the 'Advocates' for the remaining four categories. Each advocate is responsible for determining what items in his or her category deserve team attention and for coaching whoever is responsible for each agenda item. In addition, as the team considers particular agenda items, each advocate has a special responsibility for raising issues related to his or her advocacy area as appropriate.

In general, it is understood that there is a natural flow for particular agenda items from Visioning to Strategising to Implementing to Assessing and from there to the Update or Open Item categories, if further senior management attention is warranted.

The foremost challenge for the next six months is described as curing 'the lack of respect and lack of trust within the team'. The findings also show that three or more of the other members views the performance of two members of the marketing management team as sub-par, and the vice-president is one of these two. Moreover, the vice-president is mentioned only once as one of the two most effective members of the seven-person team. And he is mentioned three times as a member of a relationship that inhibits the efficacy of the team. In addition, he receives one page of positive comments about his contributions to the team and two pages on perceived areas for improvement (e.g. 'has pressured more than one of us to misrepresent issues or our opinion to senior management and has himself directly misled them').

Table 9-3   Sample of an Individual Senior Manager's Developmental Goals

1.   Consensus Building

To accomplish this goal, I will be implementing the senior management recommendations outlined during our discussion of my presentation. Specifically, if I experience opposition to a recommendation that I believe should be adopted, I will explore with individual senior management members the source of their resistance and address those concerns directly. In addition, I will try to identify those individuals who concur with my proposal and enlist their support in building consensus. Concomitantly, I will reassess my recommendations in the context of the questions raised and restructure my position to reflect my reassessment. Finally, I will solicit individual 'evaluations' of whether I have demonstrated a more effective ability to build consensus.

2.   Supporting and Managing Subordinate Development

To improve my skills in this area, I attended a management self-assessment programme in which your subordinates evaluate you. I am currently reviewing these evaluations and I will meet with the evaluator, discuss the issues raised, and request reevaluations. Concomitantly, I plan to review relevant literature and possibly attend a programme on managing professionals. Finally, I will be working with Human Resources on ways to foster employee development and to assess the effectiveness of my efforts.

3   Communication at External Meetings with Potential Strategic Allies

In response to the observation that I speak infrequently at external meetings, I will make a conscious effort to increase my input into these meetings, both to impart information and also to make known to an outside group the thinking of my department. If effectiveness at communicating appears to be a problem when I solicit team members' feedback after each such meeting, I will seek out remedial courses.

Perhaps because the feedback report contains no brief summary like the foregoing two paragraphs, but is, rather, spread across nine pages of quotations, the vice-president reviews the information with the consultant in a calm manner, with no indication that he views the situation as one of major concern. He accepts the recommendation that a half-day retreat with the marketing management team be used to create a shared-leadership structure for meetings and to get team input and buy-in to the vice-president's own formulation of his developmental objectives for the next year.

Table 9-4   Managerial Interview Schedule for Marketing Senior Team

1. What do you see as the two or three most critical strategic/business issues or managerial/process issues for your senior marketing management team to address in the next 3-6 months?

2. How would you describe the Marketing management team right now - its overall climate, sense of direction, cohesiveness, performance, ability to manage conflict?

3. How and how well do management team meetings work? Who takes leadership? How well?

4. Do any two-person relationships within the team inhibit its overall efficacy?

5. Is the managerial style of any or several of the team members a recurring problem for you and the team? If so, describe the patterns as you see them.

6. What problems, if any, do you think others on the team have working with you?

7. All things considered, whom do you see as the two most effective members of the team not counting yourself?

8. What skills do you see yourself most in need of improving in order to increase the team's effectiveness?

9. Other than changes in yourself, if two of your wishes for the team could be granted, what would you most wish changed?

At the time, the consultant is uncertain how to interpret the vice-president's calm, constructive concern during this meeting. Is the vice-president simply addressing the issues seriously? Does he not put together the pieces of evidence and therefore not yet appreciate the magnitude of his dilemma? Or is he playing his cards so close to his chest (there is a rumour he has been interviewing for positions outside the company) that he is hoping to evade the dilemma? In a sense, it doesn't matter which is the case because the president and the consultant are both committed to a process of confronting the vice-president with information and giving him new choices at each step, rather than in making untested inferences, or in manipulating a particular preconceived outcome.

In further phone conversations with the vice-president and the six marketing managers, the consultant develops an agenda for the retreat, attempting both in his process and in the meeting structure itself to model the kind of co-leadership that is being proposed for future team meetings. Each hour of the meeting is co-led by the consultant and a different member of the team. The first hour is devoted to developing an improved meeting structure and shared leadership.

The three managers viewed as most effective by the team are all asked to assume regular leadership roles for the coming year, with the notion that these roles may be redefined and will be rotated year by year to support individual managers' developmental objectives. The vice-president will continue to take leadership with regard to strategic issues facing senior management and the company as a whole. The three new roles are: 1) agenda-manager, meeting-leader; 2) executive-secretary in charge of monitoring and appraising implementation of meeting decisions; and 3) team facilitator, in charge of coaching members who so request and of intervening in cases of conflict or blockage.

During the second hour of the meeting, the vice-president introduces the new senior management development process and presents his ten goals for the coming year. His goals reflect the feedback he has received from the consultant, but in relatively vague language. The discussion reorganises these goals and consolidates them into three more concrete goals. The managers take the opportunity to press the vice-president to be sure that he recognises the pattern of difficulties that his style has repeatedly created.

Then, during the third hour, the marketing managers discuss creating their own individualised development agendas analogous to the new senior management process. In particular, the manager who has received the feedback that four members of the team experience his style as a recurring problem speaks up to express his surprise at the feedback and his desire to rectify the situation. A meeting is set for the next week among the consultant, the vice-president, and two of the managers identified as having relational issues.

This first meeting appears to have been highly successful in terms of organisational learning, in that the team is re-energised by the new structure. But the managers are not sure how confident they can be that the vice-president is learning and will change. They point to several comments he has made that seem to minimise past problems.

The president, in turn, is shocked that the vice-president says nothing whatsoever to him about the meeting the first time they see each other afterwards, and is shocked again when they meet a day later and the vice-president says simply that the meeting has been a good one and seems to have overcome all prior problems. The president, in a moment of consternation and inspiration, asks the vice-president to write down on a single page over the weekend how he has understood the feedback from the consultant and on what basis he believes that this single meeting has resolved all the problems.

On Monday, the vice-president meets, as previously scheduled, with the marketing manager who is to become the new 'team facilitator'. This marketing manager has served as team leader for several of the companies early cross-functional new product teams, so, along with the president and the manager of Employee Development, she is one of the members of the company most practised in the Strategist/Collaborative Inquiry action logic. The manager's explicit agenda is to increase the trust between herself and the vice-president, in order to increase the probability of success in her proposed role of team facilitator. The vice-president suggests that this manager is the only one who experiences the problems that she is describing. The manager, who has no knowledge of the president's request of the vice-president, responds by making an almost identical request. She asks the vice-president if he would be willing to write a short summary of how he understands the feedback he has received from the team through the consultant. For the first time, we see several of the players in an organisational episode - the president, the consultant, and this marketing manager in this case - all acting from a Strategist/Collaborative Inquiry perspective.

Within an hour of this meeting, the vice-president delivers a short handwritten note of resignation to the president. A week later, after discussion with the consultant and the senior management team, the president appoints two of the six marketing and sales managers as Acting Vice-Presidents for Sales and for Marketing and recommends that the two sub-groups (Sales & Marketing) continue their common meetings with the new shared leadership structure. The marketing manager in the foregoing story becomes one of the two new vice-presidents.

Conclusion

Clearly, we cannot know whether the vice-president who just resigned learned anything valid through this entire process. On the other hand, the two managers who have accepted the promotions to Acting Vice-President are putting themselves into position for significant managerial learning. And the president has learned a great deal. He has learned, in a way that he can feel confident, that the vice-president was not prepared to participate actively in transformational learning. At a more abstract level, the president has learned twice over now that there is a way of making difficult personnel decisions that is not unilateral but mutual. Moreover, he has learned that he can use a difficult dilemma like this one to leverage a great deal of organisational learning.

What were the organisational learnings in this case? The president, the senior management team as a whole, the consultant, and the marketing management team developed a number of organisational learning processes for both the senior managers and the marketing/sales managers: 1) the set of 'ideal' standards for a senior manager; 2) a new senior manager development process; and 3) a new shared leadership structure for the marketing/sales managers. Furthermore, several of the other vice-presidents are currently crafting shared leadership structures for their management teams.

Thus, this second case of ineffective senior manager performance shows us how the company's president is learning, not only how to solve the presenting problem, but how to use it to generate long-term Collaborative Inquiry stage structures. Now, the president no longer has any formal leadership role within the senior management meetings. Instead, he is available as an information source and coach to the formal leaders. He feels both liberated and empowered by this change, since he is now freer to represent himself as strongly as he wishes on either substantive, or procedural, or developmental issues. In other words, he wants to be as free as possible to move his attention among levels of awareness and reduce the likelihood he will become sequentially limited within single levels. At the same time, he is pleased by the new level of leadership initiative on the part of the vice-presidents because both he and they are increasingly involved in outside-the-company negotiation of strategic alliances - brief meetings with virtual strangers who are often competitors - where every possible skill in agenda management and clear communication are at a premium.

We see that the senior management of Sun Health Care is beginning to experiment with Collaborative Inquiry types of management for its own affairs. In the next chapter, we will describe a study of ten different companies (including Sun Health) in six different industries, all attempting to transform with consultative help. From this chapter's 'worm's eye' view about how transformational change occurs in one setting, we will move to a 'bird's eye' view of the regularities across a number of settings.

CHAPTER 10

THE QUINTESSENCE OF COLLABORATIVE INQUIRY

(written in association with Melissa McDaniels)

Our experience at Sun Health Care confirms for us how peer-focussed, Strategist-like leaderly action is critical in the evolution towards a Collaborative Inquiry organisational stage of development. In the previous chapter, we have already described some of the Strategist-like actions of Sun's president, its marketing manager who has been promoted to vice-president, its manager for employee development, and its consultant. In this chapter, we will continue to document Sun's evolution toward the Collaborative Inquiry mode operation and the significant roles that the Strategist-like actions of these four play. We will also try to show some of the 'rough edges' of this developmental process, so that Sun comes out sounding less like a mythic fairy tale and more like an ongoing struggle among ordinary men and women. Chapter 11 draws on wider research and confirms the vital role of senior managers in creating organisational transformations.

The manager for Employee Development at Sun has remarkably illustrated the proposition that Strategists treat their superiors in a peer-like way. He has proposed an entirely new organisational structure for the company to the senior management team. This new structure retains the existing departmental structure (in effect, the company's Systematic Productivity structure), while initiating a new system of cross-functional areas (which can become, in effect, the company's Collaborative Inquiry structure). The new, cross-functional structure includes all of senior management on different, internal policy 'boards,' which develop and implement policies in areas such as training and the continual quality improvement programme. Here is how this manager analyses Sun's recent history and current challenge in the introduction to a document presented to senior management.

> The implementation of TQM in organisations has been described in terms of stages:
> Stage 1: Awakening
> Stage 2: Activities
> Stage 3: Breakthroughs
> Stage 4: World Class
> This simple model can describe the progress of TQM at Sun, as outlined below.

Stage 1 : Awakening

The rapid growth of membership and employees raised questions about how to manage this growth. Departments had no frameworks around which to organise and plan for their growth; thus, Senior Management commissioned an operations review of two major departments. At the same time, Senior Management had a desire to push down more of the operational management of the company to the middle management and the departments; thus, the methodology chosen for the operations analysis was consistent with the major principles of Total Quality Management. This philosophy and approach focused on controlling costs while at the same time emphasising service quality.

In April 1990, design teams from Claim Services and Medical Services worked with an outside consultant, two internal consultants (one each for work redesign and training) and a management support team to complete the work redesigns. From this experience, a methodology was documented and developed into a training process so the rest of the company could continue with work redesign.

Stage 2 : Activities

Two more years were required to complete work redesign in all the departments. In each case, the following general steps were followed:

1. Identify key processes
2. Gather the facts
3. Define the current situation
4. Analyse the process
5. Define the ideal process system
6. Alpha test and convene design walk through
7. Present to the Steering Committee for confirmation.

The results of this total restructuring of departments were new or enhanced work processes (standard methods) and new organisational designs. Frequently, these new designs resulted in work teams made up of individuals who had previously worked primarily as individual contributors. Also, the departmental organisation was kept as flat as possible and cross training was stressed where appropriate.

During this stage, Senior Management developed a planning process that incorporated TQM as a primary business strategy and identified the need for a core competency in New Product Development. A new product realisation process was developed and a first new product was introduced in 1991.

Stage 3 : Breakthrough

Experience with work redesign and the use of cross-functional teams has led to the expansion of the use of this technology to resolve organisational challenges. Four new products have now been introduced, with several more in the planning stages. In addition, teams have redesigned the referral systems, identified and implemented medical cost controls, reduced the rate of abandoned calls, and have been working to redefine yet again the standard methods in most departments. Using what they have learned in training on continual quality improvement, problem-solving, and project management, employees are involved in a total of over fifty process improvement projects this fiscal year.

Significant breakthroughs are also coming as a result of our Employee Survey process. This data has enabled management to identify and respond to the areas of Compensation, Performance Management, and Appreciation and Recognition. New systems in these areas are now under development by middle management teams. Senior Management and middle management are now organised into work teams with specific roles and responsibilities.

Concrete performance improvements have also been achieved. Sun's goal for a 7.5% administrative cost was achieved in 1992-93 (down from 10% in 1990). The industry average is 12%. For 1993-94 it remains at 7.5% of revenue in spite of major investments in resources for the Medical Services department. Without these investments, administrative costs would have been less than 5%.

In addition, major breakthroughs have occurred in the medical cost control area such that our new rates for 1994 will reflect a 2% average inflation rate (down from 12% in 1992). This pricing structure will have major implications for our competitiveness in managed care markets.

Sun is on track to double its market share in five years (beginning in 1991). We have become the third largest HMO in the Southwest, with the largest number of participating physicians, and among the highest customer satisfaction ratings in the HMO industry.

Stage 4 : World Class

World Class describes an organisation whose quality management practices are recognised as being among the best in class. Sun is planning to benchmark some of its practices (Training, Quality, Costs) against the best in order to achieve World Class status. In addition, Pioneer is being recognised both nationally and locally for its quality of customer service and its overall management and is being benchmarked by others.

World Class also refers to the expansion of quality initiatives to suppliers and even customers. Pioneer is piloting a process for introducing TQM throughout a large network of medical providers and, in particular, to the management of its medical joint ventures.

Finally, World Class suggests a sophisticated measurement and information system to pinpoint both needs for and results from quality improvement activities. External customer measurement has been intensified, that has improved internal measurement at the organisational and process levels, and the Information Services function has been raised to a vice-presidential level.

The following set of recommendations focuses on developing a system of cross-functional management that directly involves Senior Management in the policy and prioritisation process for both our training and our quality process, putting company-wide needs above the functional needs of their departments...

This is the introductory section of a large book that the manager for Employee Development hands to the senior management team at the outset of his presentation to them. He has already briefly discussed his proposals with every member of the team and in great depth with several. During the presentation some of his diagrams are difficult to follow. Moreover, there is some confusion about how he is proposing to position himself in the 'new' organisation (is this just a sophisticated power grab?). In fact he has left this detail for late in the presentation and eventually offers several alternatives.

Despite these awkward moments, his overall prior track record and his careful pre-presentation briefings result in several Senior Management team members strongly supporting him at critical moments. Only a few months earlier, these same senior managers might well have had nothing to say on this topic, or else might have raised sceptical questions without recognising their effect of discouraging initiative and innovation. Now, with the new level of committed interaction that has come to characterise meetings there is animated discussion among the team, with probing questions responded to, not just by the manager, but also by various vice-presidents. The manager is not left isolated, nor the fate of his proposal determined solely by his rhetorical skills. At the end of the allotted time, all of the issues at hand have not been clarified and resolved but a subset of the senior managers volunteer for the cross-functional Quality Improvement committee, which is to continue to define itself and report back to the team as a whole.

Over and above the fact that the manager for Employee Development is measured at the Strategist stage, the foregoing events also point toward a Strategist-like action-logic. From the outset, we see that this manager has the quality of confidence, interest, and competence to create a synthetic vision for the future of the company and to advocate it to his formal superiors. The vision synthesises theoretical ideas from a variety of sources with the actual history of Sun Health Care. The manner in which he then intertwines process and content is also Strategist-like. He carefully prepares, not only in terms of the formal 'book' he presents to senior management, but even more in terms of the preliminary conversations he has with individual members. Also impressively

Strategist-like are the multiple models he offers for his own future role, showing that he is vulnerable to influence and that he is open to a variety of framings of his role.

At the same time, the overall impact of his intervention encourages the senior management team as a whole to entertain, and to begin to participate in, an altered framing of the way the company as a whole may work better in the near future, as well as an altered framing of the way the senior management team may work together as a unit.

The President's Proposal for Restructuring

There is no evidence that the manager's new model for the senior management team directly influences the president to think of new models of working together. Nevertheless, three weeks later, at the end of a meeting to begin developing the company's 1995 strategic priorities, the president, from his own perspective, and to the palpable though silent shock of the team, raises the same issue of re-forming the senior management team.

With the swirl of partnership, merger, and acquisition opportunities, he states that he would like to be able to meet with a smaller executive committee of the ten-person team in order to conduct ongoing strategising, since the smaller team can be convened more easily, can devote more time to strategising, and can presumably reach consensus more quickly. He suggests that perhaps a new role of Chief Operating Officer needs to be created to monitor the internal affairs of the company. He asks everyone to consider this type of restructuring and to suggest other ideas.

Perhaps you can imagine some of the feelings you might experience upon first hearing this proposal, if you yourself were a member of this senior management team that is working with unusual harmony and effectiveness (the company is currently experiencing the most profitable quarter of its history). Are several members of this peer-like group going to be promoted and become the others' bosses? Am I going to be asked in the group to declare my preferences in these matters? Does the president already know who he wants on this 'executive committee'? Isn't this something that he ought to decide himself and then announce? Does he feel that some of us, including me, are not performing at the same level as others? Is my job on the line here?

In a demonstration of the trust within this team, all these questions are in fact voiced, if hesitantly, at the meeting. The president responds that he has not decided anything yet and has not matched people to his suggested roles. He is acting on the basis of the recent growth in size of the team and the knowledge that no other HMO of comparable size works with such a large team. He says he genuinely wants suggestions. He is willing to make the final decision himself, but wants it to be the best informed decision possible.

The Consultant's Restructuring Proposal

After this meeting, the consultant, who has been present, independently develops a model for proceeding with this 'collaborative inquiry'. He proposes brief telephone interviews between himself and each senior management team member, followed by team meetings at which an overall summary of members' suggestions (without mentioning names of who proposes what) help to structure the discussion. Such a process permits all the relevant information to reach the table, rather than have members' fears that they are alone in their views potentially distort the information that is shared. At the same time, one can ask whether the consultant is inserting himself between the president and the rest of the team in a way that retards the vice-presidents' development of greater parity with the president by expressing themselves directly to him.

In a further move that may indicate untimely self-insertion, the consultant works through his own preliminary outline of a specific structure that may be the outcome of the foregoing process. This structure has the entire senior management team meeting together for a half-day every other week, with two subgroups of equal importance meeting on a weekly or even more frequent basis. One subgroup is a four-person Strategy Committee for external strategising, such as the president wants; the other subgroup is the Quality Improvement Committee for internal operations that is part of the Employee Development manager's suggested structure. In this way, the CEO's new structure and the manager for Employee Development's new structure dovetail together, and the two principal elements in an organisation's capacity for world class performance - its alertness and strategic relation to its external environment and its alertness and strategic relation to its internal environment - are given equal weight.

According to the consultant's preliminary model, each member of the Strategy Committee will represent one of the four aspects of the management process discussed in earlier chapters - Visioning, Strategising, Implementing, and Assessing - thus carrying forward a central structuring element with which the team is currently becoming familiar. The president can take the Strategising role. Whoever takes the new COO role will sit in the Implementing chair within the Strategy Committee and will head the Quality Improvement Committee (see Figure 10.1).

The consultant imagines that one of the two doctors on the senior management team will sit on each committee and will quite appropriately represent the Visioning process at this time when the medical profession is perforce engaged in re-visioning itself. For, what is properly occurring during this transformational period in American health care, if not a re-exploring of the relationships between the individual practice and the social institutions of medicine? What is happening if not a re-visioning of medicine from a primary mission of curing illness to a primary mission of cultivating health?

Figure 10.1 Sun Senior Management

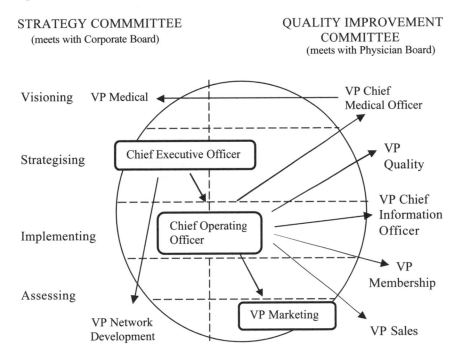

STRATEGY COMMMITTEE
(meets with Corporate Board)

QUALITY IMPROVEMENT
COMMITTEE
(meets with Physician Board)

Visioning   VP Medical

VP Chief
Medical Officer

Strategising

Chief Executive Officer

VP
Quality

VP Chief
Information
Officer

Implementing

Chief Operating
Officer

Assessing

VP Network
Development

VP Marketing

VP
Membership

VP Sales

The consultant foresees deploying one or two members of the Quality Improvement Committee to each of the same four cross-functional managerial processes. Also, because the manager of Employee Development has been mentioned more than once as a possible vice-president, the consultant foresees his promotion to a vice-presidency and a role on the Quality Improvement Committee.

We see how a collaborative inquiry about the appropriate vision for the future of the senior management team is being generated by three persons related to the company - the president, the manager for Employee Development, and the consultant. A striking aspect of these three initiators of restructuring plans is that only one of them is a member of the senior management team. Thus, the plans are emanating from very different perspectives - from a 'subordinate', from a 'superior', and from a 'bystander'.

The specific proposals are very different from one another, yet they also have much in common. All three proposals have Strategist-like qualities. All three visions are developed and presented with the invitation to a continuing conversation that will alter the initial idea in unanticipated ways as some kind of consensus is developed. Also, all three visions are so patterned that they are in fact mutually compatible, as the consultant's initial ideas illustrate. All three are patterned as uniquely crafted collaborative inquiries leading towards a uniquely crafted Collaborative Inquiry structure (although, as we will shortly see, the senior management team itself is not at all sure at the outset whether the president has a Collaborative Inquiry structure in mind, an understandable uncertainty given the hierarchical emphasis of his proposal).

Next Steps

The president is at first hesitant about the necessity for the consultant's proposed process of phone interviews with the team members during the two days prior to the team's initial meeting on the topic. But he and then the senior management team agree to it after a little discussion. (The consultant does not discuss his specific model yet, and does not know whether it will ever become relevant.)

The phone interviews reveal wide agreement that the fast growth of the company in the turbulent, unframed environment argues in favour of the president and a small Executive or Strategising Committee to devote 75% or so of its collective attention to strategising and positioning the company. Team members also generally agree that it will benefit the company to have the president become more visible on the regional and national scene and be more exposed to different innovations that are currently occurring. They also believe that the organisation will be better off if the president can reduce his attention to operational detail. Already, members feel, the president does not have enough time to mentor and coach them. Yet, at the same time, there is some concern that the group is so used to the president's leadership that it will be hard for members of the more operational group to accept another leader; they may try to circumvent that leader and still go to the president. Several members suggest that instead of one COO, three Executive Vice-Presidents be appointed, each with one or two of the other vice-presidents as subordinates.

At the same time, members are concerned not to change in ways that jeopardise the excellent overall climate of respect, mutuality, collaboration, and commitment that exists within the team at present. There is general agreement that, if there is to be a COO at all, he or she not be hired from outside because the learning curve to learn Sun's idiosyncratic culture is so demanding. Several are also concerned that the message of this restructuring to the managers in the company will be that senior management is adding a layer of hierarchy when it has been advocating reducing hierarchy; moreover, these members believe that the management level should be restructured too, if senior management is to be changed; otherwise, the managers may feel betrayed.

Shadow Issues

Another theme that emerges from the phone interviews can be introduced as an unarticulated tension between the 'insiders' and the 'outsiders' on the team.

This may properly be categorised as a kind of 'shadow' issue for the team - one that is not clearly evident to the team's own members or to anyone who might observe the team 'from the outside' - one that causes ambivalent emotions, fear, and denial even just at the mention of it. Such tension between 'insiders' and 'outsiders' had been a theme that was not publicly articulated two and three years earlier within the larger organisation, the managers at that time being viewed as 'insiders' who had often been with the company since its early days, and the senior managers being viewed as 'outsiders' hired into the company at that level. At that time, only one member of senior management was an 'insider' who had been promoted from within the company to senior management.

Now, however, there are three clear 'insiders' on the senior management team who have been promoted from within (the original 'insider' plus the two new vice-presidents of Sales and Marketing). Moreover, the president, the CFO, and one of the Medical Vice-Presidents have by now earned the status across the company as competent and loyal 'insiders' as well. The clearest outsiders are the three most recent additions to the team who have been hired into a vice-presidential role from outside the company.

In general - and it is important to the understanding of what is now being said to emphasise that the following statement has never before been explicitly stated within the company in this general way - the 'insiders' view the 'outsiders' as not well enough aligned with the improvement initiative and the general ethos of collaborative relationships within the company, and as relying too strongly instead upon hierarchical authority, delegation, and expert knowledge.

Conversely, the 'outsiders' view the 'insiders', in general, as somewhat less crisp (our summary word, not theirs) and less strategically oriented. The 'outsiders' in general lean toward introducing more hierarchy within the team (e.g., the 'three Executive Vice-Presidents' model for restructuring). This mild and unspoken disjunction between 'insiders' and 'outsiders' is made a little more prominent by two other overlapping disjunctions: the disjunction between the 'accountants' and the others; and the disjunction between two different buildings in which different members of senior management are quartered. The president, the CFO, and the two newest appointments from the outside all share accounting firm backgrounds and work in the same building. One concern within the team is that, if there is a Strategising committee and it is composed predominantly of 'outsider/accountants', and if there is a Quality Improvement committee that is composed predominantly of 'other-building/insiders', barriers between these two, so far submerged, subgroups of senior management may rise. This development would compromise the enormous comparative advantage that the president is viewed as having almost single-handedly generated for Sun by his rare capacity for mastering both the insider, detailed, 'worm's eye' view of the company and the outsider, strategic 'bird's eye' perspective on the company in its competitive environment.

Another shadow issue for the team, which members acknowledge in private, outside the meetings, but which is not discussed formally, is the increasing work load and stress levels that have accompanied the recent growth of the company and the recent turbulence in the health care environment.

These issues - in their partially submerged and fuzzy character and in the consequent difficulty of articulating them and acting upon them - are characteristic of a type of issue that arises in the evolution from Systematic Productivity to Collaborative Inquiry. During the Systematic Productivity stage, a company takes its mission and its industry environment for granted as fixed. As it evolves toward the Collaborative Inquiry stage, a company questions its mission and environment, begins to recognise that it can shape both (not merely be shaped by them), and begins to be able to articulate the way in which taken-for-granted perspectives of individuals and sub-groups within the company shape that shaping. Such 'implicit shapes' are, by their very nature, difficult and controversial to articulate explicitly, yet the failure to do so will prevent the company from evolving beyond Systematic Productivity.

The consultant follows the phone interviews by offering the above summary to the president and the senior management team. In addition, he offers the president the very specifically crafted alternative structure represented in Figure 10.1 to consider.

If you have been thinking that the consultant's model is incomprehensibly and ridiculously complex, then your reaction is similar to the president's. The president is initially cool about this model. It strikes him as too complicated to communicate easily and as unnecessarily unconventional. The paradoxical integration within the model of peer-like circularity, with horizontal division of functions between two committees, with the vertical division among the four simultaneous management processes, and with the almost hidden traditional, hierarchical lines of authority does make the model extraordinarily complex. The model displays Collaborative Inquiry stage logic, rather than the unambiguously pyramidal and deductive logic of the Systematic Productivity stage. But it may well do so in a manner that is, for all practical purposes, simply indigestible.

The president proposes still another model in response. What about reconstructing the senior management team into several overlapping subgroups, perhaps one for each of the company's three primary strategies, with no Chief Operating Officer or Executive Vice President layer?

And here we leave the process, for we have now followed Sun up until the moment of this writing. Moreover, the point of this story is more about developing a taste and a talent for the process that has just been described than it is about identifying any one particular outcome. Appreciating the significance of this kind of process is one sign of what we term the Strategist/Collaborative Inquiry breakthrough.

The Strategist/Collaborative Inquiry Breakthrough

In Chapter 9 we introduced the idea that the evolution from the Achiever/Systematic Productivity stage of development to the Strategist/ Collaborative Inquiry stage of development involves a gradual augmentation of personal and organisational awareness from a sequential version of reality, wherein one is focusing on either Visioning or Strategising...etc., toward an increasingly simultaneous experiencing of both Visioning and Strategising...etc. Now, in the context of our discussion of insiders and outsiders on the Sun senior management team and the more general notion of an insider's 'worm's eye' view and an outsider's 'bird's eye' view, we can describe the breakthrough to Strategist experiencing as the developing ability to integrate the insider, actor's 'worm's eye' view and the outsider, inquirer's 'bird's eye' view - to experience these perspectives as mutually necessary rather than as mutually exclusive. In this mode you experience yourself as simultaneously seeing from both the inside and the outside - you experience yourself as simultaneously acting and inquiring - you experience yourself as simultaneously engaging in 'business-as-usual' and in 're-visioning the business'.

Now of course, the transformations from immersion in one perspective, to the ability to alternate between one perspective and the other at different times, to the continual reality of experiencing both perspectives simultaneously are rarely sudden and final as the word "breakthrough" implies. (Indeed, one can interpret all of the developmental transformations between the Diplomat stage and the Alchemist/Witch/Clown stage as movements in this progression: from the Diplomat's total immersion in an insider's perspective, to the Expert's effort to find a formal, objective, outsider's perspective, to the Achiever's alternation between the two, etc.) But the breakthrough to both/and simultaneity is a qualitative change as the word implies and one that, according to research until the present, few human beings experience, and fewer yet experience continually.

The four Strategist-like actors who appear to be enacting the primary leadership roles in helping Sun's continuing evolution toward fuller realisation of the Collaborative Inquiry stage at first glance appear to be at different points along an 'insider-outsider' continuum. The president, who has been associated with the company the longest and has ultimate line authority within the company, appears to belong on the 'insider' extreme of the continuum. By contrast, the consultant who is not a full time member of the company at all and is retained in the first place in order to provide a more 'objective' outside perspective seems clearly to anchor the 'outsider' extreme among the four. The new Vice-President for Marketing has line responsibilities, but a staff function (marketing research), and has led the early cross-functional new product teams, as well as currently serving as agenda manager for the senior management team. Thus, he fits toward the insider end of the continuum, especially in terms of the emerging Collaborative Inquiry structures such as the new product teams which he pioneered for the company, but with some 'outside' flavours such as the staff and inquiry emphasis in marketing research. The manager for Employee Development is in effect an internal consultant and trainer, and thus an outsider/insider, though he too has line responsibilities for his department. Thus, he may fall slightly to the 'outsider' side of the centre of the 'insider-outsider' continuum, but clearly has a very strong insider flavour as well, as a full time employee and manager.

This continuum clearly captures a significant aspect of the reality of the situation; but just as clearly, when we reflect on the matter so, this is a single-visioned outside-in, structural view of the situation. As we have already seen, there is another sense, which we regard as even more significant for the future development of Sun, in which all four of these organisational actors integrate insider/outsider, actor/inquirer, and business-as-usual/re-visioning perspectives. And there is yet a third sense, we suspect, in which each of the four enacts the two different ends of the insider/outsider continuum in an un-integrated fashion.

Let us hear how persons at Sun who do not use the language of this theory speak about these four. Let us hear how their day-to-day colleagues speak of them and how they speak of themselves. Here is a senior manager speaking about the president:

> ... (the president's) support and belief are absolutely essential. He has been a real leader; he has been willing to change. He had to change some things about the way he thought about planning; he has had to learn a new system. He has had to come out and be a much more visible leader than he probably would have liked or was his natural style. He has learned a lot.

In these comments, we hear how the president has become both more outgoing and more ingoing - how he has integrated more outgoing leaderly action with more ingoing self-revisioning inquiry. As we have already seen, other members of the senior management team regard the president as having an exceptional ability to integrate the insider, detailed 'worm's eye' view with the outsider, strategic 'bird's eye' view. On the other hand, if we were to speak of insiders as 'soft' and 'subjective' by contrast to outsiders who are 'hard' and 'objective', then the president clearly favours the outsider-objective perspective.

The other Strategist-like actor of the four who falls toward the insider end of our original bifurcated insider/outsider continuum is the new vice-president for Marketing. Of her, a colleague says:

> ... the new product development process has been an enormous change effort, because it has meant substantial changes for the role of lots of managers and things that are going on in their departments. So (she) has had to be a change agent in that regard.

We hear this insider described not as a defender of the current culture and structure of the company - not as an agent of stability - but as an explorer of new ways of working - as an agent of change. Moreover, she is viewed as open to personal change as well:

> When (she) gets feedback from (the president) she knows just how to manage it, and how to deal with it within the group, and is not phased by it at all.

In describing the manager for Employee Development, whom we originally place slightly to the outsider side of the bifurcated continuum, one of his superiors on the senior management team uses almost the same sort of language as we are here:

> ... and I think his role has changed in some regards from being a singular kind of outside consultant to being really an active participant; and that is a fine line that he needs to play here because he is a manager in the organisation, and on the other hand he is an outside, you know, consultant, helping the managers develop, and playing both of those roles, depending on the project at the time. It is pretty tricky.

This theme of the trickiness of walking the tightrope that stretches in each moment orthogonally through the insider/outsider continuum is illustrated more concretely by the following comment.

> ... he is very good at finding the pace that the other people in the organisation actually learn at. And similarly, with the senior management, he is persistent about this, but he will not move ahead and get his head cut off for his troubles; he will really work patiently to bring senior management along on an issue. He is quiet, you know; he is not loud; he is not flamboyant; and I think those are important factors in his being successful as an internal change agent. If he were flamboyant, he probably wouldn't last.

This theme of the trickiness of walking the tightrope that stretches in each moment orthogonally through the centre of the insider/outsider continuum is echoed yet again in a comment about the external consultant:

> ... to play the role he is playing in many cases, in the sense that he is a consultant (yet) he is also on our board ... is a very tricky role for him.

Interestingly, the external consultant himself claims that he does not experience his simultaneous Board membership and consulting position as the 'tricky' aspect of working with Sun:

> Over the past five years, I have become both a Board member and a

consultant at all three companies with which I currently work. Given the nature of the three organisations - one is a mission-oriented for-profit and the other two are market-responsive not-for-profits - and given my personality and style of working, I find that the Board position highlights my long-term dedication to the mission of the company and that this emphasis balances my primary aim as a consultant of influencing senior management's effectiveness in the near-term. It is also important that none of the Board positions is itself lucrative and that I have an agreement with the president that I will relinquish the consulting role if a potential or actual conflict of interest is illustrated, or anytime the president so wishes.

So, what's tricky for me now, after five years of association with Sun, is not so much balancing the Board/consultant roles as it is dealing with the multitude of significant business relationships with persons and groups at all levels of the company. Although the company as a whole is my primary concern as a Board member, and the efficacy of the president and the senior management team is my primary concern as a consultant, the person or group I am currently dealing with becomes, in a very real way, my primary client at that time. For me, the really tricky part is to act in a way that is true to my current primary client and to the other two primary concerns - the efficacy of the senior management team and the mission of the organisation - at the same time.

In a sense, the external consultant is here talking about all the complex ways in which he is internal to the organisation and balances multiple long-term relationships within it. However, this consultant's appreciation for complexity seems to blind him somewhat from the simple issues. We have already mentioned how his complex suggestion for restructuring senior management 'missed' the president, who was his primary client with regard to that issue. With regard to the foregoing quotation about what is really tricky for the consultant, he may not think balancing his board and consulting obligations is tricky, but a recent evaluation by the senior managers of the consultant's performance this past year shows that the senior managers are not fully open with the consultant because of his board role.

A fitting complement to this (partially mistaken) 'insider' sense that the 'outsider' consultant ascribes to himself is the 'outsider' sense that the internal consultant/ manager of Employee Development talks about cultivating for himself:

You have to always stay fresh. You need to keep yourself fresh and your ideas fresh... so you kind of maintain the air that the external consultant brings, which makes you more... you get 'invited to the party' all the time because of that. I need some of both (internal and external consulting). I have told the company I need that; it is part of my education. It is a part of what makes me better... The contact with the academic environment, the contact with other consultants, with other clients... re-energises me. Now I can just bring all of that stuff back in here with a lot of intensity and enthusiasm.

Conclusion

This final quotation of this chapter nicely epitomises the creative intuition that draws the Strategist/Collaborative Inquiry action logic beyond itself toward the myth-making action of the Alchemist/Witch/Clown/Foundational Community stage - toward continually reframing action - which we will introduce in Chapters 13 and 14.

The accent in the very first sentence of the quotation is on continual freshness - on experiencing freshly, seeing the situation freshly, feeling afresh, feeling inquiringly, and re-conceiving one's intent in the midst of action. And the treasure such self-refreshment brings to the organisation is celebrated in the final sentence which describes the reverse of on-the-job burnout and organisational exhaustion that is so common in the demanding, globalising, continually self-reconfiguring business and professional environments of the 1990s. If Sun senior managers could all refresh themselves at work as this manager advocates, then the shadow issue of workload and stress would be less prominent.

The overall response by the Sun senior management team to its accomplishments during the year in regard to becoming more collaboratively self-managing and in regard to supporting one another's professional development, with the help of the consultant, is strongly positive. On a rating of the consultant's work between -5 ('Detrimental'), 0 ('Sometimes useful, sometimes not worth the time'), and +5 ('Of clear strategic value'), their average rating is +3.3. Members speak of "vastly improved management of the agenda and open items", of "team management actually working", and of how "getting to think strategically about one another's personal development (has been) good". They speak of the consultant as "helpful with specific management problems" and as "a good third party voice in discussions and decisions". "Suggestions concerning how to approach a particular problem were always right on target" and "helpful in controlling the emotional aspects" are additional positive comments.

Not every initiative was evaluated as successful, however. The majority of the team favours not continuing to work with the four Advocacy roles, named 'Visioning', 'Strategising', 'Implementing', and 'Assessing'. From their point of view, the four ideas never became clearly defined, nor helped the team. As one of them put it, "We got bogged down in form over substance". Or, as another one wrote, more diplomatically, to the consultant, "I did make every effort to understand the theoretical basis of your management theory. I must say some of the concepts still are difficult for me to comprehend". Still another advised the consultant simply "to make us finish what we start".

The president decided not to make any formal change in the team structure, other than to name several members to an informal strategising team. At the same time, the Employee Development manager persisted with his plan to create an internal 'Quality Improvement' Board that includes other members of the team.

Thus, the team is quietly evolving toward the Collaborative Inquiry stage, although it remains quasi-allergic to any discussion that veers toward 'process' or 'theory'. Also, we can see that some members tend to advise Achiever/Systematic Productivity solutions to dilemmas (e.g. 'make us finish what we start'). In fact, the consultant had supported a process of redefining the Advocate roles, a meeting had been held and agreements had been reached, and a member of the team had volunteered to bring the write-up to the team; but then that member had dropped the ball. Should the consultant have 'pushed' that member again? Perhaps so. But this is the subtle dance during the transformation from Systematic Productivity to Collaborative Inquiry, when the process or form of action comes to be seen as equally significant for the long-run effectiveness of the organisation as the immediate substance and short-term outcome. The team seems to be about half way there.

Before we move on to the next chapter, there is one last thing we'd like to do with you. We wish to test with you whether the story of Sun Health Care seems to you to shed light on the organisation(s) to which you belong.

Do you see a need for a process within your company, or church, or voluntary group that not only 're-engineers' existing tasks and ceremonies, not only cuts costs, and not only makes the voice of your clients or customers more influential in shaping the products or services the organisation delivers - but also re-visions and re-frames the organisation as a whole?

Does the idea of simultaneous action and inquiry - simultaneous concern with outcomes and with process - at the organisational level make sense and seem desirable to you?

Does the notion of personally integrating an outsider and an insider perspective seem feasible and attractive to you?

Do you see why it is consistent with moving in such a direction that one begins increasingly to learn about one's own and the organisation's 'shadow' or 'rough edges', as this chapter has tried to inform you about the 'shadow' and 'rough edges' of the process at Sun?

CHAPTER 11

THE IMPACT OF THE CEO'S OR MD'S STAGE OF DEVELOPMENT ON ORGANISATIONAL TRANSFORMATION

In the last chapter we have explored the connections in one organisation between the willingness of senior executives to exercise collaborative action inquiry, the success of organisational change efforts and the organisation's ability to thrive in an ever more complex business environment. In this chapter, we go from that single case study to a quantitative study of ten cases of attempted organisational transformation and of the influence of the Chief Executive or Managing Director's stage of development in the ultimate success or failure of the ten efforts.

Some researchers have argued against focusing on the Chief Executive Officer (CEO) or Managing Director (MD) in predicting a company's destiny. But we have found, through study of our own successes and failures as consultants, those senior executives at the Strategist stage of development and later are more likely to be successful in creating and supporting organisational transformation. In a hierarchical culture, a CEO's or MD's support for and legitimisation of change effort - especially when they involve new practices that aren't widely understood or practised, like the tools and concepts of organisational learning and developmental action inquiry - are critical in sustaining company wide transformational processes until results persuade an increasing proportion of the work force to commit more fully to the new order. And, conversely, a single CEO or MD incapable of exercising, recognising, or supporting transformational power can be enough of a bottleneck to undo prior organisational abilities and accomplishments. Thus, regardless of what else is happening within the organisation, a CEO can have a major influence on the likelihood of organisational transformation to a new developmental action-logic. Now that you know the results, here is a fuller description of the study (and the endnotes and reference, offer still lengthier descriptions which include the statistical results).

Studying Organisational Development Efforts

For ten years, two of us and two other consulting partners participated in and studied ten organisational development efforts, spending an average of about four years with each business. The organisations included both for-profit and not-for-profit enterprises that ranged from 10 to 1,019 employees, with an average of 485 staff members. The businesses represented numerous industries, including financial services, automobiles, consulting, health care, oil, and higher education.

Based on several criteria, we found that seven of the ten organisations, including Sun Health, prospered. They experienced significant improvements and became industry leaders on a number of key indices. On the other hand, despite our best efforts, three of the ten organisations did not progress and lost personnel, industry standing, and money.

In examining these cases retrospectively, we noticed that the companies whose CEOs or MDs had certain perspectives and values were more likely to achieve favourable outcomes in the organisational transformation process than those that didn't. We found that the more successful leaders recognised that there are multiple ways of framing reality, and understood that personal and organisational change require mutual, voluntary initiatives, not just top-down, hierarchical guidance.

In the organisations that didn't change, the CEOs actually impeded change efforts, either through benign neglect of existing learning structures or through actions that undermined the transformation process. For instance, one leader eliminated by simple disuse many of the peer learning systems built into the organisation when he arrived, gradually turning the operation into a crisis-prone, reactive entity.

Individual and Organisational Developmental Stages

Wanting to change isn't enough to guarantee personal or organisational transformation if the assumptions of one's current way of seeing, based on one's stage of development, tend to undercut efforts to operate according to the next, more encompassing developmental stage. Consequently, leaders and organisational systems that exercise inquiry-based, mutuality enhancing, transforming power, associated with the Strategist and Collaborative Inquiry action-logics are critical for transformation. For example, in the story in Chapter 9 about the two vice-presidents who were challenged to do some double-loop learning, the 'cowboy' vice-president who in effect refused and resigned called back the CEO two years later to thank him for his efforts. The former vice-president reported that his wife had criticised him for resigning. He also said that he was fired three months into his next job. Only after all this did he enter therapy and discover the degree to which he refused all well-meant influence attempts. Thus the collaborative inquiry with which that CEO and his consultant had engaged his vice-president eventually led to a transformation on that erstwhile vice-president's part.

About 39% of the adults studied in organisations operate according to the Opportunist, Diplomat, or Expert action-logics, yet it is only at the next

Achiever action-logic (where about 35% of managers are measured) that persons reliably use single-loop feedback to improve their performance. This leaves about 22% of managers who measure at the Individualist and Strategist stages. In fact, it is only at the Strategist action-logic that a leader explicitly initiates double-loop, transformational learning. Now we can understand why 'learning leaders' and 'learning organisations' are so rare.

People who develop to the Strategist action-logic or beyond can appreciate the paradoxes of exercising 'vulnerable power'. They understand that only power exercised in such a way as to make oneself vulnerable to transformation can generate voluntary transformation in others rather than mere external conformity and compliance, or resistance. For example, one MD in our study openly presented his weaknesses and shortcomings as a leader to his senior team during a time of organisational crisis. Based on this openness, the team was able to assign responsibilities so as to eliminate potential blind spots, challenge each another to develop new skills, and provide regular feedback on each other's performance. In this way, Strategists are true learning leaders.

Leaders at earlier stages of development, in contrast, would reject out of hand the actions of the Strategist MD described above. A Diplomat senior executive, for instance, would feel threatened by the prospective loss of face in publicly describing his or her weaknesses. In fact, the one Diplomat CEO in our sample companies was so unwilling to work constructively with any negative feedback from colleagues and from the market that eventually his entire strategic planning team resigned; the consultants resigned; and the organisation continued to lose money and reputation. Expert and Achiever CEOs are increasingly more likely to be able to cope with negative feedback than the conflict-avoiding Diplomat. However, unlike Strategist CEOs, who are often able to generate timely, creative actions based on the specific situation, Experts and Achievers tend to rely on 'standard operating procedures'.

Let us use Figure 11.1, below, to help us reformulate the foregoing argument in slightly different words. (The reader may want to refer all the way back to Table 2-1 and Figure 2.1 to see our original mention of the four territories of experience that appear again in Figure 9.1 and now in Figure 11.1).

One pattern of behaviour that we noticed among CEOs who successfully supported organisational transformations is that they intentionally focus the company's attention on the discrepancy between its intention to change and its actual performance. In some cases, addressing such a disparity requires nothing more than a single-loop, tactical change in *performance*, such as temporarily increasing the marketing budget and reducing the research budget. But because members of organisations are unlikely to have mastered the Achiever action-logic, where people reliably make changes based on single-loop feedback rather than defending existing practices, even single-loop changes can be difficult to achieve reliably.

In other cases, a change effort may be stymied by a team member's mental model or by conflict between a strategic priority and the organisation's culture. This level of challenge generally requires a 'double-loop' change in *strategy*. Double-loop learning is inherently transformational - it changes the form and capacity of a person's thinking or of an organisation's culture. It is a change *of* the system, not *by* the system.

Finally, a person or organisation may realise that lasting change involves continually testing one's moment-to-moment vision, thinking, action, and outcomes against a meaningful and compelling *collective vision*. Such 'triple-loop' learning goes beyond systems *thinking* to systems *experiencing*, which spans all four levels of experience. According to the developmental research, less than one percent of adults cultivate the Alchemist/Witch/Clown action-logic (which we will discuss in Chapter 13), in which individuals continually explore the interplay among single-loop, double-loop, and triple-loop learning. Yet this mysterious 'magic trick' is the ultimate key to becoming a true 'learning leader' or 'learning organisation'.

Figure 11.1   Single-Loop, Double-Loop and Triple-Loop Feedback in Full 'Systems Experiencing'

What does it mean for an organisation to progress developmentally, and how is this kind of improvement related to organisational learning? As in human development, each transformation in organisational development represents a fundamental change and increase in the organisation's capacity. As illustrated in the previous three chapters, in transforming through the first three organisational stages (Conception, Investments, and Incorporation), an organisation grows from a dream into a functioning, producing social system. If, like Sun Health in the previous chapter, an organisation transforms through the second three stages (Experiments, Systematic Productivity, and Collaborative Inquiry), the organisation gains the capacity to change its strategies and structures intentionally. Just as few persons today evolve beyond the Achiever stage, few organisations today evolve beyond the analogous

Systematic Productivity stage. But when they do (as in the case of Alcoholics Anonymous and the Jesuit Order), they become capable of helping their own members develop to the point of recognising and correcting incongruities among their visions, strategies, actual behaviour, and outcomes; that is, they become true 'learning organisations'. In short, each organisational transformation from one stage to the next represents major organisational learning, and beginning at the Collaborative Inquiry stage, an organisation explicitly and intentionally generates ongoing individual and organisational learning.

Obstacles to Change

In the ten organisations that we studied, all of the CEOs and many members of the senior management teams completed the Leadership Development Profile that we use in our research and consulting. Five of the CEOs measured at the Strategist stage or later, and five measured at pre-Strategist stages. In all five cases in which the CEO was found to be at the Strategist stage, the organisation transformed in a positive way - the business grew in size, profitability, quality, strategy, and reputation. Moreover, trained scorers agreed that that these CEOs supported a total of 15 organisational transformations. (All but one of the Strategist CEOs supported at least two transformations during the four years we worked with them.)

Conversely, in the five cases of organisations with pre-Strategist CEOs, there were a grand total of zero organisational transformations (a three-stage regression in one case, two cases of no change, and two cases of positive transformation [one one-stage chance and one two-stage change]). In the three cases with no positive transformation, the organisations experienced crises and highly visible performance blockages. The correlation between later CEO stage of development and positive organisational transformation is statistically significant beyond the 0.05 level and accounts for an unusually large 42% of the variance.

This finding is further strengthened by another analysis of the data. All four of the consultants were measured at the Strategist stage or beyond. Three were measured at the Strategist stage and one at the Alchemist/Witch/Clown stage (to be described in Chapter 13). Developmental theory predicts that actors at later stages will be more effective in supporting developmental transformation even when persons or organisations are at earlier stages. Consistent with this prediction, the Alchemist/Witch/Clown consultant played the lead role in the two cases where pre-Strategist CEOs participated in successful transformation. If we add together the developmental scores for the CEO and the lead consultant in each of the ten cases, and if we correlate the rank order of the resulting numbers with the rank order of the number of successful transformations achieved by each organisation, we find that this correlation is significant at the .01 level and accounts for 61% of the variance.

A closer retrospective look at these two anomalous cases is also interesting. In both instances, the CEO treated the outside consultant and the one or more team members measured as Strategists as close confidantes. In one of these cases, the CEO stopped working with the consultant and became CEO of another organisation (after the original research had been completed and reported as above). Rather than discovering what would be timely and creative in the new setting, this CEO tried to reproduce what worked in the previous organisation. The organisation regressed, lost hundreds of millions of dollars, and the CEO was fired.

We can also look a little more closely at the three examples in which the organisations did not transform in a positive direction in the original study. In each of these cases, the pre-Strategist CEOs had increasingly distanced themselves from the consultant and from senior management team members who measured at the Strategist or later stage. In one case, the CEO alternated between, on the one hand, highly valuing his internal consultant/senior manager and the change process and, on the other hand, trying to displace her from the senior management team altogether while freezing the change process. Not surprisingly, the organisation did not transform during this period.

Leverage Points for Organisational Development

So, what do the results of this study mean for other organisations that may be embarking on, or are in the midst of, a transformation process? First of all, they indicate that any business that is serious about achieving organisational transformation should carefully consider the significance of the CEO's or MD's role. Our results challenge common assumptions such as 'Change can start anywhere in the organisation', or 'Bottom-up change is what we want'. At least initially, the CEO's support is necessary in order to create a culture in which change can start anywhere within the organisation.

Second, if the senior executive him or herself is unwilling to assume a leadership role in the transformation or is unable to accept feedback from others, our results support raising this issue with him or her as early as possible to highlight the potential impact of this behaviour on the change process. Different CEOs are likely to respond as differently as the two Sun Health Care vice-presidents in Chapter 9.

Third, the results of this study indicate the usefulness of diagnosing the current developmental stage of the organisation as a whole, in order to understand the challenges it faces and to outline strategies for moving to the next level. Certainly, we as consultants did so in each case and tested our tentative diagnoses and strategic prognoses with members of the organisations (adapting the language we used to the context we were in). We found that our diagnoses gained us legitimacy and helped focus the transformation process.

Fourth, developmental theory holds that a person operating from a later stage can play a positive role in supporting transformation of a person or organisation at an earlier stage of development. Thus, an MD at the Achiever stage can help an organisation at the Experiments stage or earlier to transform. Likewise, as we found in the two organisations that transformed without the guidance of a Strategist MD, a pre-Strategist MD may successfully partner with others from within or outside the organisation to support organisational learning.

Fifth, members of the senior team can engage in a self-diagnosis process (with the help of the references listed in the Endnotes), or it can solicit outside help to evaluate the current level of individual and organisational development. At first blush, it may seem unacceptably risky to attempt two change processes - of senior management team members and of the organisation - at the same time. Why not work first with the senior management team and later with the wider organisation? This may be possible and preferable in some cases, but often the organisational and environmental conditions that call for organisational transformation will brook no delay. Also, the awareness of organisational members that the senior executive and senior managers are facing the same vulnerabilities, uncertainties, experiments, and transformations as they are can become a potent force for widespread buy-in, as was the case at Sun Health Care.

Finally, as the cases in Chapter 8 illustrate, organisational retreats to engage in 'systems experiencing' across the four territories of visioning, strategising, performing, and assessing can sometimes transform the stage of development of an organisation in as short of a time as a single weekend.

Conclusion

So far as we know, these are the only ten cases in which the developmental stages of senior managers and organisational transformation have been studied together. Our results suggest that CEOs or MDs at the more mutual, more learning-oriented later developmental stages help an organisation evolve through earlier stages up to the Collaborative Inquiry stage, where organisational learning becomes the regular mode of doing business. Recently, in *Good to Great*, Jim Collins isolated 11 companies that transformed from good to great and sustained the new levels of performance for long periods of time. He found the quality of their CEOs to be a critical factor in the transformation. Although he is unable to explain the qualities of these CEOs in theoretical terms, we suggest they sound developmentally like Strategists and recommend that interested readers see for themselves.

In the face of perpetual transition, the great challenge is how to interweave productivity and inquiry in the short and long-term. This process entails interweaving productivity and inquiry in the organisation's vision (e.g., SAS airlines' motto 'Moments of Truth'), strategies (e.g., 3M's formula for increasing a division's funding as it increases the percentage of its ROI from recent innovations), operations (e.g., meetings that encourage frank inquiry and dialogue as well as decisiveness), and assessments (e.g., 360-degree feedback).

This challenge is at least as great as the Achiever/Systematic Productivity struggle to gain unilateral political, economic, and technological control over nature and society that has preoccupied us for the past 500 years. As more and more of us become aware of the dignity of mutual, transformational relationships, rather than unilateral, exploitative relationships, within organisations and polities, between men and women, and between society and nature, we will become increasingly inspired to devote our daily lives to these means and these ends. We will see in the next chapter that when one undertakes such a quest, one heightens the potential not only for the transforming of institutions but also for one's own personal fulfillment.

CHAPTER 12

SEEKING THE GOOD LIFE - A
DEVELOPMENTAL INQUIRY

Now, as we near the end of this book together, we wish to ask you, our readers, one of the most profound questions it is possible to ask: "What is the good life and what is the path toward it?"

It is timely to ask explicitly "What are our different versions of the good life?" because the path of action inquiry described in this book is one that includes repeated radical transformations of our own experiencing. One question that naturally arises is, "Where are these changes ultimately taking me?" Another is, "Are there any ultimate values that remain constant throughout this journey and are they values that I can ascribe to?"

Or, the question may arise in a more skeptical form for you, such as, "Is not the question of the good life more like a religious question?" - a question that is one's own private business, rather than one to be addressed in the context of management, organisations, and economics?

Still other readers may chime in, "Doesn't the market system and market theory presume that each consumer has his or her own utility function, which is not the business of economic theory per se?" The simple answer to this question is, 'Yes'. Market economics has assumed that it need not concern itself with people's utility functions. Market economics 'works' (according to the theory) no matter what you like or value. But this book argues that companies can make significant long-term progress toward improving the quality of their products and services and of their market and financial positions, only if a very special process occurs. In short, they must value one particular dynamic – 'self-questioning-in-action'- as perhaps no one has since Socrates and the philosopher kings whom he imagined as the best possible executives.

The vast majority of all managers (the large proportion at the Achiever stage or earlier) must somehow, paradoxically, be open to a level of questioning that more than once leads them through upending developmental transformations that recast their assumptions about the aims of life and work before they become fully open to moment-to-moment questioning that can improve performance. During such developmental transformations, the very meaning of questioning itself, the very sense of how time works, and the feel for what kind of exercises of power generate action inquiry all change in ways that the person rarely if ever imagined before the change.

Put still differently, our argument is that, unless the managers, senior executives, and Boards of organisations fundamentally reconsider the value of self-questioning-in-action in attaining the good life for themselves, the globes economic, political, and spiritual problems and polarisations will not abate. Our grotesque inequalities of wealth and power will continue to become more extreme. So too will the more subtle, but even more significant, inequalities among peoples of the world in their positive sense of the meaningfulness of their lives.

Yet virtually all persons tend to resist the disorientation and suffering of periods of upending questioning. Few leap at the opportunity to repeat the upending sense of their teenage years, especially when they hold major corporate responsibilities. Perhaps the only way to become enamoured of questioning-in-action is to make questioning-in-action the primary commitment and practice in one's personal search toward the good life - as we will suggest toward the end of the chapter.

You will have the opportunity to wrestle with the question of how much to value what kind of questioning as the chapter continues. By way of preview, we propose that a good way to approach the good life is to see it as composed of four primary goods - namely, good money, good work, good friends, and good questions. As you can by now imagine, these four goods relate closely to the 'four territories of experience' we have been discussing throughout the book - the realms of outcomes (money), actions (work), thoughts and feelings (friends), and intuitive vision (inquiry). But before turning to the discussion of good money, good work, good friends, and good questions, and of why they may be good candidates as criteria to focus upon in the search for the good life, let us examine some other areas of life that need to be addressed anew today by a constructive definition of the good life.

Communism's claim to have a workable answer to the 'good life' question is no longer at all credible. At the same time, in America, fewer feel wealthy, or even comfortably middle class. In the U.S. the gap between the richest fifth of the population and the poorest fifth has been widening for the past generation. Cynicism, discontent, and disillusion with regard to virtually all professions permeate broad layers of our population, especially in the wake of the corporate ethics crises of 2001-2003.

From another angle, we are increasingly realising that the entire modern way of life, with its predominant emphasis on the values of production and consumption and its odd and explosive mixture of spiritual relativism, fundamentalism, and terrorism is endangering the planet. This clear and present danger stretches from the Himalayan forests, to Madagascar's waters, to the powder keg of Middle Eastern fundamentalisms, to Brazil's plant and animal life, to Mexico City's air, to the regressive, relativistic, postmodern, floating exchange-rate monetary system we now endure, to the thinning ozone layer over the North and South Poles. From the point of view of the market model of economics, these are mere 'external diseconomies' in our quest for the good life. But since these effects of our actions may threaten our very survival, surely an appropriate definition of the good life and of the path toward the good life will properly subordinate both production and consumption to higher values.

At the outset of the third millennium, the global nature of the political economy and of its environmental effects dictates that our answers to the perennial question about the good life will this time have global consequences - not just local or national consequences. Therefore, this additional question arises: is there a way of defining the good life that can have global validity - leading, for example, to a more just global monetary and banking system and to meaningful environmental treaties - without obliterating justifiable differences in values?

Another question, yet more ambitious: is there a way of answering all these questions that leaves the market system intact as a method of determining prices and that leaves broad leeway for different individuals and societies to evolve distinctly, while simultaneously posing a challenge to all individuals and societies to evolve constructively? This would be the most conservative possible path toward the good life from our present condition.

We believe that there is an answer to these questions that is at once immediately practical within the melange of market-like systems that now exist, broad enough to allow for infinite variety among personal and societal value systems, deep enough to embrace many transformations of understanding, and mysterious enough to allow each a lifetime of continuing questioning. The most succinct way of stating this answer is that the good life consists of an appropriate blending of good money, good work, good friends, and good questions. Toward the end of the chapter, we will ask you whether any of these four goods are among the goods that you consider primary, and what other goods strike you as among your primary few. Now, let us examine more closely what we mean, and what each of you may mean, by each of these four criteria that we claim constitute the good life when appropriately blended together.

Good Money

We will be surprised if very many of you who have ever tried to make ends meet don't agree that making good money represents positive net personal and social value.

But some of you are probably aware of the ambiguity in the cliche 'good money'. When we say that someone makes good money, we typically mean simply that he or she makes quite a lot of money. There is an implication that the person makes more than an average amount of money, an ample amount of money, comfortably enough money, maybe more money than we can imagine we would really 'need'.

In the context of talking about the good life, however, the phrase 'good money' also carries an ethical overtone of some initially unclear sort. Can we imagine making 'bad money'? Perhaps such a phrase applies to illegal profits, such as those of Michael Milken based on insider information in the Wall Street junk bond market of the 1980s. But not all of us would agree that all illegal profits are 'bad money'. In the Soviet Union of the 1970s, the only free markets were illegal black markets, yet some would argue that such illegal profits contributed more to personal and social net value than the money made by legal means under that system.

No. According to the four criteria of the good life that we are here proposing, what is ethically good about making good money is that one makes money in a way that blends best with the other three criteria of the good life. One can see plenty of examples of persons who accept jobs they don't regard as good work in order to make more money. One can also see examples of persons whose dedication to making more money leads them to sacrifice more and more of the leisure time during which one can cultivate good friends and good questions. Although there may be extenuating considerations in particular cases and for short periods of time, in general making more money in these ways reduces rather than increases the overall goodness of one's life. Hence, no matter how great the amount of money made in such cases, they are not examples of 'making good money,' according to this definition of the good life. (Of course, these arguments only have weight if you agree on the importance of the other three criteria of the good life. Since we have not yet discussed the meaning if these other three, you are quite right to feel tentative about accepting our claims at this point.)

Another way of putting this is that, of the four criteria of the good life, three of them - good work, good friends, and good questions - are intrinsically valuable (we value the time actually spent engaged with them). By contrast, good money is only extrinsically valuable (valuable as a means to obtain other values, not as an end in itself). Therefore, any time we spend making, managing, or spending money - when we are not simultaneously doing good work, meeting good friends, or raising good questions - is not intrinsically valuable time. Indeed, every moment we spend in this way reduces the amount of intrinsically valuable time in our life.

At one extreme, according to this definition of the good life, if the richest person in the world spent all his time making money in the way just described - thereby leaving no time for good work, good friends, and good questions - he would have the 'poorest' life of anyone. He would be making absolutely 'bad money' and he would be living an ideal case of 'the bad life'. The reclusive, addicted, suicidal millionaire Howard Hughes seems to have exemplified this case.

At the other extreme, making no money at all could be an ideal case of 'making good money', if one's entire life were spent doing good work and engaging with good friends and good questions. (This extreme may initially strike readers as even more unlikely than the other. In fact, however, it is much more likely, since whole cultures have functioned altogether without the symbolic token of exchange value that we call money.)

Turning away from these extremes to the vast middle range of situations that virtually any adult reading this book inhabits, one can be said to be making good money insofar as one spends the least amount of attention to making, managing, and spending money consistent with spending the greatest amount of attention to doing good work and engaging with good friends and good questions. Note that this way of defining making good money says absolutely nothing about how much money one makes. Note also that this way of defining making good money is perfectly consistent with spending as much time as one wishes making money, so long as one constructs such money-making activity in such a way that it simultaneously involves doing good work, engaging good friends, and asking good questions.

In any event, this gives you a sense of what we mean by 'making good money'. Does it sound more - or less - like what you mean by 'making good money'?

Good Work

Of course, we would all rather make good money by doing good work than by doing bad work. But what do 'good work' and 'bad work' mean, and how important is good work?

To us, good work means work that invites the development of craft-like skills and aesthetic judgment (whether in the realm of materials, of relationships, or of language). Such work calls for a kind of mastery that is never fully achieved, in the sense that it can thereafter be exercised in a rote, repetitive, or mechanical fashion. Instead, good masterwork requires and reflects an active attention by the masterworker at each moment to the interplay between one's own body-in-action and the material. This active attention integrates knowledge and application, prior experience and future ideal, disciplined sobriety and spontaneous responsiveness. In the case of soccer the World Cup competition exhibits the ideal of grace and social artistry that masterworks can achieve. In the case of executive level work, the principally influential artistry is exhibited, for better or worse, each time the executive speaks. Hence, the importance of crafting effective, artistic speech as we began to study in the early chapters of this book. In short, good work raises the consciousness of the worker. It generates mind-body integration and good health.

But our description of good work is still radically incomplete. Left as it is, this definition can give the impression that good work is good just for the worker - is nothing more than a form of narcissistic self-stimulation. Such an imp lication does violence to our most primitive intuitions about what work is - namely, that it produces something of value to someone(s) other than the worker. And indeed, this is another essential element of the definition of good work advanced here: good work produces something of value to someone(s) other than the worker. Everything in the prior paragraph about good work actually implies this without making it explicit.

Another way of seeing the social nature of all craft mastery is to remember that such mastery is defined in relation to a tradition (even when it redefines the tradition in creative ways). All craft traditions represent at once sacred and social trusts: they are dedicated to the creation of genuine, rather than false, social value. (Of course, how to differentiate genuine from false value in particular cases - whether in food, in works of art, in legal arguments, in accounting audits, in political candidates, or in spiritual teachers, to mention only a few - is among the best and most difficult of good questions... a matter to which we will return below.)

Furthermore, the masterworker can only properly appreciate all of his or her own prior experience and future intention in their embeddedness within social relations - relations to mentors, peers, and apprentices within the craft tradition, relations to specific clients and the general public who receive the work (be it product or service), and relations to past and future generations.

'Delighting the customer' - one of the current clichés about how to succeed in business - is certainly one of the alchemical outcomes of good work, according to this definition, and one of the ends toward which the masterworker aims. But it is just as certainly not the only end. 'Delighting the customer' is a great phrase in that it evokes the spontaneous enthusiasm of response - the raising of consciousness and the arousing of appreciation - which the very best products and services generate in their recipients. On the other hand, 'delighting the customer' can become a murderously narrow and inadequate criterion of good work when it becomes the only or the overriding criterion. Witness NASA's not delaying the Challenger flight, in an effort to be responsive to its major client - the Office of the President. The result? The death of seven astronauts, and, for years, of the credibility of the agency.

All of human history in any field of endeavour instructs us that there is no simple public measure of good work. In the short term and even in the middle term, good work may or may not be rewarded by good money, by promotions, by awards, or by positions of communal esteem and trust (e.g. Board memberships). Nevertheless, doing good work is a more significant criterion of the good life than making good money for two reasons. First, as already stated, it is intrinsically valuable, not just extrinsically valuable. Second, good work can generate good money; by contrast, good money can only support, not generate, good work.

The public judgment of good work is so problematic because the very best work does not generate a passive result, but rather acts on the public - raises consciousness and questions about the very boundaries of the product, service, or medium. This is most evident in the realm of the creative fine arts. But it also occurs in the most down-to-earth products such as shoes, filled with air and advertised as vehicles for flight by Michael 'His Airness' Jordan and other colleagues of his craft tradit ion.

We know best the cases when such boundary-questioning-and-crossing experiments succeed in commercial terms. But such success hardly proves that those experiments provide much genuine value (as the rapid succession of fads suggest), and many more such experiments fail than succeed. Many of the failures deserve their fate. Others have simply asked questions for which the public is not yet ready. Recognised geniuses integrate an enormous span from indigestible questions to delighting the customer (and they often exhibit extraordinary endurance throughout their lifetimes in their experimenting toward such a span of consciousness). Think of Edwin Land of Polaroid, or Shirley MacLaine of Hollywood and various astral dimensions, or Pablo Picasso, or Marguerite Yourcenar, the first woman elected to the French Academy .

As the foregoing paragraphs suggests, good work unveils quootions that evoke wonder in the worker, in coworkers, and in the audience. But wonder is a gentle word, and questions sometimes act more roughly. The commitment to do good work can badger and bedevil the worker with such questions. A final criterion of good work is that, through such questions, the work remains lively for the worker and keeps the worker lively till death doth them part (at least insofar as those of us still living can see). And a brief postscript: If an increasing proportion of the members of a society seeks to live a life that includes good questions, good friends, and good work, then good work that raises good questions is increasingly likely to generate good money and esteem for the masterworker.

Such, then, is the definition of good work offered here. This definition emphasises the challenge of developmental action inquiry inherent in good work and shows that this is not just measured by an increase in the external quality of the product, but also by the vivification of the awareness of the worker. This more vivid awareness is particularly characteristic of the rare Alchemist/Witch/Clown frame that we will be illustrating in the next chapter.

How do these ideas accord or not accord with your own sense of good work? To what degree do you experience yourself as currently doing good work and preparing yourself to further improve the quality of your work, either by this definition or by your own?

Good Friends

A common way of describing good friends is to speak of buddies who have a lot in common (like to shop together, or play basketball together, or get along at work). They can trust one another's reliability. They support one another - perhaps casually, but nevertheless reassuringly. And they don't get into arguments... (too often).

What do you mean by good friends?

This common way of describing good friends is emphatically not what we mean by good friends. No. We mean more nearly the reverse.

Good friends, as we understand the relationship, are persons who wish to meet and celebrate their differences, in part because these differences clarify who each is and what each values. Good friends often act unpredictably because they are growing and seeking to promote one another's growth. Good friends actively develop trust by disclosing their own efforts to grow, by supporting the other's efforts, and by getting into fights of a certain kind - by struggling together over what each means by the good life and by confronting one another when possible contradictions appear between a person's espoused principles and actual practices.

'Buddies' share norms and values that remain implicit. They thus tend to become more alike, or at least appear to become more alike, until some rift separates them. By contrast, good friends, as here understood, explicitly test their differences and become more different from one another - stranger and stranger - even as they also develop shared aims, respect, and love at the deepest level. e.e.cummings' lines about friends and lovers bespeak this kind of love:

> *love's function is to fabricate unknownness...*
> *how lucky lovers are (whose selves abide*
> *under whatever shall discovered be)...*

This kind of friendship is highly challenging and dynamic. It is essential for discovering and defining for oneself what the good life is and what one's own particular good work is. Persons who begin to taste and value this kind of friendship tend to be attracted to, rather than repelled by, strangers who come from different cultures, generations, sexes, religions, or races. And because such friendships are rooted in concern for one another's development, they tend to become lifetime friendships that can span great distances and long periods of absence, rather than temporary friendships founded around some specific age-related activity. Developmental transformations tend to occur within the friendship rather than ending the relationship.

No matter what the beginning circumstances or formal roles of the participants in such a friendship - even when they are hierarchically related as mother-daughter, boss-subordinate, or teacher-student - the friendship evolves toward a peer relationship in its maturity.

By this definition, family relationships are a sub-category within friendship. Marriages and parent-child relationships at their very best cultivate mutual development and, over twenty-five year time periods, peer relationships can evolve. According to this definition of the good life, the proper aim of marriage and family life is to generate the kind of friendship described here.

Many persons in today's world have no friendships of this kind. Others have one or two friends with whom, on rare occasions, they border on the kind of experience described here. Because the kind of friendship we are talking about does not treat either person's current equilibrium as sacred, it can feel threatening. Persons frequently shy away from this type of friendship without fully realising it - for example, laughing away the beginnings of what for the other would have been a significant disclosure. The degree of male violence against wives and of parental abuse of children is one raw indication of how far many families are from creating the conditions for true friendship.

Who do you count as good friends? Do the names differ if you use your own prior definition and if you use the definition presented here?

The definitions of good work and good money offered earlier are probably fairly easy to understand and probably contain some attractive elements, whether or not you fully agree with them. By contrast, the definition of good friends offered now is more likely to seem strange and problematic. Although this definition contains echoes that go back at least as far as Plato's dialog Lysis on friendship, this kind of friendship has never flourished widely in any society. It has often been regarded as dangerous to family, church, and state because it generates a deeper loyalty to e.e.cummings' "whatever shall discovered be" than to any taken-for-granted, pre-structured institutional authority. It is a late-stage, Alchemist/Witch/Clown/Community of Inquiry experience of friendship as will be explored in the next two chapters, an experience that only a minuscule proportion of the human race has initiated before now.

Whereas it is at least conceivable that global consensus could be achieved about the positive value of good work and good money, as we are defining them, it seems much more likely today that global consensus would form against our definition of good friends than for it. Neither American individualism, nor European postmodernism, nor Middle Eastern fundamentalism, nor Japanese clannishness predisposes persons toward such friendship.

But this is just the (paradoxical) point. No taken-for-granted culture can generate such friendship. The aspiring inter-cultural friends must generate such friendship for themselves by offering their allegiance to good questions. This kind of friendship is not personality-bound and culture-bound, but personality-transforming and culture-transforming.

This kind of friendship welcomes strangeness (weirdness, queerness) and transformation (so long as these present themselves in a mutual and vulnerable manner), rather than protecting against strangeness. Hence, such friendship is consistent with a global society that allows for local and personal differences.

This kind of friendship is also just what you'd want in a Board of Directors, or a senior management team (or a team at any other organisational level). For a work team's ultimate constructive purpose is surely to question whether its members, both collectively and individually, lead/act in ways consistent with the organisation's mission.

Good Questions

Which leads us, in a more general way, to the role of good questions in the good life. Most people treat questions as leading toward answers - the point being to discover the correct answer. In such cases, questions serve at best as a means to an end. From this point of view, it will no doubt seem peculiar at first to hear our claim: that good questions are intrinsically valuable - indeed, more valuable to someone aspiring to the good life than good work or good friends (though truly good questions often insinuate themselves through good work and good friends).

Of course, what we mean by good questions are not mere questions of fact, e.g. 'Where's the bathroom in this place?' To such a question, we want an answer - pronto. Nor are good questions mere questions of theory that deserve and repay eternal rumination. Good questions are intrinsically valuable because they heighten our awareness of external facts, of our own acts, of theories, and of our own attending in the moment - make us more alive and more related to the rest of our own lives and everything else.

Good questions, insofar as we can attend to them, connect us to a wider, living universe. Every time that the scene before our eyes comes to life and we really see the colour, the movement, and the relationships - every time looking becomes seeing - we are looking with a question. Every time we truly listen to the sounds reaching our ears, we are hearing with a question. Every time we actually taste the food we are eating, we are... actually tasting.

To taste is to test. To test is to question. To question is to taste. The subtlest taste of all, and the trickiest to develop, is the taste for continuing questioning. Initially, we can't help hoping that we'll find an answer that ends our agonising questions. We'd rather not be that alive! We're anything but sure that we want to learn how to see answers as leading to better questions. Questioning may or may not be translated into words. In poetry, at its best, every word is tasted as it is written (and as it is read). In prose, too.

An organisation's mission or purpose is, properly, an undying question - sometimes prodding, sometimes alerting, sometimes guiding its members. But how many members of an organisation treat it this way? How to focus, how to formulate, how to wake up to an organisation's mission is itself a good question. How to wake up others to this questioning is another good question. Is anyone in the organisation awake to these questions?

What are the questions guiding your life (or that you are trying to evade)? What is the single question that integrates those different questions? Are you asking every day? Every moment? Are you fully alive - let alone living the good life - when you are not tasting your experience? Are you embalmed within your thoughts right now, or are you tasting your thinking along with your embodiment, outcomes, and your changing quality of attending?

Inquiry and Faith

Perhaps you are a committed believer, with a deep, embracing, and comforting faith. Whether your faith is in the Koran, or in the miracle of Jesus' birth, death, and resurrection, or in a-theistic scientific method, or in constitutional democracy, you may feel that you have passed beyond this 'adolescent theology of questions' to a wonderful, well-founded answer.

Yes. But if your answer is truly wonder-ful and you are truly alive to its wonder now, then you are wonder-ing and wonder-ful - alive to its mystery - questioning. To advocate scientific method without question, or Christ's resurrection without appreciation for the mystery, are grand self-contradictions indeed!

Good questions never die. It is only our attention that dies to them. Good questions enliven parties (even political parties!), organisations, and each of us individually (even those of us who avowedly and emotionally hate to be put into question). Good questions grow relationships ('What thoughts, feelings, and actions are truly loving now?'). Good questions grow vocations ('How can I excel my current attention in the service of excellent work?'). And good questions grow wealth ('Who are my customers and what will tickle them pink?'). Whereas 'right answers' have a way of growing armies and generating destruction, good questions generate conversation and good spirits.

Good questions rise outwards toward the very nature of nature, toward the very nature of the universe. Good questions deepen inwards toward the very mystery of one's own and others' human being, attending finally to one's own and others' attending, bestowing the gift of developmentally meaningful glances, silences, words. Good questions expand flirtatiously along the boundaries and surfaces of the present. We can only work, love, and question in the present. Can we remain present to the present, even as our hearts remember the past, our minds roam the future, and our bodies fall toward sleep?

As we grow older and begin to stiffen physically, are our questions becoming increasingly lively? Do they guide us toward increasingly fluidifying exercise?

Not all questions become increasingly lively. Not all questions awaken us to the present. Not all questions meet any of the criteria for good questions advanced in the foregoing paragraphs. Indeed, the experience of good questions is likely to be relatively rare, and may be felt as somewhat illicit or dumb in a society such as ours in the West, conditioned for the past five hundred years by the quest for scientific certainty.

If you immediately and fully agree with our sense of what good questions are and with our sense of their centrality to the good life, we will be astonished. For we have never seen the matter presented so. Moreover, we have heard many initial reservations and objections to these ideas when we share them verbally - objections that are by no means fully dealt with in this brief introduction to the notion of good questions. So... what are your initial responses to this notion?

Prioritising and Blending the Four Goods

In beginning to draw together the thoughts you have had as you have read the foregoing pages, you may wish to consider the following questions:

1. What additional criteria for the good life - besides good money, good work, good friends, and good questions - have occurred to you?

2. How do you prefer to reformulate the four goods we have tried to describe?

3. How do you prioritise the four goods presented here and/or the goods that seem primary to you?

4. Which of these primary goods have you concentrated upon in your life more than others?

5. How successful do you feel you have so far been at generating each good that seems primary to you?

6. When you share such reflections with your friends, or the members of an inquiry group, what do you and they together come up with as the most significant blocks for you to overcome, or dissolve, or accept as of now and the nearest future, if you are to make your way toward your version of the good life?

We have been quite explicit about our rank ordering of the four goods that we believe are conducive to the good life. Good questions, we have asserted, grow relationships, vocations, and value/wealth. Good questions are, therefore, in our understanding and experience, the primary aim of anyone seeking the good life. As strange as it may sound from the modern point of view, a practitioner of this path toward the good life might say - even cheerily, "Good questions bedevil me; therefore, my life is good."

Good friends are the second highest priority in our version of the good life, and friendships are good to the degree that they are based on good questions. The more you take the risk to bring the questions that be-devil, be-wilder, and be-muse you to your friends; and the more you take the risk to listen to their questions; the better your friendships will become, even when the questions are addressed to the friendship itself. (Along the way, you are likely to lose some 'friends' who don't want to face such questions, at least not just now or not in just such a way).

Good work is the third priority among our four primary goods. Work is good to the degree that it revivifies good questions (raising the worker's awareness); to the degree that it spins off good friends and the leisure to enjoy them (indeed, the best work, and all truly artistic work, is itself leisurely in this respect); and to the degree that it embodies itself in ways that others, including Mother Earth herself, value.

Money, we have asserted (including bankable credit, which it is far more useful to have, in most cases, than mere literal cash) ranks lowest of the four goods, having no intrinsic value. Money, therefore, functions as a good only insofar as it supports the other three goods.

The very best way for money to support the other three goals is to make it (enough of it so that one is not distracted by its absence) by doing good work with good friends addressing good questions. To create such conditions is a high challenge indeed! If one succeeds, the issue of how to divide one's time among the different priorities obviously fades, since one is attending to all four goods at once. This represents the ultimate blending of the four goods - the good life. At least, this is our current belief. We are in the midst of testing it - each in our own different ways - in the daily living of our own lives.

Conclusion

These pages have attempted to raise questions with you about what you regard as the good life and as the path toward the good life. We have attempted to provoke you in two different ways:

1. by asking you what approach to the good life is compatible at one and the same time with a market economy, with cultural and personal diversity, and with the developmental transformations that adulthood can entail; and

2. by offering you a set of four, rank ordered criteria for the good life and the path toward the good life for you to compare to your own evolving criteria.

We have not attempted to make a strong, closely-knit argument in favour of our particular criteria. Instead, we have attempted to say just enough to display the outlines of each criterion, the outlines of their overall coherence with one another, and the outlines of their consistency with a globally universalisable definition of the good life that does justice to local differences.

Of course, you may not agree that we have succeeded in displaying either the beneficence, or the coherence, or the universal applicability of our four criteria for the good life. We will welcome your comments to that effect, since it is altogether in our own self-interests to improve our approach. Please tell us also how your favoured criteria fare in response to the demand for beneficence, coherence, and universalisability?

Good wishes on your path. If you believe you are choosing something like a path of developmental action inquiry, we hope you are beginning to find the approach that we have introduced in this book of use. If you practice this action inquiry 'gait' very far along the personal development path, we hope this book will serve as a kind of companion through one or more significant transformations in your relationship to the rest of the world.

If you pursue developmental action inquiry until you are practising the Strategist action-logic and organising with others in a Collaborative Inquiry fashion, the possibility of a still more penetrating inquiry may begin to reveal itself to you. Our final chapters offer what little evidence we have been able to gather about frames that are even rarer today than the Strategist/Collaborative Inquiry frames.

CHAPTER 13

THE 'CHAOTIC' ACTION AWARENESS OF TRANSFORMATIONAL LEADERS

When we were consulting to Sun Health Care, the organisation described in Chapter 9, Sun's manager of Employee Development described his unusual contract with the organisation to work one day a week as a consultant outside Sun and the health care industry. He was illustrating his view that he needed a number of practical strategies to help him move back and forth between a 'worm's eye' view and a 'bird's eye' view of the challenges he faced. Then, he said, as a kind of logical conclusion, "You know, you need to keep yourself fresh and your ideas fresh". It sounds like an attractive idea - especially to those of us who feel as though we are run a bit ragged by the demands of our work and our life!

A simple idea - an obvious idea - and an enjoyable experience: keeping fresh. Wouldn't we all rather feel fresh than stale? Isn't it obvious that improving the quality of our actions depends upon fresh awareness of what's at stake, fresh, new ideas about how to operate more effectively, and fresh, new energies for actually doing so?

But, if keeping oneself fresh is such an intuitively appealing idea, why is it so rare to find anyone amidst the power brokers of organisational life who seems genuinely fresh, authentic, unassuming, good humored, timely, and acting to align personal, organisational, societal, and global goods? Why do we usually have to resort to the names of a few historical figures - Gandhi, or Pope John XXIII, perhaps Nelson Mandela, or Eleanor Roosevelt? Why is this eternal freshness at the heart of the Alchemist/Witch/Clown frame (to be illustrated in this chapter, to the best of our abilities) and its social parallel, the Foundational Community of Inquiry stage of development (to be introduced in the next chapter) so rare?

Why, if refreshing oneself is such a simple and appealing idea, are the names we use to describe this stage of development so strange and unfamiliar? Why do we use a range of names such as 'Alchemist, Witch, Clown, Sibyl, and Wanderer' for individuals and 'Foundational Community of Inquiry' for the social engagements of such people?

Why is development to this stage so rare that six different studies by different researchers in different industries have found no managers whatsoever who score at this Alchemist level?

Why is it so rare that even when we set out to search for innovative leaders who might measure at this stage, we find that fewer than half of the extraordinary persons who take the measure score at the Alchemist action-logic?

We will offer a series of diverse illustrations throughout this chapter in an effort to catch brief glimpses of the answers to these questions. We can begin by explaining why it must be true that 'brief glimpses' are the very best we can hope to achieve in this regard. Think about it this way: once an answer to these questions becomes a settled intellectual truth - a mindset - it is no longer fresh; it is no longer in contact with the color and the shock and the feeling of a fresh perception.

At this developmental point, neither the person, nor the organisation, is based on, or finds its identity in, a particular mindset or structure. Instead, the person or organisation continually re-tastes the four 'territories of experience' - freshly seeking harmony among them. For the person, the four experiential territories to be alchemically blended at each moment are: (1) the living fire of intuition/intention/attention, (2) the clear winds of critical, strategic thinking, (3) the liquid currents of compassionately attuned, relaxed, and vigilant actions, and (4) the gravitational, grounding, material world, object of our perceptions, craftwork of our hands, 'signed' by the effects of our acts. For organisations, within whose bounds most people of the developed world work, the four experiential territories that all leadership interweaves, whether intentionally or unintentionally, whether congruently or incongruently, are: (1) visioning, (2) strategising, (3) performing, and (4) outcomes-assessing.

The transformation from the Strategist frame towards this most elusive and malleable of the action-logics we have so far encountered in this book is, like all other developmental transformations to later stages, a movement from *being* something to *having* that kind of thing. The person ceases to be subject to the Strategist action-logic and comes to have that and all the earlier action-logics as moment-to-moment options. This time one can say the transformation is from being *in the right frame of mind* (e.g. having the 'right' theory of timing, the 'right' names for the four territories of experience, etc.) to having a *reframing spirit*.

A reframing spirit continually overcomes itself, divesting itself of its own presuppositions. A reframing mind continually re-attunes itself to the frames of reference held by other actors in a situation, and to the underlying organisational and historical developmental rhythms, seeking the 'common sense' of the situation, seeking to discover and articulate the motivating challenge of the situation in a language accessible to all participants.

Discovering this motivating challenge can create a social jiu-jitsu effect: just as total disintegration is threatening, the person or organisation or nation suddenly fluidifies and acts with unforeseeable vigor and resolve. For this reason, this vulnerable power is often experienced as alchemist-like, witch-like, or clown-like.

Figure 13.1 is curvy, complicated and unclear. It provides a good analogue for the transition between different frames of meaning making. The early part of the journey is portrayed as a sequence of somersault-like transformations from the Opportunist perspective to the Diplomat and on to the Expert and Achiever; but then becomes infinitely more complex in the movement through Individualist, which is and isn't a stage, to Strategist and finally to Alchemist. The Ironist stage is not revealed to us but lies somewhere within the whole. This tantalising map, which has no 'top' and invites the reader to turn the page in order to find each frame at the 'top' of any imagined hierarchy, captures some of the transitory, chaotic and profoundly up-ending qualities which may attend the actual experience of transition beyond its intellectually and calmly imagined process, which calls, normally for greater neatness and linearity.

Figure 13.1   Later Stage Representation of the Dynamics and Up-ending Qualities of the Transformational Journey Through and Between Different Frames.

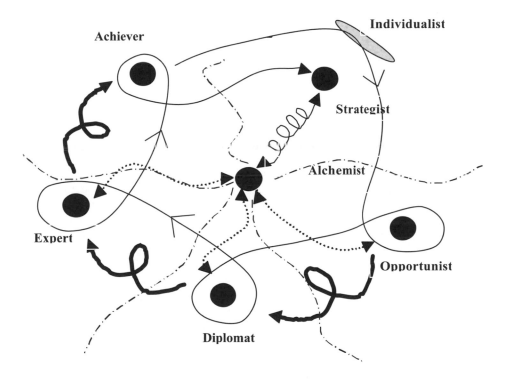

The transformation to this managerial style requires facing and learning how to transform the entire dark side of the human condition as that manifests itself in oneself and one's surroundings. Unlike the Strategist, who may believe that he or she is on the side of good and can beat evil, the Alchemist recognises that the polarisation between good and evil - between victory and defeat, between the sacred and the profane, between classes, races, and sexes, between I and Thou - is recreated at each moment by our relatively fixed and one-sided perspectives on the world. Evil emanates from the character of our own fallen, passive attention; it cannot be permanently defeated. Indeed, to fight against it as though it were only outside us is to reinforce it.

Action inquiry becomes, for the Alchemist, not so much a theory of managing as an ongoing jousting, at one and the same time, with one's own attention and with the outside world.

Such a person requires no official role. His or her power and authority derive from listening to developmental rhythms. By virtue of this four-territory listening, he or she takes the 'executive role', a sense of responsibility for the whole that is open to anyone, regardless of official role. Listening in this way, with a sense of wonder repeatedly reawakening in body, heart, and mind, the Alchemist experiences the rhythms of a particular conversation, of the lives of the individuals conversing, of the particular organisational setting where the conversation is occurring, and of still wider historical circumstances as radiating from the past and the future into the only time when awareness and action are possible: this inclusive present.

A Study of Six Alchemists

Let us explore further whether and how these theoretical speculations are illustrated in the activities of several late-stage executives. Because of the difficulty in finding managers in large samples who measure at the Alchemist and at the still later Ironist stages of development, we searched out persons who, on the basis of public reputations for uniqueness and unusual success, or on the basis of personal testimony by close associates, might be operating at later developmental action-logics. More than half of theses people did *not* measure at the two latest stages; but we have observed in great detail a half dozen who have measured at the Alchemist or Ironist stages. Of these, some agreed to tape their predictions and reflections on work days for a week on their drives in and out from work. Some have agreed to let one of us dog their footsteps for whole days at a time. And all participated in two or more hours of interviewing. In four of the six cases, one of us has had long term contacts with the persons, in one or more of the following roles: consultant, member of a Board of Directors, teacher, friend, fellow participant in a spiritual community.

For our present purposes, we wish to provide a few glimpses of these people in action, in an effort to convey the sense of moment-to-moment attention, unpredictability, uniqueness, and cross-level analogising that characterises much of their work and play. (Indeed, a telling characteristic of their work and play is that they cannot really be distinguished; 'work-play' is a conjugation that comes closer to describing the actual interweaving of business, art, and leisure in their lives).

Brief Glimpses of Alchemist-like Experiencing

The first thing that struck us forcibly as we became more intimately connected with our subjects' workdays was that they were key players, not in one organisation, but in *many*. Their days were unpredictably divided into initiatives and responses across a number of organisations. Perhaps the most extreme example of this was the woman who interacted with between five and seven organisations each day of the week that she documented. Her primary organisational affiliation was as a member of a global consulting firm, and she acknowledged that when she was visiting a particular client, she would occasionally have brief contact by phone with no more than one or two other organisations in the course of a day.

But this week she was at her own firm's offices throughout. There she: 1) trained junior consultants, 2) served on a performance evaluation committee, 3) developed an affidavit for a suit against a Board of which she was a member, 4) billed 37 hours to three different direct client firms as well as five other engagements that she more indirectly supervised, and 5) initiated 42 telephone calls and received 19 on behalf of a newly organising industry trade association (she called this effort 'market development'). In addition, she offered two different, ongoing workshops from 8-10pm on two of the evenings. The participants in these workshops included former and current organisational clients who wished to engage in their own personal and professional development at a deeper level.

Although this illustration is offered from the outside in, giving no direct taste of this woman's experiencing, it suggests to us one way that persons who measure at the late stages of development tend to live at once 'symphonically' and 'chaotically'. In our next illustration, we look at this same phenomenon from the inside out perspective of another one of our Alchemist executives.

This second illustration highlights a second thing that struck us when we observed these executives directly: that, within a given day, their pace varied enormously. From the prior illustration, one might mistakenly conclude that these people are in a constant rush. Quite the contrary. We found in all of them a sense of leisure, playfulness, or meditativeness at times; a sense of urgency, fierce efficiency, or craftlike concentration at others. Indeed, in this particular case the two types of responses coexisted simultaneously. This CEO intentionally works and lives in a different city from his corporation's headquarters. His office takes up parts of two floors in a large Victorian house, the rest of which is his home. The first floor office consists of an impressive, but more or less normal, outer office for the secretary and visitors, along with his inner office, including an informal seating area, a working table for meetings of up to eight or ten people, and a private bathroom. Within the bathroom is a spiral staircase to the second floor.

A large exercise mat, a wall of books, and comfortable seating, dominates the second floor room. A speakerphone makes it possible for this man to be exercising or lounging in a totally relaxed fashion, yet project his voice over the phone in a rapid, staccato fashion. This technique, he explains, encourages callers to come to the point more quickly and seems to increase their cooperativeness when he slows down, momentarily, to give them what they can appreciate as 'quality attention'. Even in his busiest times in the office downstairs, this executive escapes upstairs for two or three minutes each hour to do sit-ups, pushups, Aikido, or yoga postures.

Challenged about the manipulativeness of his telephone technique, he responds unabashedly,

> "I *am* giving them quality attention. In fact, I am giving them a far higher quality attention than most of them can imagine. This way of working increases the quality of my attention, saves their time and money, and apparently serves them well, since many of them are long-term clients of our firm. My closest colleagues are aware of the set-up and joke over the phone about what I'm probably doing as we speak, and that seems to heighten the creativity of our exchanges as well".

The World Bank Executive

A third element in common among all six executives is their apparently equally deep fascination with three different sociological levels - with personal detail at the individual level, with the dynamics of group and organisational issues, and with how the organisations of which they are members, or of service, relate to national or international developments. We have already seen this pattern in our first example of the global consultant who attends to personal development, organisational development, and inter-organisational networks. Another dramatic example of this theme was the World Bank executive from Sweden, with whom we conducted our research during the 1980s, when former US Congressman Conable was serving as president of the World Bank and launched a major re-organisation and downsizing.

Conable's procedure was to redraw the organisation chart, with far fewer positions, and invite everyone in the organisation to become a candidate for any position, thus effectively 'killing' the former structure (and generating skyrocketing anxiety among World Bank professionals). Conable himself hired fewer deputies than he had had previously, and they in turn followed suit, hiring their reduced number of subordinates, and so on. Although the espoused theory of this change was to profoundly shake up the perceived complacency of the World Bank while downsizing, the actual outcome was in no way transformational. Because of the intense anxiety and politicking and the lack of any formal performance evaluation procedures, former bosses hired back former subordinates for similar positions as before, with few exceptions.

The late-action-logic Swedish executive whom one of us was observing and interviewing at the time took a different tack, however, and became one of those exceptions. She began by telling her current subordinates that the problem of personnel evaluation and organisational transformation were, in her view, the bottlenecks that most frequently inhibited success in third world development programmes. Therefore, she regarded a person's ability to solve the current organisational dilemma in a way that could be applicable to third world projects as a primary (but not the only) criterion for rehiring. She therefore asked her subordinates, as part of their job application process, to propose methods to resolve this kind of dilemma in a transformational fashion, *as well as other persons in the World Bank whom they regarded as most highly qualified.*

Initially, most of the former subordinates did not recommend any other candidates for the positions, evidently regarding it as contrary to their career interest to do so. Only one of the former subordinates met the executive's request. This person also offered some inventive structural suggestions for how to proceed. The Swedish executive hired this person and let the rest of the group know the basis for her decision, as well as the additional structural features for the remainder of the selection process. One of these features was that, in order to be considered for any of the remaining three positions, each of the remaining five former subordinates absolutely must recommend the most qualified person outside the group for the particular position, documenting the process that she or he had used to reach that determination.

Three of the five subordinates felt trapped, insulted, and/or betrayed by this procedure. Two of them refused vociferously to participate, while the third masked his alienation (although the Swedish executive was well aware of it). This person 'pretended' to participate, but in a way that was ineffective. The constructive, negative feedback from the Swedish executive persuaded this person to change his strategy for his continued search within the World Bank for a position, and he ultimately won one. The two 'vociferous refusers' never did get a new position. The Swedish executive invited each of the remaining two persons (who responded positively to the Swedish executive's second 'wake up call') to take the position for which, based on prior experience, they were *least* qualified. She explained her decision to them as a challenge to increase their attention to teamwork and to learning from others, and both accepted. The final position was offered to one of the candidates recommended by the three rehired subordinates. Perhaps there *was* a good analogy between the skills and strategies this executive was trying to cultivate and the skills and strategies needed for success in third world development. In any event, at the end of the following three years, this group had one of the best performing loan portfolios among all the area groups within the bank.

This story not only illustrates a manager's analogical attention to individual, group, and international issues, but also illustrates, from a distance, a fourth theme in common among the later stage managers we researched. This theme is the charismatic quality of their personal relationships, but in the service of challenging others, even at the risk of significant conflict, rather than generating worshipful subservience. These women and men Alchemists seemed to use their sensitivity to initial conditions, to the particular language meaningful to their interlocutors, and to new initiatives throughout ongoing encounters, along with their capacity for intelligent analogy and an evident relish for unpredictability, in a way that increased their own and others' alertness, learning, and sense of mutuality.

Chaos Theory as a Map of Late-stage Action Awareness

How are we to understand the kind of strategising and action awareness that these unusual leaders cultivate? Chaos theory has recently become fashionable in the natural and social sciences. Chaos theory highlights processes that are non-repetitive and unpredictable - apparently irrational - when mapped in two dimensions, but which reveal astonishing shape, order, and singularity when mapped in three dimensions. Instead of learning the truth by dividing the phenomenon into parts, the chaos theory approach is to look at the phenomenon as a whole from a higher dimension. In this regard, chaos theory is about how apparently formless qualities like smoke and clouds, ocean currents and weather, moods and organisational norms can be seen as moving rhythmically and taking shapes, when viewed mathematically as $(x+1)$ dimensional phenomena rather than as x dimensional.

Chaos theory also introduces the notion of fractals - self-similarities or analogies across micro, meso, and macro scales. The idea here is that you can't measure many shapes precisely (such as the shoreline of England, or the surface area of a mountain, or the play of a person's stream of consciousness) because the more closely you focus on an area of detail the more squiggles or bumps you can see and measure. Therefore, what becomes important is not precise measurement, but an equation for the overall quality of the shape. What is remarkable is that for some phenomena that shape is reproduced at whatever scale of size one examines the phenomenon. Approximate analogies for wholes become more important than precise measures of parts.

Let us say a little more about chaos theory, not only because it relates to inside-out, Alchemist-like awareness, but also because it will help us to reconsider the nature of developmental theory, which, until this chapter has been presented as though it is a Strategist-like, right-mind-set. (The reader may want to flip back to Figure 13.1 for an exception that conveys a more analogical, chaotic, alchemical flavor.)

Another characteristic of chaos theory is that it focuses on a system's enormous sensitivity to initial conditions in its further development. Small differences in initial conditions can generate great differences in the eventual shapes of two systems. Moreover, activity and inactivity, meaningful communication and noise (as, for example, over a phone line), are not evenly distributed in such systems. Therefore, averages or means are not particularly meaningful ways of summarising, and evenly spaced interventions will not generate calculably cumulative effects. On the contrary, activity and noise occur in spurts. Consequently, no overall equation is sufficient for predicting when to act to effect a certain change. The actor also requires awareness of initial conditions and of the ongoing syncopation in the system's development, since the effect of a given action will be determined in part by whether it occurs during a spurt or a pause in the system's activity. To act in a timely, transforming fashion requires a free attention at all times, more than a predictive theory of when to intervene.

At first glance, all three of these qualities of chaos theory -

1. shape as discernible from a higher dimension when treated as x+1 dimensions
2. fractal self-similarities across scales, and
3. sensitivity to initial and ongoing conditions -

appear disconnected from, or directly contrary to, the developmental theory that we have used throughout this book. Does not developmental theory suggest a predictable, orderly development through tightly defined stages, whatever the initial conditions?

If we consider further the illustrations of late-stage executives just offered, we will find that there is not just a strong contrast between developmental theory and chaos theory, but also a close kinship between the two. In fact, the chaos theory propositions presented in the previous paragraphs and the version of developmental theory that corresponds with Alchemist-like awareness are strikingly self-similar - like fractals.

With regard to the notion of shape as discernible from higher dimensions, if we think of each of the four territories of experience as a different dimension, things that appear shapeless and arbitrary at an earlier developmental action-logic gain shape when viewed from the next higher dimension. For example, behavioral norms don't mean much to a person at the Opportunist stage who is mastering the outside-world territory by means of his or her own actions. Such behavioral norms become meaningful at the Diplomat stage, when a person is gaining control of the personal action dimension by conforming to the normative patterns that he or she infers in the social setting s/he is currently acting in. However, for this person at the Diplomat stage, the world of systemic logic is still only implicit, not yet controllable. He or she is ruled by cultural or peer-group convention, not by an independent application of an explicit and internally consistent logic, a dimension that the Expert will seek to master.

With regard to seeing self-similar fractals at different scales, only at late stages, when a person seeks to experience the different territories of experience simultaneously, can he or she see whether there are successful analogies - self-similar fractals - or significant incongruities across the territories. Only at late developmental action-logics, for example, do executives see, care about, and attempt to create fractal-like relationships among mission, strategy, operations, and outcomes, as the Swedish World Bank executive does in the earlier illustration. At earlier stages, executives are more likely to care only (or primarily) about outcomes, or only (or primarily) about operations, or only (or primarily) about the internal logic of a strategy.

Finally, with regard to the issue of sensitivity to initial and ongoing conditions, developmental theory appears invariant only when considered as an abstract theory. In practice, persons spend longer or shorter periods of their lives at different action-logics, spend longer or shorter times in the 'chaotic' transitions between action-logics, and conclude their development at different points along the developmental continuum. Moreover, at later action-logics a person's attention becomes both more inclusive and more dscriminating. From the perspective of an earlier action-logic, "nothing" happened at an hour-long meeting, implying that it was boring and that s/he takes no responsibility for the overall shape of the event. From the perspective of a late action-logic, the same meeting may have seemed an intense drama with several interweaving developmental processes and much at stake, during which s/he failed to find the moment and the action that could transform an inconclusive process into a more meaningful and creative event. In short, the drama of development, influenced by the tone set at the outset, perhaps even by the arrangement of furniture in the room, and by each wisp of interruption, is occurring at many intersecting scales for the Alchemist on a daily and hourly basis - not just over a lifetime.

Why is there such a strong contrast between the initial view of developmental theory as a rigidly sequential, linear theory, and the view of developmental theory offered here as opening towards chaos. One way of embracing both horns of the dilemma is to interpret the 'rigid' version of developmental theory as resulting from taking a reconstructed, outside-in perspective on development - a type of perspective consistent with the overall outside-in, bird's eye approach of the Expert and Achiever stages of development and of contemporary mainstream social science. At the same time, the dynamic/chaotic version of developmental theory presented in this chapter can be interpreted as corresponding with a constructive, late-stage, inside-out-and-outside-in perspective on development. This type of perspective is consistent with the actual action/inquiry awareness of late-stage transformational leaders, as illustrated in the previous section.

From Chaos Theory to Chaotic Action Awareness

What the chaos theorists' elegant theorising does not address is how human beings in their day-to-day organisational and family lives can come to appreciate the complexity, indeterminacy, and higher-order orderliness that the theory of fractals reveal - and that effectual organisational management in turbulent times demands. Developmental theory, which at first blush contradicts chaos, actually describes how persons and organisations can evolve toward just the complex, analogical appreciation of experience, *in the very midst of that experiencing*, that chaos theorists *speculate* about or measure through a retrospective empiricism.

In a passage on improvisational flute playing, written before chaos theory was formulated, mathematician Michael Rossman brings chaos theory to life in a description of the interplay of the four experience-able territories; external sound, the hand working the flute, the pattern of the past music, and the intuitive intervention of each next note, which destroys the previous 'whole' and creates a new one:

> Sometimes the music itself leads me forth, embracing even my tremors and contradictions in something whole. Playing free, every so often I realise that the note I have just begun is not the one 'I' had intended

and sent out orders to produce, but a different one chosen confidently by my body to extend the music - quite independently of the listening-and-scheming me who flashes with resentment at the mistake.

...When I am free to uncover in the instant the dancing logic of those next notes that will weave the slip into consonance, make it have been inevitable, I feel involved in some transcendent mathematics. To reduce it to the simple case of improvising alone, it is as if, on some cosmic abscissa and ordinate, I were living out the construction of a complex curve while simultaneously deriving its equation, unifying induction and deduction in a way inverse to their unity while playing Bach. The curve comes to a point not predictable from the equation known up to that moment; rather than reject the point as anomalous, a discontinuity, I continue the curve through it and beyond in a way which yields a new equation, one containing its previous version as a limiting case valid up to that odd point, and embodying a deeper notion of continuity. And so it goes, when I am moving in the spirit of a world in which chance and accident and will are subsumed in a higher order.

Seen from the inside-out, developmental theory is the story of how consciousness of four territories of experience and of the harmonies and disharmonies across them can evolve. We can hear in Rossman's improvisational flute playing the 'freshness' that we connected to the Alchemist action-logic at the outset of this chapter. In the sentence that starts 'Playing free...' he provides as clear a word-illustration of the 'free attention' that can 'see' the other three territories of experience at once as we have so far seen in this book. These qualities, as well as the fact that Rossman combined mathematics, music, and political organising at the time he wrote this, makes him sound as though he is operating from the Alchemist frame. He is not a person for whom we have a Leadership Development Profile, so we cannot confirm our qualitative observations with a quantitative finding.

This example again raises the question, why is this freshness so difficult to rediscover in the ongoing struggles and tensions, habits and comforts, of our lives? One answer is that the optimistic language we have used about harmonising the four qualities of experience from intent to affect - hides as much as it reveals. What it hides, when that is made explicit, will go another long step toward making clear why so few people and organisations move toward this kind of continually-quality-improving-experiencing.

What the language of harmonising the four territories of experience hides is: the distances, disharmonies, and incongruities among these different qualities of experience that are revealed to a widening awareness. To experience such incongruities is not just an intellectual exercise, but is an existential, emotional shock. For example, to experience oneself as lying when one believed oneself honest, or as acting unilaterally when one advocates acting collaboratively, generates suffering. Who wishes voluntarily to take on the continual suffering of witnessing the gaps in oneself, in others, in organisations, and in larger social processes between intentions, espoused values, actual practices, and outcomes? Who knows how to transform such suffering, not into imprisoning neuroses, but rather into emancipating consciousness that graces each meeting afresh?

One answer, we believe, is: a person at the Alchemist stage who is intuitively trying to create a business or a family setting where inquiry about the most difficult issues is valued and practiced. We call such a setting a Foundational Community of Inquiry and will be giving it fuller description in the next chapter.

Conclusion

We have offered glimpses of evidence from a small sample of late-stage executives. They provide suggestive illustrations of what 'chaotic' action-awareness looks like. Since these illustrations all occurred among persons measured at the Alchemist/Witch/Clown stage of development, and since earlier studies of managers at earlier stages have generated no such illustrations, the data is consistent with, and therefore not disconfirming of, the hypothesis that development to the later stages generates 'chaotic' action-awareness.

Obviously, much more research is necessary to generate confidence in the general validity of this hypothesis (and some of it has already been done, as the endnotes for this chapter indicate).

To determine whether this hypothesis is valid, not just generally, but also in your case will require still further research by you, in the action inquiry mode.

CHAPTER 14

CREATING FOUNDATIONAL COMMUNITIES OF INQUIRY

In this chapter we address ourselves to the future. If you and we agree enough in our visions of the good life as described in Chapter 12, then it is likely that you will want to join us in spirit and in your own practice. Our shared challenge will be to work toward creating real-time cultures of inquiry, mutuality, and timely action at work, in personal relationships, and in spiritual, political, and artistic actions.

Here we offer brief glimpses of what such inter-organisational cultures of inquiry may look like, as we discuss the Foundational Community of Inquiry stage of organising that parallels the Alchemist/Witch/Clown stage of personal development. We are hampered by the fact that we have only shadowy and fragmentary exemplars to help stimulate your imagination, for we believe that no fully embodied exemplar of this stage of organising has ever existed historically.

Table 14-1 shows the theoretical characteristics of the Foundational Community of Inquiry stage. This name for this stage of organising suggests two apparently opposite qualities - foundational stability and transformational disequilibrium. It is the union of these opposites in a Foundational Community of Inquiry that we are seeking.

Boards of Directors function, by intent and at their best, as foundational communities of inquiry for their organisation, testing the clarity of, and the congruity among, mission, strategy, operations and outcomes and creating a learning community for the CEO. A Board of Directors is less likely to realise its potential if the Chairman of the Board is the CEO or if the majority of the Board is employed by the organisation. In such cases, the power asymmetry in favour of the CEO is likely to dampen both the sense of mutuality and the sense of inquiry on the Board. In 2001 and 2002, the US economy has reeled under the impact of companies, like Enron and Global Crossing, whose Boards failed to function as foundational communities of inquiry.

The Society of Friends - commonly known as Quakers - is another peer-like organisation that illustrates characteristics of a Foundational Community of Inquiry. Its members place themselves in permanent political tension with their own countries by refusing to engage in war, seeking to become conscientious objectors and peace mediators in times of war. They have no official or professional ministry. Their meetings for worship, as well as their business meetings, are characterised by a silent, inquiring listening by each for an inner voice or Inner Light that may correspond to what we are calling in this book intuitive, multi-territory awareness. The occasional messages that participants offer gain dignity and resonance within this culture of intentional listening.

Table 14-1   Characteristics of a Foundational Community of Inquiry

1. Political friction among different paradigms/frames/stages within the organisation and between the organisation and the wider environment; all fundamentalist, universalistic ideologies are challenged by the community's emphasis on peer-like mutuality and on the humble, vulnerable practice of timely action inquiry.

2. Ongoing, experiential-empirical participatory research on relations among spiritual/intuitive visioning, theoretical/practical strategising, timely performing, and assessing outcomes in the visible, external world; such research generates sense of mutuality.

3. Collaborative Inquiry structure fails ('dies') because it does not meet the alchemical challenge of timely transformational, emancipatory, collective action; pre-verbal, shared purpose is revealed as sustaining and as generating multiple momentary structurings that invite enactment choices and feedback on the consequences of such choices from all participants.

4. Appreciation of continuing interplay of opposites: action/research, sex/politics, past/future, symbolic/diabolic, etc.

5. New experiences of time: his-story becomes my-story; interplay of time bound needs, timeless archetypes, and timely creativity.

Another example that suggests at least the shadow of a Foundational Community of Inquiry is an organisation conceived at a picnic one day in the 1500s. Six University of Paris students who did not all know one another were brought together that day by a former Spanish soldier, Ignatius of Loyola. Together, they dedicated themselves to founding the Society of Jesus, the Jesuit Order. Within a decade, Jesuits were beginning to travel, often alone, to the far corners of the world, in order to immerse themselves in the cultures of India, China, the Paraguayan natives, and others. Rather than seeking to impose the European structure of Catholicism, they sought to reconceive how the Christian spirit could be communicated in each distinctive culture. So influential and so controversial did the Jesuit Order become in global exploration, politics, education, and science, as well within the Catholic Church itself, in theology and in spiritual exercises, that it has twice during its history been proscribed and later resurrected. Its womanless, non-procreative aspects obviously restrict the generalisability of this quasi-illustration of Foundational Community.

During the late 1960s, the Beatles provided a window into Foundational Community. Exploring the meaning of life, both individually and corporately, the Beatles inspired a more far reaching - certainly a more artistic – Cultural Revolution than Mao. Or was that the Rolling Stones who were the shadow community? Or is the Grateful Dead really the example that we are looking for? In any event, all of these are peer organisations with global impact in both economic and cultural terms (and, like the Jesuits, none of them included women members).

Triangular Friendships

Let us turn now to the simplest possible ongoing form of a Community of Inquiry - a triangular friendship in which each of the three members is consciously and explicitly related to the other two members and committed to ongoing mutual transformation. Unlike the single relationship between a couple, which can easily become habitual or polarised, there are four relationships to be balanced and transformed within a triangle, three couple relationships and one three-person relationship. Such triangular, mutually transformational friendships are today unnamed, unknown, and scarcely practiced by anyone. Indeed, our arithmetic of friendship has focused throughout the modern era, almost solely, on the simplest possible form of friendship - the couple or best friend, the two-person male, female, or inter-gender relationship. By contrast, the human subconscious during the modern era is constantly seduced and obsessed by covertly triangular dynamics - for example, the husband, the wife, and the lover; the boss, the favoured subordinate, and the more competent subordinate; or the parents taking out their problems on one of their children. So common are such implicit triangulations, that many therapists take as a prime directive to seek them out in their clients' practice and unmask them, with the intention of eradicating them.

But what if good friendship is really about cultivating an awareness of one's limits and shifting emotional alchemy? What if good friendship is really about enacting mutuality across different preferences, feelings and intellectual assumptions? What if good friendship is about exposing one another's verbal maladroitness and learning sharper, more caring, more transformative speaking? Would not explicitly triangular relationships, much more easily and continually than couple relationships, test one's ability to maintain a changing balance, to fall gracefully out of balance, and to rebalance? Might not aspiring members of a Community of Inquiry choose to hone their relational abilities and awareness in several experimental triangular friendships prior to, or after completing, a lifelong couple commitment?

What may motivate the development of organisations that cultivate adult development and triangular (or communal) friendships? As modern medicine invents new ways to help people live longer, two issues arise. First, half of each married couple is likely to live longer, alone and lonely, after the other's death. Second, rituals for helping people to die voluntarily, with dignity, and in community become increasingly desirable. The following future scenario envisions a new international form of not-for-profit foundational communities of inquiry in health care and other institutional fields. This scenario was produced in the late 1990s as part of a year-long visioning and strategising process of a leading US health management organisation:

Philadelphia Quaker Health in 2025

In 2025, Philadelphia Quaker Health is the most trusted and respected name in health care. It is one of the Nine Majors - the nine largest Not-for-Prophets (NFPs) in the world. (Of course, just as many for-profit entrepreneurial ventures fail, many organisations have failed in the attempt to create liberating developmental disciplines analogous to those of successful NFPs).

Philadelphia Quaker Health has close to one billion members globally, and, of these, more than nearly 100 million are fully vested. (Once fully vested, members' income and life care through death is guaranteed and at least half of their economic assets become fully integrated into PQH's Intergenerational Trust.)

Together, NFPs now account for approximately one-third of global annual revenues. Unlike for-profit corporations and government agencies, Not-for-Prophets, like Arborway Investing and Drug Lords and Ladies, have become global, multi-sector organisations by accepting the challenge of cultivating, not just the negative freedoms so well managed by the U.S. Constitution (under which all of the top 500 NFPs are incorporated), but also and in particular:

the balanced adult
eco-spiritual, social, physical and financial development
of members and clients

Philadelphia Quaker offers personal budgetary options in regard to elective care for members who successfully maintain their health (and more than 80% of the membership in every age group of the octave does). Currently, the *Mass-age Mess-age* unit receives the largest proportion of the elective budget.

'Friendly Quakers' - as we playfully call ourselves, whether we are doctors, business associates, member beneficiaries, or even mere clients of the enterprise - are all committed to personal, family, and organisational initiatives to increase good health and prevent disease. For example, every Friendly Quaker belongs to an 'Active Health Triangle'. The Triangles meet at least once every three weeks for exercise and conversation, to address each member's spiritual, organisational, and physical health dilemmas. In these Triangles members typically discuss their most perplexing and troubling issues and share suggestions, via the Web and the Intranet, about alternative resources they can access from other PQH services.

The opportunity to join a different Triangle each year is what initially attracts most clients to become members of PQH. As everyone is well aware, the Triangles shift membership each year based on the stated partner-preferences of each member. 'Free love', new PQH members fondly imagine. But, as they learn, and as another of the Nine Majors advertises: *'Dreams do come true... Dis-illusion-ingly... Trans-form-ingly...'*!!!)

Like the others of the Nine Majors in relation to their original sectors, Philadelphia Quaker Health is far and away the largest and most respected player in the health care industry globally. It is also a Liberating Discipline that generates enormous trust and longevity among its doctors, business associates, member beneficiaries, and clients. Indeed, the organisation is more likely to choose to discontinue its relationship with members prior to their final, full vesting (after as many as 21 years) than the members are to discontinue their relationship with PQH.

In the wider global market and in the US political process, there is great controversy about the adult development orientation that all the successful Not-for-Profits share. Spiritual, scientific, political, and economic fundamentalists -- those who wish to preserve traditional forms of religious authority, empirical validity, individual rights, and property rights – tend to regard the Nine Majors as emanations of the Great Satan (the more so, as members of their own families join an NFP and their family inheritance is threatened).

Why do the Not-for-Profits generate such contestation and consternation? Because the NFPs' 21-year vesting process for adults tests whether members will voluntarily undergo more than one developmental transformation, and these transformations challenge a person's inherited, fundamental, taken-for-granted beliefs and practices. For example, most of the Nine Majors put primary emphasis on Triangles and Quartets rather than Couples. Also, they divert wealth by inheritance from the blood family to the NFP community. Moreover -- and worst of all from the perspective of the three dwindling monotheisms -- they encourage 'Fast Forwarding' (a fasting and communal celebration process through which Senior Peers choose their time of death).

Religious and individual rights fundamentalists decry such transformational initiatives, arguing they are often cult-inspired or cult-manipulated (most people, though, think that's like the pot calling the fairy godmother black). In any event, during the past twenty years the Nine Majors and the next 491 of the 'Good Life 500' have continued to gain market share by comparison to the Fortune 500, the global governmental sector, and the traditional religious and educational not-for-profits.

An Evolving Foundational Community?

Let us now turn from imagining the future to look at a contemporary home-grown exemplar of a Foundational Community of Inquiry. This organisation is a relatively small investment advisory firm named Trillium Asset Management, founded by its continuing CEO, Joan Bavaria. Starting in the early 1980s, Joan invited each employee who so wished - whether secretary, computer programmer, or president - to buy (at a nominal price) one share of stock and thereby gain an equal vote with the president at the quarterly shareholder meetings. These shareholder meetings, in turn, elect the Board of Directors, including two employee members, and either confirm, disconfirm, or direct other Board actions. (Today, the one-employee-one-share structure has been modified to recognise longevity and level of decision-making responsibility. Also, about 30% of the stock has been sold to another company, in order to create a friendly strategic alliance and to give the shares redeemable market value.) This collective ownership structure, along with the actual mutuality of day-to-day business relationships within the company has resulted in extraordinarily low turnover over the past twenty years.

But the collective ownership structure is not the only unique quality of this for-profit investment company. It is also unusually mutual in its customer relationships and in its methods of analysing whether companies represent good investment opportunities. Trillium's investment strategy directly contradicts the conventional financial wisdom that your investment portfolio ought to be determined solely on criteria of financial return, starting from the widest possible universe of companies. On the contrary, the Trillium advises its clients on ways to limit the universe of companies in which they consider investing on the basis of non- financial factors, such as the social, political, and environmental effects of the companies. Thus, Trillium caters to clients concerned with the ethical impact of their investments and works to identify companies that take responsibility for their ethical impact on their employees and the environment while operating profitably. Thus, Trillium seeks a peer-like mutuality both with its clients (inquiring into their investment criteria) and in companies' relationships to their employees, communities, and environments. Trillium's corporate vision is expressed in its motto: 'Investing in a Better World'.

A decade ago it was self-evident to virtually all financial experts and professionals that Trillium's investment strategy guaranteed lower than average financial returns (not to mention that its one employee/one vote structure seemed the knell of doom for managerial discipline). The conventional wisdom 'on the street' was that only a small market segment of quirky idealists would choose to lose money like that. But it turns out empirically that, for some reason that is incomprehensible to market economic theory as currently formulated, a lot of potential clients (a rapidly growing number of whom are now becoming actual clients of Trillium and the other social investing advisors that have been springing up) are interested in integrating their spiritual, political, and economic commitments. Moreover, it turns out that if you choose the best financially performing companies from among the narrower universe of companies that show signs, not only of a healthy short-term interest in profits, but also of a longer-range interest in integrating their mission with their internal structure and their community and environmental effects, you get more reliably positive long-term financial outcomes. In late 2002, during the continuing stock market downturn, when many investors are leaving the stock market for bonds, Trillium continued to attract new clients.

In addition to founding Trillium, Joan Bavaria is also one of the founders of the national association - called the Social Investment Forum - that has helped to define and redefine this new sub-industry over the past decade. She is also on numerous Boards and is one of the writers of the environmental principles (originally called the Valdez Principles, now the CERES principles) that companies like Sun Oil and General Motors have signed. Moreover, she has played a major role in the creation of the UN-funded Global Reporting Initiative that is currently developing social and environmental measures for companies worldwide. In short, like the Alchemist/Witch/Clowns described in the previous chapter, Joan plays a role in multiple organisations and balances her attention among micro-, meso, and macro-scales of activity (15 years ago she scored at the Strategist frame when measured).

Today, Trillium competes on even terms with the traditional investment houses; it has spawned a whole sub-industry of social investing; and all the mainstream financial houses are developing social screens for investing groups. Moreover, Trillium has accomplis hed all this while shadowed by a lawsuit that threatened the survival of the company for several years in the early nineties before being settled to all parties' satisfaction. Thus, Trillium has survived a prolonged 'near-death' experience, as well as significant political and economic friction with the dominant paradigm of the financial industry.

Conclusion

How will all these examples of incipient Foundational Communities of Inquiry - real and imaginary - spiritual, political, and financial - affect you? How will this book as a whole, about the multiple personal and organisational transformations that we invite if we commit ourselves to the path of developmental action inquiry, affect your life? That is, of course, for you to determine. Your decision will, in turn, depend on the degree to which you come to share or do not come to share the underlying values that guide one towards a Foundational Community of Inquiry.

CHAPTER 15

LIBERATING DISCIPLINES – THE LATEST ORGANISATIONAL STAGE OF DEVELOPMENT

This final chapter offers a definition and illustration of the latest stage of organisational development, according to the theory espoused in this book. Few organisations in history can be said to have approached this stage, yet it is important to say something about this stage, for it represents the most complete realisation of a learning organisation that we can imagine. We call this stage Liberating Disciplines.

Liberating Disciplines cultivate a spirit of inquiry and transformation among organisational members who may first enter it at very different stages of personal development. Gradually, the organisation's overall mission becomes a question that alerts and guides its members at each moment. Such an organisational structure does not just implement particular strategies and projects, but also questions whether given strategies, actions, and outcomes truly further the mission. The leadership of an organisation at the most advanced Liberating Disciplines stage of development can only sustain this subtle structure if the leaders themselves are at the parallel Ironist stage of development and have generated their own Foundational Community of Inquiry. Only then will the organisation cultivate, not members' obedient conformity, nor merely competent performance by members, but rather their continuing transformation from stage to stage of adult development as they increase their capacities to join in the inquiry.

The Societal Role of Transforming Inquiry

For a society to be truly and fully self-transforming and self-renewing, institutions at the Liberating Disciplines stage of development that cultivate transforming inquiry must exist at the centre. For example, is it mere coincidence that during that most creative and enduring of social transformations - the American Revolution - most of the signers of the Declaration of Independence belonged to the world's largest organisation for adult inquiry at that time - the Freemasons? Today, if we know of this organisation at all, we imagine it as a kind of glorified fraternity based on silly mumbo-jumbo. But at the time of the American Revolution it was a genuine esoteric society wherein one built one's own independence by developing an inner, self-transforming conscience (Adam Smith's 'spectator within the breast', symbolised on U.S. dollar bills as the eye atop the pyramid [itself a Masonic symbol]).

Likewise, at the centre of India's transforming inquiry that restructured it from a British colony to an independent nation stood...Gandhi's ashram. Gandhi's unique fusion of political and spiritual action inquiry between 1918 and 1948 not only generated a process of adult moral development for thousands and thousands of practitioners of 'Satyagraha' ('Truth Force'), and not only led to India's independence, but also produced the leaders of every single major political party in India during the 1950s.

An analogous process would occur in a truly self-renewing organisation. In such an organisation, the senior management and board of directors properly engage, not just in strategic planning and management, but also in a transforming inquiry that gradually aligns the organisation's structure, performance, and outcomes with its mission. The board, in particular, properly plays a role that can be described as 'a community of inquiry within a community of social practice'.

Likewise again, an analogous process would occur in a fully self-transforming institution, such as the ballet or finance or social science. For example, a social science committed to self-transforming inquiry would engage, not just in empirical and theoretical inquiry, but in inquiry that challenges its own paradigm and assumptions. Indeed, each study in such a science would not only offer new empirical and theoretical results, and would not only challenge the received paradigm of social science, but would illustrate how the author/scientist challenges his or her own paradigm of thought and action. It would serve not only as a Liberating Discipline for others, but also as a Liberating Discipline for the creator of the scientific project. (As we shall see, this is one aspect of the general character of Liberating Disciplines - that they can transform the 'boss' as well as the 'employees'.)

Figure 15.1 shows how the institutions of an ideal, self-critical, self-renewing society can be conceived as interrelated (the cone is intended to represent a section of a circle, with periphery and centre). At the periphery, the military guards against threats from without - against intrusion by destructive forces. Just inside the periphery, prisons, asylums, police, and the court system maintain the internal boundary against threats from within. At the other extreme - the centre - operate the creative, flexibility-enhancing institutions that foster the spiritual exercise of transforming inquiry. Such is the function not only of the Freemasons and of Gandhi's ashram, but also of Quaker meetings, of Native American medicine lodges, of Yoruba trance dances, and of Hindu sexual yoga, among the many attempts to institutionalise transforming inquiry.

Between the stability-maintaining institutions near the periphery and the flexibility-enhancing, transforming institutions near the centre lie the self-reproducing institutions of the commercial, industrial, and entertainment sectors. (Each distinct institution and organisation can be characterised along this periphery-centre model as well.)

**Figure 15.1   Creating and Maintaining Institutions in a Self-renewing
Society Guided by the Spirit of Inquiry**

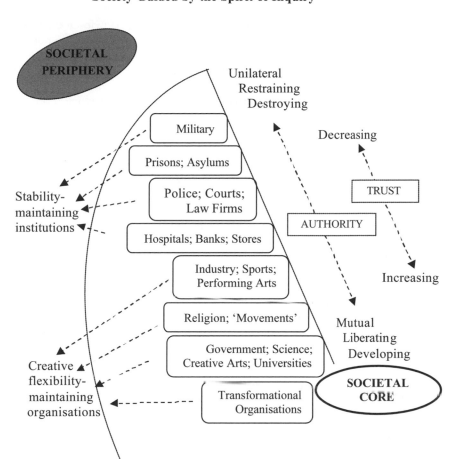

Despite the examples already offered, most readers will no doubt feel
unfamiliar with and skeptical about the very possibility of Liberating
Disciplines. There are three reasons why institutions that cultivate transforming
inquiry are relatively unknown and usually invisible. First, such institutions
may simply not exist in a given society. Second, even though such institutions
may exist in a given society, they may cloak themselves or be suppressed
because they question central values. For example, Alcoholics Anonymous is a
partially cloaked society. Third, even if such an institution is not cloaked, it
may in effect be invisible from the developmental point of view of most
members of the society. Most people may interpret the conflict associated with
any paradigm-challenging institution as simply distasteful to them, make a
negative judgment about the institution, and thereafter simply look the other
way.

With regard to the first reason, can the reader point to many schools that cultivate transforming inquiry? Illich suggests that schools today function more like prisons, places of incarceration. Freire suggests they function more like banks, helping the already well endowed to get ahead. Bowles and Gintis suggest they function more like factories, reproducing the existing social norms rather than challenging and transforming them. Thus, even though we presume that schools and universities cultivate developmentally transforming inquiry among students, few do. Interestingly, the only university that has been able to show empirically that it does cultivate developmental transformation is Maharishi International University in Fairfield, Iowa (the university associated with Transcendental Meditation). There can be little question that this university is outside the received paradigm for American universities.

The second reason why institutions that cultivate transforming inquiry are relatively unknown and rarely visible is that, because they cultivate inquiry into the most sacred and taken-for-granted of social values, they are frequently regarded as dangerous and subversive by most persons and institutions. They therefore frequently cloak themselves from public view. Thus, for example, the typical architecture of Zen monasteries was of courts within courts, the inner courts often unknown to novices and the public, accessible only to senior adepts. Gaining entry even to the outermost court was not automatic, but rather required commitment and persistence. Similarly, many of the Sufi schools in the Islamic world remain hidden to this day, so unorthodox does their teaching-learning process appear from the point of view of the literal, hierarchical monotheism of official Islam. Both Zen and Sufi practices are precisely assumption-testing and assumption-transforming practices.

When institutions that cultivate transforming inquiry among their members have been publicly visible for a time, they have frequently been suppressed. Examples include Socrates' teaching, the Whirling Dervishes in Turkey, and the Jesuit Order within the Catholic Church, which has twice been suppressed.

The third reason why institutions that cultivate transforming inquiry may be invisible is that their role and purpose is not seen or understood by the majority of individuals. They re-present - and cultivate development toward - the later stages of personal development. Each later developmental perspective introduces a person to a new way of tasting and organising experience, a way relatively inaccessible and invisible to persons at earlier stages, as illustrated throughout the earlier chapters of this book. According to developmental theory, with guidance we can each understand - though not initially reproduce in our own, real-time action - the perspective one stage beyond our current position. But we are less likely to glimpse perspectives two or more stages later than our own. Instead, we are likely to distort and reinterpret them.

The Organisational Design of Transforming Inquiry

The foregoing discussion will suggest that it must be difficult, if not in principle impossible, to describe the internal structure of an organisation that truly enacts the mission of cultivating transforming inquiry. Certainly, it must be the opposite of a constraining, inflexible, bureaucratic structure. An organisational structure that cultivates transforming inquiry must be liberating, flexible, paradoxical, and self-transforming. Such a structure falls altogether outside the boundaries of what is commonly defined as an organisation. In other words, as we ought by now to begin to expect, the idea if liberating structure challenges our very paradigmatic assumptions about organisation. Listen to Katz and Kahn's definition of organisation in their *Social Psychology of Organisations:*

> The organisational context is by definition a set of restrictions for focusing attention upon certain content areas and for narrowing the cognitive style to certain types of procedures. This is the inherent constraint. To call a social structure organised means that the degrees of freedom in the situation have been limited. Hence organisations often suffer from the failure to recognise the dilemma character of a situation and from blind persistence in sticking to terms of reference on the basis of which the problem is insoluble (p. 277).

Let us attempt to create the mirror image opposite of this definition of organisational structure, in order to define an organising process that truly cultivates transforming inquiry through Liberating Disciplines. For the notion of 'constraining organisational structure', with its connotation of an objective, external, social boundary being superimposed upon undisciplined, subjective persons, we can substitute the phrase 'liberating social psychological discipline'. The word 'liberating' mirrors the word 'constraining'. And the words 'social psychological discipline' mirror the words 'organisational structure', though less obviously so. Persons voluntarily 'take on' (become disciples of) a discipline based on internal commitment, rather than 'submitting and externally conforming to' a structure. The words 'social psychological' indicate that the social and the psychological interpenetrate one another, whereas the word 'organisation' suggests discontinuity between the person (psyche) and the social (organisation).

But the phrase 'liberating social psychological discipline' is really too awkward to use. Let us shorten it, therefore, to 'liberating discipline' - a felicitous paradox that may open us to the mystery of effective organising. Now we have some of the reasoning that leads to the choice of name for the Liberating Disciplines stage of organising.

Let us continue in this fashion to create a mirror image of the Katz and Kahn definition. With some poetic license, we produce the following initial definition of a 'liberating discipline' on the left hand side of the page, with the Katz and Kahn language on the right side:

A liberating discipline	(not) An organisational context
is by experience	(not) is by definition
a set of challenges	(not) a set of restrictions
for questioning	
(the quality of one's) attention	(not) for focusing attention
and widening it and	(not) narrowing

one's cognitive-emotional tracking to include the enacted task, process, and mission.	(not) the cognitive style (not) to certain types of procedures.
This is the enacted dynamism. To call	(not) This is the inherent constraint.
a social psychological process	(not) a social structure
liberating means that	(not) organised means that
the degrees of freedom and discipline	(not) the degrees of freedom
in the situation are expanding.	(not) in the situation have been limited.
Hence organisations that cultivate transforming inquiry rarely suffer from the failure to recognise the dilemma character of a situation and from blind persistence in sticking to terms of reference on the basis of which the problem is insoluble.	(not) often suffer from the failure

What can this strange arrangement of words mean? The reader may wish to try translating this somewhat mechanical aping of the Katz and Kahn definition into more congenial language. For example, our colleague Peter Reason of the University of Bath suggests beginning like this: "We can only fully comprehend a liberating community or organisation as we experience it. However, we can say that such communities encourage their members through a discipline of practice to question...". Jay Conger of University of Southern California suggests that it sounds as though an organisation that cultivates transforming inquiry is like a spiritual practice of individual growth within a supportive community. (But our personal experience suggests that the word 'supportive' is a little cosier than the atmosphere generated in a community of inquiry.)

Once we domesticate the definition of Liberating Disciplines sufficiently to mean something to us (and we suspect such an effort will include a good three readings of this chapter as a whole and some experience in an organisation that at least aspires in this direction), the more important question becomes: What will a pattern of organising based on this definition look like?

First, the definition means that a leadership intent upon generating Liberating Disciplines will regard every organisational dilemma, directive, task, or encounter as an opportunity to challenge the attention of self and others. The aim of each action is never merely to accomplish a predetermined end, but equally and simultaneously to widen the attention of participants to question and see whether mission, strategy, present action, and outcome are congruent with one another or not. At its most challenging, such leadership action generates tasks that are incomprehensible and undoable without ongoing awareness of the accompanying social psychological processes and purposes.

Second, Liberating Disciplines are inherently dynamic. Whatever structure is created at a given time is meant to evolve over time as the membership's overall awareness and initiative increases. Indeed, the leadership may initiate radical changes in structure as much to heighten inquiry as to accomplish predetermined ends more effectively. Both leaders and members properly challenge the passive tendency to treat a given organisational structure as ultimate and encourage instead a continuing search for a thread of meaning from sense of mission or source purpose, through cognitive structuring and restructuring, as well as through passionate and dispassionate embodied action, into visible events and products.

Two further corollaries about Liberating Disciplines follow directly from these comments. First, the appropriateness, legitimacy, or efficacy of the given organisational structure is open, in principle, to challenge by any organisational member at any time. Such challenges can function both to heighten vigilance of the members and to better align organisational purposes, processes, practices, and profits. Incongruities among mission, strategies, operations, and outcomes are inevitable. The leadership gains legitimacy and the organisation as a whole gains confidence and efficacy by seeking out such incongruities and correcting them.

The second corollary points to the obverse condition: the leadership becomes vulnerable, in practice, to public discrediting if it acts inauthentically. That is, the leadership rapidly loses legitimacy if its tasks, processes, and purposes become incongruent with one another and it refuses to acknowledge and correct such incongruities.

Table 15-1   Eight Characteristics of Liberating Disciplines

1. The leadership practices deliberate irony

2. Tasks are constructed to be incomprehensible and undoable without reference to accompanying processes and purposes

3. Structural evolution over time is premeditated and pre-communicated

4. A constant cycle of experiential and empirical research and feedback is generated

5. The leadership uses all available forms of power to support the previous four qualities, consistent with also meeting the next three conditions

6. The organisational structure is open, in principle, to inspection and challenge by organisational members

7. The leadership becomes vulnerable to attack and public failure in practice, if tasks, processes, and mission become incongruous and leadership does not acknowledge and correct such incongruities

8. The leadership is committed to, and highly skilled at seeking out, recognising, and 'correcting' personal and organisational incongruities.

Thus, there is a very real sense in which the leadership of an organisation that cultivates transforming inquiry puts itself in a very vulnerable position. It is no doubt the dim intuition that such is the case that keeps most organisational leaders from adopting this whole approach to organising. On the other hand, we may predict that organisational leaders who have participated in Liberating Disciplines for a generation or more of their adulthood will actively seek out such conditions in order to keep themselves vigilant - in order to support their own ongoing efforts to interweave moment-to-moment action and inquiry. Moreover, they will understand that their social authenticity and mutuality with persons at all levels of conventional hierarchies, as well as their organisational transforming power, derive from their vulnerability.

At the same time, there is another side to this leadership vulnerability. Especially when organisational members are young in their commitment to Liberating Disciplines and their attention is therefore still predominantly restricted to what William Blake called 'single -vision(ed)...sleep' (seeing the outside world as the only objective territory of experience, and not witnessing their own acting, thinking, and attending as equally real). Such members may levy charges of leaderly or organisational incongruities that may well be invalid and untrustworthy. Such charges may reflect their inability to apply Blake's 'fourfold vision' (simultaneous awareness of purpose, process, action, and outcome) to themselves and the organisation. A fourfoldedly attentive leadership will turn such conflicts into educational opportunities, challenging the 'charging' members to 'retreat' and to taste and digest unexpected feedback. Indeed, the more adept the leadership is in interweaving action and inquiry, the more it will risk using all available forms of power to create a rich context for transforming inquiry, recognising as it does so that no genuine personal or organisational transformation can be forced.

An Organisational Leadership Serving the Spirit of Inquiry

Let us examine, though no more than briefly and very incompletely, an organisation that we judge offers the best example we have ever found of a multi-generational set of male and female leaders and leadership groups dedicated to cultivating the spirit of inquiry. The organisation spans some eighty years at present and consists of tens of thousands of members globally. It includes many persons of international repute in the fine arts and the performing arts, in the gamut of scholarly disciplines, and in the professions, as well as members of every race and social class and many ethnic groups.

The mission of this not-for-profit, global, educational organisation is to re-present and cultivate a kind of playful awareness and action in its members' lives - a kind of spiritual and mundane inquiry on a moment to moment basis - that makes them more awake, more conscious, more true to themselves (selves whom they increasingly realise they have yet fully to meet).

In *Spiritual Choices: The Problems of Recognizing Authentic Paths to Inner Transformation,* Anthony, Ecker, and Wilber compare this organisation to others that are explicitly concerned with members' spiritual transformation, and they offer a comparative critique of these organisations' different practices. In addition, a wide range of books by and about several of the organisational leaders provides different views of the organisation's history and purpose. One of us has also participated in the organisation for over a quarter century, but stopped doing so ten years ago in order to pursue his spiritual inquiry in a more singular fashion for a time.

This organisation - or, better, this set of Liberating Disciplines - is commonly named The Gurdjieff Work, after George Gurdjieff, the Greek-Armenian who first gathered students about him in Moscow in 1913, after having explored esoteric schools from Egypt to Tibet during the previous twenty years. Gurdjieff continued to create unusual conditions for learning until his death in Paris in 1949.

Gurdjieff - like Plato - held that we are habitual creatures who wander dreamily or blinkered through our days - which our ordinary waking state is as far short of full, inquiring consciousness as our nighttime sleep is from daytime awareness. The inquiry activities within the Gurdjieff Work include meetings at which members have the opportunity to review their internal efforts at observing the quality of their own awareness and performance throughout the preceding week, while simultaneously engaging in such self-observation at the meeting itself. Another inquiry activity is for all members to take on a particular internal inquiry task ('Listen to how you listen') while performing an external task of some kind (e.g building a stage and arranging the lighting). For example, one such inquiry activity, which sounds absurd outside the context of studying the quality of one's own awareness, is to brush one's teeth with the unaccustomed hand holding the brush. Setting this small task for oneself can show how difficult it is even to remember what we intend to do, can highlight how habitual most of our actions are, and can show how difficult it is to continue for long with a true spirit of inquiry.

Gurdjieff mounted various public presentations with students on different continents (music, dance, lectures, etc.), among the many vehicles he generated for challenging students toward a more active awareness. One unusual sociological characteristic that members of this organisation uniformly report is that the leadership provides consistent, though surprising, direction in the inquiry domain, but not in the task-oriented domain. Occasionally, as when preparing for one performance or another, there is a strong, task-oriented demand. But at other times the quality of performance is left very much up to the individual members. This inconsistency of task-orientation is highlighted by the fact that there are continual, highly consistent inquiry activities.

A second striking sociological characteristic of this organisation is that the leader - Gurdjieff - intentionally generated conflict with some of his leading students, who in turn set up their own distinctive versions of these Liberating Disciplines. Then, after the Gurdjieff's death, many of these erstwhile apparently divergent 'sects' reunited into a single enterprise. In this way, conditions were created both during and after the founder's lifetime that raised questions about the legitimacy of each leader's approach.

At first hearing, this situation of divided leadership no doubt sounds counterproductive. It directly violates the military/bureaucratic dictum about unity of command. But remember that one of the oldest and most stable polities in the world - namely the United States of America - is organised to institutionalise conflict among its three branches and its two parties. As a result, the legitimacy of each President's actions is constantly being questioned and tested, which increases the legitimacy of the system of governance in the long run. Given this enviable record, one begins to wonder whether international corporations should consider institutionalising a more public struggle within their leadership groups. Apparent unity of command may be a necessary feature of an organisation at society's periphery whose primary concerns are efficiency and unity against outside competitive threat (e.g. the military). But a core social organisation whose primary concerns are continuing dialog among multiple cultures and continuing inquiry about how to improve quality - an organisation closer to the other end of the sociological spectrum shown in Figure 15.1 above - may require a more contentious internal environment.

A third surprising and paradoxical sociological characteristic of the Gurdjieff Work is that it has never advertised itself in any way or sought to attract and convert new members. Instead, it remains cloaked, thus posing the potentially empowering challenge to all who come into contact with the rumour of the organisation's existence to find their way into it, if they so wish. So begins the study of what one truly wishes. To find the organisation, one must truly wish to do so.

When one begins to ponder this anomalous characteristic, one realises that a slightly less extreme version of this phenomenon of intentionally difficult entry is characteristic of many of the highest quality organisations. Consider Alcoholics Anonymous (you have to get there by yourself), the New York City Ballet or the United States Marines, the Boston Consulting Group or Yale's secret society Skull and Bones, to which the Presidents Bush, as well as their nemesis and national court jester, Doonesbury cartoonist Gary Trudeau, belong.

A fourth surprising characteristic of the Gurdjieff Work's web of Liberating Disciplines is that - unlike more commercial self-help organisations or evangelical sects - the new members do not in effect support the leaders. On the contrary, as one takes more leadership responsibility within the organisation, one is expected to make more significant financial contribution as well. Leaders show their fitness to lead in small part by their enhanced ability and commitment to balance high achievement in the everyday commercial world with a deepening commitment to this liberating discipline.

Taken together, these unusual approaches to organising generate a frequent 'dilemmic' sense for members. That is, the members frequently experience themselves as facing a relatively unstructured dilemma, rather than a well-defined problem, and a dilemma that demands a higher awareness than their wavering efforts at self-observation show them they are generating. Such a repeated sense of dilemma can be defeating to anyone accustomed to external success, or accustomed to avoiding responsibility for one's own performance. On the other hand, how else can one cultivate a moment-to-moment taste for transforming the quality of one's own awareness and action?

The Film *Groundhog Day*

If the example of the Gurdjieff Work seems too distant to teach us much, let us consider the story of the film Groundhog Day as another example of Liberating Disciplines.

In Groundhog Day, comedian Bill Murray plays an insufferable, egocentric TV weatherman who reports on the annual appearance of the ground hog in a small western Pennsylvania town. One year, the weatherman gets caught in a peculiar time warp whereby he begins that same day over and over again. At first, he is terminally depressed; then he gradually, gleefully, and sophomorically realises he has license to do whatever he wishes; still later, he begins to take the eternally repeating day as a liberating discipline that permits him to raise his awareness and his timely presence from one version of the day to the next. See the movie for details.

If this interpretation of the comedy as a liberating discipline appears a bit like reaching, consider the story behind this story: Consider the similarity between the Groundhog Day story and the novel entitled *The Strange Life of Ivan Osokin* by Gurdjieff's prime student, Peter Ouspensky, a Russian mathematician and philosopher. In that story, an Alchemist gives the central character, Osokin, a chance to re-live twelve years of his life and correct his mistakes. But can the man correct his mistakes, or is he doomed to repeat them? Can he escape the coil of eternal recurrence through special disciplines of awareness and timely action? Read the book for details.

If this connection between the Gurdjieff Work and the film Groundhog Day appears even more like reaching for a connection, consider a story behind that: Bill Murray has been a longtime member of the Gurdjieff Work.

Now, what is the story here? Where does truth end and fiction begin? And how can stories themselves serve as liberating disciplines?

That in itself is a long story. We can start by examining the traditions of Hasidic and Sufi stories. The Disney cartoon Aladdin is a Sufi story...

Conclusion

Overall, this brief overview of the Gurdjieff Work, along with the even briefer references to other historical examples and contemporary films, can offer an impression of organising and leadership that generate Liberating Disciplines -

that invite each participant to join in an inquiry that can transform one's present awareness.

As international organisations such as the United Nations and the World Bank struggle with the questions of how to generate a new world order both politically and economically, is there a spirit more likely to increase peace, productivity, tolerance of diversity, creative tension, transformation, and harmony than the spirit of inquiry?

As organisations attempt to operate in a manner that fosters sustained organisational learning, is any approach less centrally dedicated to inquiry in the moment of action likely to draw us toward that grail?

As persons seek understanding, mutuality, and intimacy across boundaries of race, culture, age, and sexual orientation, can we conceive of an authentic, mutually empowering and dignifying, covenantal relationship that does not invite and welcome an ever deepening, ever lighter and more illuminating inquiry in the midst of our relational actions?

These very questions (not the answers to the questions) can guide us toward a wider awareness. Can we see through our impatience to have answers and gradually acquire the taste for incompletion - the taste for being present at the very leading edge of our personal development and the very leading edge of a process of organisational transformation? Will our leadership in our managing, our parenting, our teaching, our consulting, or our writing, generate Liberating Disciplines and a spirit of inquiry?

ENDNOTES

The Leadership Development Profile

The concept of ego development has its roots in ancient Greek, Hebrew, Hindu and Buddhist cultures. Early this century development aroused interest as people sought to understand the consequences for humans of Darwin's work. Freud, Adler, Jung and others have all contributed enormously to our understanding of the development of the 'ego' in mature humans. Drawing on these sources and on original research in the 1960s and 1970s, Jane Loevinger put forward a developmental framework which became the Washington University Sentence Completion Test. This instrument is one of the most widely used and validated in the field of personality assessment with thousands of research projects carried out worldwide.

Bill Torbert and Susann Cook-Greuter adapted Loevinger's instrument for professionals and explored its use with managerial populations. The resulting Leadership Development Profile has been used to 'measure' the meaning making frames of managers and leaders since 1990. Further information about the research base of this framework can be found in the Endnotes for Chapter 4, on the next page.

The Leadership Development profile is determined by the skilled analysis of a subject's responses to 36 unfinished sentence stems. In contrast to many forced-choice psychometrics subjects often find the sentence completion process to be interesting, amusing, challenging and developmental in its own right.

The Profile has been used to support individual development, and has also been used in team development and other OD interventions.

Details of the Leadership Development Profile can be found at www.harthill.co.uk

Chapter 1

In addition to this book, two other books published 2000 develop the notion of action inquiry in more scholarly language and with a much wider list of references than will be found in these Endnotes. One of these is the *Handbook of Action Research* (Peter Reason and Hilary Bradbury [eds.], London, Sage), which includes a chapter by Torbert called 'The practice of action inquiry' along with many other closely related chapters. The other is *Transforming Social Inquiry, Transforming Social Action* (Francine Sherman and William Torbert [eds.], Boston, Kluwer Academic Publishers).

The course syllabus for the Leadership Workshop at Boston College, in which practising managers begin the journalising and experimenting reported throughout this book, is available on the web at www2.bc.edu/~torbert

Chapter 2

The Continental Illinois information and quotation at the beginning of this chapter are from *The Wall Street Journal*, 30th July 1984. The manager-subordinate conversation about the widget delivery problem is from David L. Bradford and Alan R. Cohen *Managing for Excellence* (New York, Wiley, 1984, pp.37-38).

The four categories into which speech acts may be divided are based on prior theory and research found in Chris Argyris and Donald Schön, *Theory in Practice: Increasing Professional Effectiveness* (San Francisco CA, Jossey-Bass, 1974); C. Argyris *Reasoning, Learning and Action* (San Francisco CA, Jossey-Bass, 1981); D. Schön *The Reflective Practitioner* (New York, Basic Book, 1983); W. Torbert *Managing the Corporate Dream* (Homewood IL, Dow Jones-Irwin, 1987); and W. Torbert *The Power of Balance* (Newbury Park CA, Sage, 1991).

Chapter 3

The four action inquiry exercises introduced in this chapter are, of course, only a few of the thousands of exercises available through different traditions of spiritual practice in everyday life.

In order to go very far in developing action inquiry awareness, skills and transformations, it will be necessary to find more companionship, challenge and support than this or any other book can provide. Only a few courses at a few universities around the world today directly support such learning. Some spiritual traditions like the Gurdjieff Work (see Chapter 16) offer weekly group meetings and exercises to be tried on a daily basis. It is also possible for four or more persons to create or join co-operative inquiry groups for this purpose (for guidelines see Peter Reason's *Participation in Human Inquiry* [London, Sage, 1994] and John Heron's *Co-operative Inquiry* [London, Sage, 1996]).

Chapter 4

The developmental frames described in this chapter correspond closely to adult developmental stages identified by Susann Cook-Greuter, Robert Kegan, Lawrence Kohlberg, Jane Loevinger, Robert Selman, and others. See, for example, S. Cook-Greuter *Postautonomous Ego Development* (Cambridge MA, Unpublished Harvard doctoral dissertation, 1999); R. Kegan *The Evolving Self* (Cambridge MA, Harvard University Press, 1982); L. Kohlberg 'Stage and sequence: The cognitive and developmental approach to socialisation theory and research' in D.A. Goselin (ed.) *Handbook of Socialization Theory and Research* (Chicago IL, Rand-McNally, 1969); J. Loevinger *Ego Development: Conception and Theories* (San Francisco CA, Jossey-Bass, 1976); and R. Selman *The Growth of Interpersonal Understanding* (New York, Academic Press, 1980).

Studies of the numbers of managers holding the various developmental frames include J. Davidson *The effects of organisational culture on the development of nurses* (Chestnut Hill MA, Boston College School of Education, Unpublished doctoral dissertation, 1984); Aaron Gratch 'Managers' perceptions of decision making processes as a function of ego development and of the situation', (New York, Teachers College, Columbia University, Unpublished manuscript, 1985); J. Hirsch *Toward a cognitive-developmental theory of strategy formulation among practicing physicians* (Boston MA, Boston University, Unpublished doctoral dissertation, 1988); R Quinn and W. Torbert 'Who is an effective transforming leader?' (Ann Arbor MI, University of Michigan School of Business, Unpublished paper, 1987); S. Smith *Ego development and the problems of power and agreement in organizations* (Washington DC, George Washington University, Unpublished doctoral dissertation, 1980); W. Torbert 'Identifying and cultivating professional effectiveness at one professional school' (New York, Paper presented at the annual meeting of the American Society for Public Administration, 1983).

Even more impressive, an entirely different set of developmental studies using different measures, (R. Kegan *In Over Our Heads* Cambridge MA, Harvard University Press, 1994) found the same percentages of adults as the studies just mentioned in the Expert or prior stages (58%), as well as 35-36% at the Achiever stage.

Chapter 5

The descriptions of the Individualist and Strategist frames offered in this and the next chapter are drawn from our own experience and from the work of S. Cook-Greuter, *Postautonomous Ego Development: A Study of its Nature and Measurement* (Cambridge MA: Harvard University Doctoral Dissertation, 1999); L. Hy and J. Loevinger *Measuring Ego Development, second edition* (Mahwah, NJ: Lawrence Earlbaum Associates, 1996); B. Lichtenstein, B. Smith and W. Torbert, 'Leadership and ethical development: Balancing light and shadow' *Business Ethics Quarterly* (5, 1, 1995, 97-116); J. Loevinger, *Ego Development* (San Francisco: Jossey-Bass, 1976; and J. Loevinger and R. Wessler, *Measuring Ego Development, vol 1* (San Francisco: Jossey-Bass, 1970).

Chapter 6

In our study of Strategists and pre-Strategists, we asked our interviewees to select two recent incidents to describe in detail, one where they felt they had been effective, and another where they had been less effective. We occasionally asked questions for clarifications, but mainly left it to the interviewees to organise their responses. The transcribed interviews were separated into two categories: pre-Strategists and Strategists. A different research assistant analysed the transcripts in each category, locating themes and exploring how common each themes was within that category. Then the research assistants identified common themes (themes clearly illustrated more than half of the transcripts in that category) among the transcripts in the other category. It turned out that no themes common among the Strategists were also common among the Achievers, and vice versa. This research was reported in D. Fisher and W. Torbert 'Transforming managerial practice: beyond the Achiever stage' in R. Woodman and W. Pasmore, *Research in Organizational Change and Development,* Vol.5, (Greenwich CT, JAI Press, 1991, 143-173). The present chapter is adapted from this article, and contains excerpts from it, with the permission of the publisher.

Research results showing a link between managerial effectiveness and developmentally later stage frames are reported in B. Hall and H. Thompson *Leadership Through Values* (New York, Paulist Press, 1980); K. Merron, D. Fisher and W. Torbert 'Meaning making and management action' *Group and Organization Studies* (12, 3, 1987, 257-274); S. Smith *Ego development and the problems of power and agreement in organizations* (Washington DC, George Washington University, Unpublished doctoral dissertation, 1980). Further information on the sentence completion test we used to identify our interviewees' frames my be found in Jane Loevinger's body of work, most of which is cited, and then supplemented and superceded, in Susann Cook-Greuter's *Postautonomous Ego Development: A study of its nature and measurement* (Cambridge MA, Harvard University, doctoral dissertation, 1999).

Single-loop and double-loop learning are discussed and illustrated in detail in C. Argyris *Reasoning, Learning, and Action* (San Francisco CA, Jossey-Bass, 1981); C. Argyris and D. Schön *Organizational Learning* (San Francisco CA, Jossey-Bass, 1978); M. Rein and D. Schön *Reframing* (New York, Basic Books, 1994); D. Schön *Reflection in Action* (New York, Basic Books, 1983).

The ability of individuals to accommodate diverse frames as an essential ingredient in organisational transformation is discussed in W. Torbert, 'Leading organizational transformation' in R. Woodman and W. Pasmore (eds.) *Research in Organizational Change and Development*, Vol. 3, (Greenwich CT, JAI Press, 1989, 83-116); and W. Torbert 'Managerial learning and organizational learning: a potentially powerful redundancy' *Management Learning* (25, 1, 1994, 57-70).

The two studies discussed toward the end of the chapter are: (1) J. Bartunek and M. Moch *Creating Alternative Realities at Work: The Quality of Work Life Experiment at FoodCom* (New York, Harper Business, 1990) and (2) R. Krim *The challenge of creating organizational effectiveness: labor-management cooperation and learning strategies in the public sector* (Chestnut Hill MA, Boston College, Department of Sociology, doctoral dissertation, 1986).

Chapter 7

Table 7-1 is reprinted by permission of the publisher from W. Torbert and D. Fisher 'Autobiographical awareness as a catalyst for managerial and organizational development' *Management Education and Development* (23, 3, 1992, 184-98). A full chapter of description and illustration for each organisational stage is offered in W. Torbert *Managing the Corporate Dream* (Homewood IL, Dow Jones-Irwin, 1987). (This book is now available from Torbert, copyright holder, Carroll School of Management, Boston College, Chestnut Hill, MA 02467, or torbert@bc.edu.)

Chapter 8

Two of the organisational transformations described in this chapter originally appeared in Torbert's *Managing the Corporate Dream* (Homewood, IL, Dow-Jones, 1987) and in his article 'Managerial learning, organizational learning: a potentially powerful redundancy' *(Journal of Management Learning,* 25, 1, 1994, 57-70) and are edited and re-presented here with permission.

Chapter 9

Most organisational development and quality improvement models in the late twentieth century have not addressed the earlier organisational transformations discussed in Chapter 8 but rather the transformation from Systematic Productivity of large, established companies to Collaborative Inquiry addressed in this chapter and the next. It is not surprising, therefore, that they tend to view the transformational issue as a one-time 'breakthrough' issue (e.g. the breakthrough stage in Juran's *Quality Control Handbook* (New York, McGraw-Hill, 1951) or the change from Model I to Model II in Argyris and Schön's work (e.g. *Organizational Learning* [Reading, MA, Addison Wesley, 1978]). This focus on a single transformation obscures not only other organisational transformations before and after this one, but also the ongoing, imperfect, stumbling, self-redesigning process illustrated in these two chapters.

Chapter 10

Seven of the managers and senior managers at Sun volunteered to take the developmental measure during the consulting process. Of these, the manager of Employee Development was the only one to score at the Strategist stage. The marketing manager who became the new vice-president for marketing at the end of Chapter 9 scored at the Individualist transition between Achiever and Strategist. The consultant who worked so closely with the CEO and the team scored at the Alchemist/Witch/Clown stage, which is more fully described in Chapter 13.

Susann Cook-Greuter's work most comprehensively describes the theory and validity testing underlying the developmental measure we use. Her work is aggregated in her Harvard doctoral dissertation *Postautonomous Ego Development: A study of its nature and measurement* (Cambridge MA, Harvard University, Unpublished doctoral dissertation, 1999).

Chapter 11

The full original study on which this chapter is based is written by Rooke and Torbert and appears in the *Organization Development Journal* (16, 1, 1998,11-28) under the title 'Organizational Transformation as a Function of the CEO's Developmental Stage'.

Chapter 12

Another related theory of what anyone can be presumed, minimally, to mean by the good life is offered by John Rawls in *A Theory of Justice* (Cambridge MA, Harvard University Press, 1971). While his theory is not synonymous with the one offered here, it is not fundamentally inconsistent with it either (see W. Torbert 'Doing Rawls justice' *Harvard Educational Review* (44, 4, 1974, 459-469). Rawls' candidates for the four primary goods are: (1) self-esteem; (2) a rational plan of life; (3) the opportunity for good work; and (4) wealth. The last two are obviously closely relate to the ideas of good work and good money.

Many writers have addressed the social issues of inequalities of wealth, of meaning-making difficulties that result in extremes of cynicism and fundamentalism, and of ecological dangers that are summarised at the outset of the chapter. For example, the well-known conservative Kevin Philips has written two books on the topic *The Politics of Rich and Poor: Wealth and the American Electorate in the Reagan Aftermath,* (New York, Random House, 1990); and *Boiling Point: Republicans, Democrats and the Decline of Middle Class Prosperity* (New York, Random House, 1993).

The distinction between individualistic capitalism and clan capitalism is based on William Ouchi *Theory Z* (Reading MA, Addison-Wesley, 1981); William Lazonick (1991) *Business Organization and the Myth of the Market Economy* (Cambridge UK, Cambridge University Press, 1991); and Lester Thurow *Head to Head: The Coming Economic Battle Among Japan, Europe, and American* (New York, Morrow, 1992).

Best known among the recent cultural critiques of the US is Robert Bellah et al. (1985) *Habits of the Heart: Individualism and Commitment in American Life* (Berkeley CA, University of California Press, 1985). More recently, there is Donald Kanter and Philip Mirvis *The Cynical Americans: Living and Working in an Age of Discontent and Disillusion* (San Francisco CA, Jossey-Bass, 1989).

The most provocative extended treatise on the relation of money to the good life that we have encountered is Jacob Needleman's *Money and the Meaning of Life* (New York, Doubleday, 1991). Although the flavour and style of that book are very different from our brief comments here, we do not sense any fundamental inconsistency in the underlying argument.

The lines from 'Love's function is to fabricate unknownness' are reprinted from *Complete Poems, 1904-1962,* by e. e. cummings, edited by George J. Firmage, by permission of Liverright Publishing Corporation and W.W. Norton and Company. Copyright © 1935, 1963, 1991 by the Trustees for e.e. cummings Trust.

See Carey McWilliams *The Idea of Fraternity in American* (Berkeley CA, University of California Press, 1973) for a prolonged meditation on the value, and the perceived dangers to church and state, of good friends.

A fuller and different discussion of questioning occurs in Chapter 15 'Living Inquiry' of W. Torbert *The Power of Balance: Transforming Self, Society, and Scientific Inquiry,* (Newbury Park CA, Sage Publications, 1991). Consistent with the value of inquiry, we are currently arguing together about whether 'good sleep' should be considered the fourth primary good, thereby reordering 'good money' to the fifth rank among primary goods. Arguments in favour of 'good sleep' over 'good money' include: (1) good sleep is an intrinsic good; (2) good sleep implies a '"free' conscience; (3) good sleep requires good exercise; (4) good sleep implies learning from altered state experiences not bounded by one's habitual, waking assumptions; (5) good sleep implies being on relatively good terms with developmental transformations, such as the transformation from life to death can be. The conversation continues...

Chapter 13

The 'alchemist' quality of Alchemist/Witch/Clown is well developed in M. Yourcenar *The Abyss* (New York, Farrar, Straus & Giroux, 1976).

The sense of the sybil is conveyed by William Golding's final book *Double Tongue* (New York, Farrar, Straus & Giroux, 1995) about the Delphic Oracle and by Per Lagerkv ist *The Sybil* (New York, Random House, 1958).

The Wanderer is one of the 64 hexagrams of the Chinese Book of Changes called *The I Ching* (R. Wilhelm [trans.], Princeton NJ, Princeton University Press, 1967). The notion of a community of inquiry is incomp letely illustrated in W. Torbert *Creating a Community of Inquiry* (London, Wiley Interscience, 1976).

Chaos theory is described and illustrated in F. Dubinskas 'On the edge of chaos: a metaphor for transformative change' (Las Vegas NV, Academy of Management Symposium paper, 1992); in J. Gleick *Chaos: Making a New Science* (New York, Penguin, 1987); in B. Mandlebrot *The Fractal Geometry of Nature* (New York, Freeman, 1977); M. Wheatley *Leadership and the New Science* (San Francisco CA, Berrett-Koehler Publishers, 1992). See particularly the photos and models in Gleick.

R. Evered and M. Louis (1992) discuss the distinction between 'outside-in' and 'inside-out' social science in Evered, R. & Louis, M. 'Alternative perspectives in the organization sciences: 'inquiry from the inside' and 'inquiry from the outside'' (*Academy of Management Review,* 6, 3, 1981, 385-395). Torbert and Reason discuss the action inquiry approach to social science. See W. Torbert *The Power of Balance: Transforming Self, Society, and Scientific Inquiry,* (Newbury Park, CA: Sage Publications, 1991); P. Reason 'Three approaches to participative inquiry,' in N. Denzin and Y. Lincoln (eds.) *Handbook of Qualitative Research,* (Thousand Oaks CA: Safe, 1994, 324-340).

Our approach builds on the developmental theories of Perry and Kegan. See R. Kegan *The Evolving Self,* (Cambridge MA: Harvard University Press, 1982); R. Kegan *In Over Our Heads: The Mental Demands of Modern Life,* (Cambridge MA: Harvard University Press, 1994); W. Perry *Forms of Intellectual and Ethical Development in the College Years: A Scheme,* (New York: Holt, Rinehard & Winston, 1978). Kegan and Perry have also focused more on the dynamic process of transformation among stages than on the formal logic of each stage. They too see development as a movement in the direction of an increasing openness to context, to relationship, to the limits of formal reasoning, to moment-to-moment primary experience, and to the inescapable process of commitment and responsibility to particulars across time. Interpreted in this way, developmental models appear to be telling a story of movement by living systems from relatively inadequate, overly static and simplistically deterministic logics to perspectives compatible with chaos theories.

Finally the quotation about improvisation flute playing and mathematics comes from M. Rossman 'Music lessons', (*American Review,* 18, 1971, 21-31).

Chapter 14

Of the unusual organisations cited in the beginning of the chapter as pointing toward Foundational Communities of Inquiry, twelve-step programs like the Alcoholics Anonymous are today rather widely known, and in England and the USA Quaker meetings can be found in most major cities. But few are familiar with day-to-day events during the Chinese Communist revolution; William Hinton's *Fanshen: Documentary of Revolution in a Chinese Village* (New York: Monthly Review Press, 1966) provides a detailed view. To learn more about the Jesuit spiritual practices and political influence on history we suggest R. Fulop-Miller *The Power and the Secret of the Jesuits* (New York, Viking, 1930) and Ignatius of Loyola *The Spiritual Exercises* (London: Burns & Oates, 1900).

Mihaly Csikszentmihzalyi's proposal for quartets of activist-inquiry can be found in his book *The Evolving Self,* (New York: Harper Collins, 1993, pp.285ff.)

Chapter 15

The notion of 'liberating disciplines' has previously been described, in more scholarly detail, in Torbert's *The Power of Balance* (Thousand Oaks CA, Sage, 1991).

Adam Smith's notion of 'the spectator within the breast' appears in his book before *The Wealth of Nations,* called *The Theory of Moral Sentiments* (Indianapolis IN, Liberty Classics, 1759/1969).

The ambiguities and power of Gandhi's work are well highlighted in Erik Erikson's *Gandhi's Truth: On the origins of militant non-violence* (New York, Norton, 1969).

The research showing that Maharishi University of Management encourages developmental transformation among students, whereas other universities do not, is Howard Chandler's 1991 unpublished doctoral dissertation, *Transcendental Meditation and awakening wisdom: A ten-year longitudinal study* (Fairfield IA: Maharishi University of Management).

Katz and Kahn's definition of 'organisation' is found in their book, *The Social Psychology of Organizations* (New York, Wiley, 1978).

The Anthony, Ecker, and Wilbur book, *Spiritual Choices*, was published in 1987 by Paragon House in New York.

Of the constantly increasing number of books appearing about the Gurdjieff Work, the following offers various perspectives:

Bennett, J. 1973. Gurdjieff: Making a New World. New York NY: Harper & Row.

Collin, R. 1954. The Theory of Celestial Influence. New York NY: Samuel Weiser.

deHartmann, T. 1964. Our Life with Mr. Gurdjieff. New York NY: Cooper Square Publishers.

Gurdjieff, G. 1963. Meetings with Remarkable Men. New York NY: Dutton.

Gurdjieff, G. 1975. Life Is Real Only Then When "I Am" . New York NY: Triangle Publications.

Mairet, P. 1936. A. R. Orage: A Memoir. London: Dent & Sons.

Moore, J. 1992. Gurdjieff - The Anatomy of a Myth. Rockport MA: Element.

Ouspensky, P. 1949. In Search of the Miraculous: Fragments of an Unknown Teaching. New York NY: Harcourt, Brace & World.